5-6-7-8
out

D1206223

A HISTORY OF AMERICAN LIFE

IN

TWELVE VOLUMES

ARTHUR M. SCHLESINGER
DIXON RYAN FOX
Editors

ASHLEY H. THORNDIKE   CARL BECKER
Consulting Editors

A HISTORY OF AMERICAN LIFE

To complete the series there will appear subsequently Vol. IV by Evarts B. Greene covering the period 1763-1790; and Vol. V by Dixon R. Fox covering the period 1790-1830.

A Seventeenth Century Home

The Whitman House
Farmington, Connecticut

1664

A HISTORY OF AMERICAN LIFE
Volume II

(THE
FIRST AMERICANS
1607-1690)

A. M. Schlesinger

BY
THOMAS JEFFERSON WERTENBAKER
EDWARDS PROFESSOR OF AMERICAN HISTORY
PRINCETON UNIVERSITY

New York
THE MACMILLAN COMPANY
1938

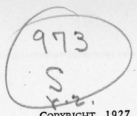

A Plantation seems a fit place for those Ingenious Spirits that being low in the World, are much clogg'd and oppress'd about a Livelyhood, for the means of subsisting being easy there, they may have time and opportunity to gratify their inclinations. . . .

WILLIAM PENN, Some Account of the Province of Pennsylvania (1681).

But . . . being thus passed the vast ocean, and a sea of troubles before in their preparation (as may be remembered by that which wente before), they had now no friends to welcome them, nor inns to entertain and refresh their weatherbeaten bodys, nor houses or much less townes to repaire too, to seek for succoure. . . . May not and ought not the children of these fathers rightly say: Our fathers were Englishmen which came over this great ocean and were ready to perish in this wilderness; but they cried unto the Lord, and he heard their voyce, and looked on their adversitie.

WILLIAM BRADFORD, History of Plymouth Plantation (1648), chapter ix.

58 4-12

CONTENTS

ILLUSTRATIONS
(By the Editors)

1672). Our reproduction from the Brinley copy in the New York Public Library. Chauncy had been a professor of Hebrew and Greek in Oxford, coming to Plymouth in 1638, after refusing to read Laud's "Lawful Sunday Sports" aloud in his church. He was president of Harvard from 1654 to 1672. Samuel Green (1615-1702) was one of the first printers in America, having a career at the press of over fifty years. Most of his nineteen children became connected with the printing trade.

(c) The "Old Tunnel" Meetinghouse, Lynn, Mass. (1682-1827). From Alonzo Lewis, *History of Lynn, including Nahant* (Boston, 1844), 99. This is a good example of a seventeenth-century New England meetinghouse, better, in fact, than the "Old Ship" at Hingham, which, though built the year before and now the oldest New England church in use, was thrown out of its original proportions by two extensions during the eighteenth century, about doubling its floor area. The Lynn church was so called because its cupola was shaped like an inverted "tunnel" (*i.e.*, a funnel). It was 50 x 44 feet, with galleries on three sides, the top unceiled, and the bell rope hanging down in the center. Pews were built when and as owners desired in shape, size, decoration and fitting! One was maintained for Negroes. Town meetings were held in this meetinghouse until 1806. See Lewis, *Lynn*, 166-167.

(a) James Blair (1656-1743): missionary to Virginia, 1685; commissary, 1689; president of William and Mary College, 1692-1743. Detail of a portrait hanging in the chapel of the college. The whole portrait is three-fourths length, both hands spread, one resting on an open book. Reproduction in Bolton, *The Founders*. Another portrait hangs in the college library, and a miniature belongs to the Virginia Historical Society.

(b) Old Trinity, Dorchester County, Md. (about 1680). Section of illustration in Swepson Earle, ed., *Maryland's Colonial Eastern Shore* (Balt., 1916), 87. It was originally cruciform, but one wing has been removed. It received its present name in 1853.

(c) St. Luke's, near Smithfield, Isle of Wight County, Va. From illustration in *The Colonial Churches in the Original Colony of Virginia* (Richmond, 1907), 51. The roof fell in 1887, soon after which a workman found a brick, thus dislodged, marked 1632, and this date is now claimed for the church. The shape of the windows and the triangle over the door point to an early origin, though the Gothic persists here less rigidly than in the later Old Trinity.

modern collectors. See G. A. Plimpton, "The Hornbook and Its Use in America," Am. Antiq. Soc., *Trans.*, new ser., XXVI, 264-272 (Oct., 1916). Some hornbooks had also figures and simple syllables.

(b) Title page of John Cotton's *Milk for Babes* (London, 1646). From P. L. Ford, *The New-England Primer, A History of its Origin and Development* (N. Y. 1897), plate xxi. Cotton's book probably appeared in 1641, but the first edition now extant is that here represented. Other editions followed with varying titles, such as *Spiritual Milk for American Babes*, etc. It was not so lively as its catchy title might imply, being largely questions and answers on religious doctrine, written at the request of the general court. "The children of New England," wrote Cotton Mather in 1697, "are to this day mostly fed with his excellent catechism, which is entituled *Milk for Babes*." Mather, *Magnalia Christi Americana* (Hartford, 1820), I, 255. The *New-England Primer* was scarcely begun in the period under review, but the *Bay Psalm Book* circulated after 1640. Education was chiefly religious.

X. JOHN COTTON ON PLAYING CARDS AND DANCING *facing*   274

From a tracing of an unsigned rough draft of a letter by the Reverend John Cotton (1585-1652) in reply to inquiries by the Reverend R. Levett, March 3, 1625/6; Massachusetts Archives, CCXL, 1-2 and 3-4. Photostat copies kindly furnished for this work by Frederic W. Cook, secretary of the commonwealth. These are the oldest original manuscripts in the Massachusetts Archives, the letters having been written before Cotton fled to America from the Laudian persecution in 1633. A modernized transcription in the Mass. Hist. Soc., *Colls.*, ser. 2, X (1823), 183-184, reads, for this extract, as follows:

"Carding I take to be unlawful and [as?] containing in it a lottery, at least in the shuffling and cutting and dealing. And a lottery also it is to choose Valentines in that sort you mention. Where man and his action is only causa per accidens of an event (as in carding and in choice of Valentines) God is the only and immediate causa per se. Now to appeal to him and his immediate providence for dispensing these ludicra, seemeth to me a taking of God's name in vain.

"Dancing (yea though mixt) I would not simply condemn. For I see two sorts of mixt dancings in use with God's people in the Old Testament, the one religious, Exod. XV, 20, 21, the other civil, tending to the praise of conquerors, as the power of God, 1 Sam. xviii, 6, 7. Only lascivious dancing to wanton ditties, and in amorous gestures and wanton dalliances, especially after great feasts, I would bear witness against, as a great flabella libidinis."

    (a) The growth of a house—plan of Hempsted House (1643–), New London, Conn. Reproduced by permission from J. Frederick Kelly, *The Early Domestic Architecture of Connecticut* (Yale University Press, New Haven, 1924), 11. This shows how some houses grew from a one-room area with the chimney in the corner to a balanced plan with the chimney in the middle, and finally to a house of five or six rooms on the main floor by the addition of the lean-to. The chimney, which is about ten feet square at the bottom, tapered toward the front as it went up so that it reached the open air at the ridge pole. After the evolution of this house plan had been completed many New England houses were built in this form from the first. Note the boxed-in stairs.

    (b) A betty lamp. It was suspended from a hook which might catch into the mantel or elsewhere. The chief fuel of such lamps was pitch, grease, vegetable oils, fish oil, and finally whale oil. Before 1680 probably all lamps were imported, but about that time a Newburyport tinsmith began to make them. Early in the next century upright lamps became common, especially after improved by the Franklin burner, but pine knots and tallow candles continued to be the chief reliance in many homes. For numerous pictures, see H. M. Cordell, "The Evolution of Artificial Light," *Mich. Hist. Mag.*, IX, 338-356 (July, 1925).

    (c) The kitchen in the "Old Ordinary," Hingham, Mass. From a copyright photograph kindly furnished by William Wallace Lunt, clerk of the Hingham Historical Society, which now maintains the house as its headquarters. He writes, "The older portion of the house was built in 1649-1650 and became a hostelry about the 1690's, continuing so until the death of the last landlord, Abiel Wilder, in 1838." It will be noticed that this room contains no Windsor chairs, rockers or other eighteenth-century intrusions, but does exhibit a wide variety of the wooden, pewter, earthen and iron ware used by the "first Americans." On the crane are the hooks and trammels holding the pots and below the spiders, trivets, footstove, "Dutch oven," etc. On the dresser is a broad display of utensils. Note the bake oven at the left.

    (a) Jeremiah Dummer (1645-1718), silversmith, by himself in 1691. From a photogravure loaned by Charles K. Bolton, librarian of the Boston Athenæum. This portrait and that of Mrs. Dummer, same artist and date, both of which belong to Paul M. Hamlen of Boston, are discussed by Frank W. Bayley in *Old-Time New England*, III, 696-699, and by F. W. Coburn in *N. Y. Times Magazine*, July 24, 1921. There probably exists no portrait by a native American up to this time which surpasses this in feeling and technique. There is no evidence that Dummer ever went abroad. Some portraits of immigrants were painted in England before the embarkation; some colonists were painted in America by itinerant painters of English birth and training; some were painted in England during visits of the subject; some were painted there by artists who having never seen the subjects relied on written descriptions sent over.

(b) Seventeenth-century chairs, etc.

(1) High chair. Note slightly raked legs, no foot platform, curved arms, top slat pierced for hanging up on the wall. Owned by Herbert Osgood Fox, Scarsdale, N. Y.

(2) Pieces in Metropolitan Museum of Art, New York City. A wainscot chair (more common in the South) is shown at the left. Note the sturdy construction below the seat. "It is not a bad rule to remember that the heavier the underframing of a chair, the earlier its possible period." Edwin Foley, *The Book of Decorative Furniture* (2 vols., London, n.d.), 187. A Carver chair (so called from one brought from England by Governor Carver) at the right. The trestle table is of oak and pine. The Bible box is decorated with carving.

(3) Chair said to have been owned by Dr. Christopher Witt, the mystic of the Wissahickon; see *A History of American Life*, III. From Esther Singleton, *The Furniture of Our Forefathers* (Doubleday, Page & Co., N. Y., 1913), 51. This style was frequently used with cloth upholstery, sometimes decorated with "Turkey work" or other species of embroidery. Property of the American Philosophical Society.

(c) An oak court cupboard, New England, about 1650. From [Anderson Galleries], *Fifth Sale of Fine Early American Furniture gathered by Jacob Margolis, Cabinet Maker of New York City* (N. Y. 1924), 107. 63½ in. high, 47¼ in. long, 23 in. deep. This piece illustrates the massive architectural character of early furniture in showing both arched and angled panels and robust balusters. The ornaments (split spindles and bosses) are applied as to a wall; these were oftentimes painted black, while brick red was also used for decoration.

(d) A high chest of drawers, near the end of the seventeenth century. From L. V. Lockwood, *Colonial Furniture in America* (2 vols., N. Y., 1913), I, 72. New woods became fashionable toward the end of the century, this piece being of walnut, maple and pine. Design had now

become quite detached from architecture.   In its graceful
trumpet legs and drawer heads of beautifully matched grain,
softly lustered, it shows a growing refinement in England
now imitated in the colonies.

EDITORS' FOREWORD

"PLANTATIONS" being, as Lord Bacon observed, "amongst ancient, primitive and heroic works," the circumstances of their founding command attention far beyond what may be warranted by the number of those concerned or the bulk of records that remain; certainly the beginnings of the thirteen English colonies, so big with destiny, have stirred the reverent curiosity of American historians, generation after generation. Professor Wertenbaker, tracing how seventeenth-century Englishmen became the "first Americans," has worked through an old field in the sense that many of his materials have been used before, but in examining them from a different point of view he has revealed new color and new value for the student of American civilization. Even such well-known sources as Cotton Mather's *Magnalia* and Alsop's *Province of Maryland* yield riches unnoticed by political historians. Occasional levies upon local history bring forth striking illustrative data; in the state of health in Hingham, Massachusetts, for example, we see the hazard of all colonial life as through a reducing glass.

Pioneer work in the social history of the period was done by Philip A. Bruce for the Old Dominion and by William B. Weeden for New England, but the present study makes a fresh contribution by constantly comparing the two societies, showing incidentally how much they were alike at first and how their differences grew under different geographic influences. It may be noticed in passing that the author brings into brief summary for the first time the results of his researches in Virginia land papers in London and in Richmond, going far to dissolve the traditional picture of the old South as settled mainly by Cavaliers, always ready to defend their sensitive honor in a duel, who came as gentlemen capitalists and set up impressive establishments sustained by large retinues of servants.   The comparative method is employed, too, in describing the seventeenth-century folkways in these far outposts against a background of contemporary English custom, as in such varied concerns as witchcraft, medicine, crime and punishment.   Any fact of American social history of that time, as Edward Eggleston once demonstrated, must be related to this background, rather than to the prevalent notions of the present day, if it is to take on real significance.   It is pleasant to follow the author into his conclusions that in most human interests these adventurers bettered themselves by their arduous voyage across the Atlantic, though there were many who failed to survive in the wilderness struggle.

Comparison may go further.   In the preceding volume of this *History of American Life,* Professor Priestley showed the immense power of the Christian church in other European colonies in the New World, especially the Spanish.   It is interesting, with this in mind, to note the points of similarity and of contrast with the ecclesiastical establishment of New England. Here, too, tithes were collected, education controlled, heresy punished and books censored; here, too, as time went on, the traders and the clergy grew jealous of each other.   It is true that in New England the church amassed no comparable hoard of property, and, restrained by Protestant renunciations, indulged in no such proud display as did its contemporary in New Spain. But in part these differences could be explained on the score of environment: the stubborn fields of New England could have yielded no such opulence to the sacred institution as did the mines of Nueva Viscaya, no matter what ambitions the ministers might have cherished, and they could have raised no great and gorgeous edifices, had they wanted them, without cheap labor like that supplied to the Spanish by the sedentary Indians. Whatever their causes, the contrasts are striking, and we understand each civilization better by comparing the tiny town of Boston with the great capital at Mexico; or the plantations on the James with the haciendas of Sonora, the Dutch manors on the Hudson and the seigniories along the St. Lawrence.

The eighty-three years before 1690 were a period of community beginnings, one after another, along the coastal plain. Some communities, indeed, as those in the Carolinas and Pennsylvania, began so late in the period that they are left for treatment in the next volume.[1] Nevertheless, despite the difficulties of tracing in an orderly way the evolution of a society yet in the making, Professor Wertenbaker has written what is essentially a history of development. Growth and change are traced in many phases; in the sphere of intellectual culture, perhaps some losses as well. His accounts of the Anglican church in Virginia, as profoundly modified by the circumstances of topography, and of New England Calvinism, affected almost as much by the increase of commercial prosperity, will afford some happy illustrations to the social philosopher. As

[1] J. T. Adams, *Provincial Society* (*A History of American Life*, III).

the final chapter eloquently shows, by 1690 a great work had been accomplished that would have astonished the most sanguine prophet of the age of Hakluyt. A creditable sum of wealth had been created and a civilization blocked out, which, whatever its ultimate origins, is to be recognized as distinctively American.

A. M. S.
D. R. F.

THE FIRST AMERICANS
1607-1690

THE FIRST AMERICANS

CHAPTER I

A New World Makes New Men

WHEN the English people first planted themselves in the New World, they had very definite ideas as to the character of the industrial and social life which they were to establish there. The settlements at Jamestown and Plymouth were not, as is so often supposed, isolated enterprises, carried out in the one case solely for private gain and the other for religion's sake. It is well to remember that neither the London Company nor the Pilgrim Fathers could have succeeded in their perilous ventures without the consent and support of the crown, and the crown acquiesced in each case because of the benefits which were expected to accrue to England. In fact the founding of colonies in America was but the fruition of hopes and plans nourished for a full half century before Captain Christopher Newport set sail in late 1606 upon his first memorable voyage to Virginia. These plans envisaged the creation of industrial communities to supply England with various commodities which she herself could not produce, to create a market for English manufactures and to provide a stimulus for English shipping.

But in attempting to devise in advance a workable social and industrial scheme for far-off colonies, Sir Humphrey Gilbert, Captain Christopher Carleill, the indefatigable Richard Hakluyt and other able publicists had set themselves an impossible task.   They might propose what they would, but in the end the character of their colonies would be determined largely by geographic conditions, by the location of their settlements, the configuration of the country, its climate and its soil.   To understand the history of the English in America, one must study those great natural features which the mother country could neither change nor fully reconcile with what became her fixed colonial policies.

The determining factors in the life of the English colonies were the Atlantic Ocean, the character of the coastline from Maine to Florida, the great coastal plain and the Appalachian range.   All-important was it to the Englishmen who settled on the banks of the James or the shores of Massachusetts Bay that three thousand miles of water lay between them and Europe.   Despite their sentiments of loyalty this made it impossible for them to remain Englishmen; slowly, but inevitably, it transformed them into Americans.   Before the seventeenth century had drawn to a close Virginia and New England had developed types of men distinctly their own, with occupations, manners, dialect, interests and outlook upon life different from those of Englishmen.   The government at London awoke gradually to the fact that England after all had not been extended to the shores of the New World, but that her settlements there were things apart, with separate economic and, therefore, with separate political and social interests.

Even in the most homogeneous nations various sections, because of different geographic conditions, often develop divergent economic interests which lead to bitter political strife, if not to civil war.   But if these differences are not too profound, if they are not racial, for instance, it is often possible to remove them and so to restore unity. The freeing of the slaves in the United States and the resulting collapse of the peculiar economic and social structure of the South has eliminated, perhaps for ever, the only deep-rooted cause of hostility between that section and the rest of the country. But the separateness of Britain and her colonies was based upon conditions beyond the power of man to change, upon the broad expanse of the Atlantic, upon soil, climate and geography.

It was this fact which made the American Revolution inevitable. Edmund Burke well understood this at the time and explained it in simple terms which should have given pause to the government of George III. "The last cause of this disobedient spirit in the colonies is . . . deep in the natural constitution of things. Three thousand miles of ocean lie between you and them. No contrivance can prevent the effect of this distance in weakening government. . . . Nothing worse happens to you than does to all nations who have extensive empire; and it happens in all the forms into which empire can be thrown." [1]

In the present age, with its swift ocean steamers, its submarine cable and its wireless, it is difficult to realize the degree of isolation entailed by migrating to America in the seventeenth century. The only means of communication was the crude sailing vessel of the day. Not only did it require from four to eight weeks to make the voyage from England, but one might have to wait for months before finding a ship bound for his place of des-

---

[1] Edmund Burke, "Speech on Conciliation with America," *Works* (rev. edn., Boston, 1866), II, 125-126.

tination. The merchantmen trading to the Chesapeake Bay colonies usually made one trip a year, sailing from England in September and October, and returning after they had taken on their cargoes of tobacco. So general was this custom that an impression prevailed that a voyage of six or eight months was required to reach America.

Correspondence was carried on with great difficulty. If a dispatch was too late to go out with the fleet, it might not reach its destination for a full year. When charges were brought against Sir Francis Nicholson by members of the Virginia council of state, so many months elapsed before his answers could be received by the board of trade, that they became tired of waiting and removed him unheard. It was the custom for officials in the colonies to write to the board concerning important events as they occurred, so that their letters would be ready for the first sailing. Often a large number of communications would pile up in this way. In the meantime, the British government would remain in ignorance of what was taking place in the colony. Months passed after the outbreak of Bacon's Rebellion before any official report reached England, and Charles II did not know the extent of the uprising or whether it would be necessary to send troops.

It was impossible for the mother country to offset the lack of common interests by the strictness of her control. The all-powerful arm of Britain became weak and nerveless when extended across the Atlantic. The local assemblies took advantage of their isolation and resorted to a policy of delay in their struggle with the crown. Massachusetts in this way postponed the full establishment of the royal power in that province for two decades after the Restoration; and, had it not been for the second Stuart despotism and the extraordinary efficiency of its agent, Edward Randolph, she might have prevented indefinitely the loss of her charter.

The Atlantic actually tended to nullify the king's veto, for the colonial legislators made it a practice to put their statutes into operation immediately after their passage, pending advice of "his Majesty's pleasure." When the royal disapproval arrived, perhaps a year or eighteen months later, the law would be reënacted in some other form and again put into effect. The board of trade prohibited this subterfuge, but they were never able to stop it entirely. The colonial governors, upon whose shoulders rested the burden of upholding the royal authority, felt keenly the disadvantage of their isolation. Unable to consult the board of trade in case of a sudden crisis, and hampered by instructions from a government often ignorant of local conditions, they fought a losing battle.

As the years passed, England and her colonies drifted apart. The American community grew as family after family was established. Despite the common heritage of blood, language, political institutions and traditions, the line of development for each led in different directions. After the lapse of a century and a half England awoke to the realization that she was trying to govern a foreign people, that the British child had grown into the American man.

It must be remembered, however, that though the Atlantic separated mother country and colony, it also served as the only highway between them, the highway over which passed immigrants and merchandise and all communications of whatever character. It was vital, then, that the settlements should be made upon or near its shores. For decades after Jamestown was founded the colonies were but infants, requiring the support of the Old World for nourishment and protection.

It was fortunate that the eastern shore of North America from the Gulf of Mexico to the Gulf of St. Lawrence should be so admirably suited for a seafaring people. At every point its lines are broken by sounds, bays and wide river mouths, large enough to harbor the greatest fleets. Massachusetts Bay, Narragansett Bay, Long Island Sound, New York Bay, Raritan Bay, Delaware Bay, Chesapeake Bay and Albemarle Sound afford natural shipping points for transatlantic traffic. Had it not been for this fact, it is probable that the English would have failed in their attempt to colonize this region. It is noteworthy that the character of the shores of Palestine, which contain not one harbor worthy of the name, has shaped the history of that land by turning the faces of the people away from the sea, and making of them an Asiatic rather than a Mediterranean folk. In sharp contrast to the course of events in the Holy Land, the inviting doors of the northern Atlantic Coast of America beckon always outward and thus made it possible for the struggling colonies to keep their saving contacts with the Old World. Virginia and Maryland sent out their tobacco fleet each year and received in return the manufactured products of England; New York sold her furs in the European market; and New England found her prosperity in the carrying trade, shipbuilding and fishing.

The navigators of that day did not always cast anchor at the coast ports, for the rivers with which the country abounds gave them ready access to the interior. The Connecticut, the Hudson, the Raritan, the Delaware, the Susquehanna, the Potomac, the Rappahannock, the

York, the James, the Roanoke, the Santee were all navigable for many miles for the ocean-going vessels of the day. The Dutch masters often took on their cargoes of furs at Fort Orange, where Albany now stands, while the tobacco traders ascended the great tributaries of Chesapeake Bay and tied up at the private wharves of the planters. And above the fall line were long stretches of river, deep enough for the shallop or the canoe, which served as avenues of approach to deep water. Had man himself planned this system of waterways, it could hardly have been better suited for the needs of foreign trade.

It was inevitable that the settlements should first group themselves around the bays and push up the river valleys. In 1665 the colonies could be divided into six distinct geographic units, all shaped by considerations of transportation: the Massachusetts Bay group, the Narragansett Bay group, the Long Island Sound and Connecticut River group, the New York Bay and Hudson River group, the Delaware Bay and Delaware River group, and the Chesapeake Bay, Potomac, Rappahannock, York and James group. At this date hardly a settler had planted his home more than a dozen miles from deep water, and many could step directly from their own wharves upon the vessel which conveyed their produce to Europe.

By the end of the century two new groups had been formed, one around Albemarle Sound and the other around Charleston Harbor, while in the older communities the settlements had in a few cases extended some distance inland. All central New Jersey had filled up, Penn's Quaker colonists were pushing northward and westward from Philadelphia, the Virginians were seeking new lands above the falls of the Rappahannock, the Matapony and the Pamunkey. But even at this late date, nearly a century after the establishing of Jamestown, most of the colonists were still clinging to the coastal waterways, and their settlements formed a narrow fringe along the shore of the great body of water which connected them with the Old World. In the eighteenth century came a remarkable growth of population and wealth, which made it possible for them to break in part this dependence on Europe and for the first time to turn their faces westward. In another hundred and fifty years they were destined to push out three thousand miles until they had covered the central parts of the continent and had reached the Pacific Ocean.

It is misleading to say that the colonists, during this first century, were prevented from spreading into the interior by the great mountain chain which extended from Maine to Alabama. Except in New York and New England, their settlements in no place approached the mountains, while in the South they were still hundreds of miles away. The colonists did not move westward in this their formative period, because there were no great rivers leading in that direction which they could follow without getting out of touch with the Old World. It was the mountain barrier, of course, which shaped the rivers, making them short and swift, but we must not lose sight of the fact that the all-important consideration with the settlers was the question of foreign communication. A great plain would have blocked their expansion as effectively as the mountains, had it been destitute of navigable rivers.

The French, in marked contrast to the English, placed their seventeenth-century colony on the one waterway which leads westward into the heart of the continent. The St. Lawrence, together with the Great Lakes, constitutes a vast highway, which could not fail to shape the life of the colony which was planted on its banks. To the explorer its lure was irresistible. Decades before Alexander Spotswood led his Knights of the Golden Horseshoe to the summits of the Blue Ridge Mountains, Joliet, Marquette and La Salle had explored the waters of the old Northwest and followed the Mississippi into the Gulf of Mexico.

Close upon the heels of the French explorer came the trapper and the trader. Having a position of advantage for the traffic with the Indians in furs, the French made the most of it. They established their posts far out in the wilderness and attracted to Montreal and Quebec the trade of the northwest for a radius of a thousand miles. As New England based its life on farming, fishing, commerce and shipbuilding, as the Chesapeake Bay colonies were bottomed on the culture of tobacco, so Canada thrived on the accumulation and shipment of peltries. This fact in itself was unfortunate. The fur trade, while lucrative, was limited in scope and transitory in character. With the advance of the whites it was inevitable that the area available for hunting should be restricted and game become scarce. The Englishmen who settled upon the Atlantic Coast placed their dependence on industries more capable of expansion and therefore more suited to a growing population. It is this which in large measure explains the fact that, at the outbreak of the French and Indian War, the English colonists outnumbered the French at least fourteen to one.

The far-flung line of the French colonies was a source of great weakness. The century in which the English remained on the shore gave them an unshakable grip upon that region, a grip which made it possible for them later to strike out irresistibly to the west. The French settlements, on the other hand, stretching out for many hundreds of miles into the wilderness, were at all points loosely held. With the founding of New Orleans and the extension of the Canadian outposts to link up with a new line of forts upon the Mississippi, this weakness was further aggravated. The French colonies became but an attenuated chain from the Gulf of St. Lawrence to the Gulf of Mexico. This chain passed around the English colonies to the north and west, barring them from expansion into the territories beyond. Sooner or later the English advance would run afoul of it, either to be hurled back by it or to break it asunder. It was a perilous situation indeed, one which was directly responsible for the ultimate triumph of the English. In a very real sense, the collapse of French civilization in North America was the result of the chance which led the French discoverer Jacques Cartier into the mouth of the far-penetrating St. Lawrence.

Not less important than the Atlantic and the river systems in shaping the destinies of the English colonies in America was the great coastal plain which stretches from northern New England to the Gulf of Mexico. Here the settlers, their children and their children's children were to remain and make their homes. This plain presents in its different portions wide divergences in configuration, soil and climate. In New England the belt of lowland is narrow, varying in width from fifty to eighty miles; in New Jersey, Delaware and Pennsylvania it widens to a hundred miles or more; while in the Carolinas the mountains recede a full two hundred miles from the shore.

The New England soil is largely of glacial origin, most

of it boulder clay, not infertile, but difficult to cultivate. In the southeastern part is a wide strip of sandy land which is almost useless for agriculture. The summers are comparatively short and the period of cultivation restricted; the winters are long and severe. With a small agricultural area, a stubborn soil and a harsh climate, the region is not well adapted to farming. To hard labor and intelligent management the land will yield a fair return, but for extensive agriculture, for great staple crops produced with cheap labor, it will not do. Although the Puritan settlers succeeded in producing food in abundance, New England was not intended to be a great agricultural region and their utmost efforts could not make it so. For commerce, however, there were splendid opportunities. Harbors abounded. In the extreme north, it is true, the lack of fertile back country and the extremely high tides offered serious obstacles to trade, and Maine and New Hampshire were slow in filling up. But Massachusetts, Connecticut and Rhode Island, because of their great protected bays, had every facility for commerce.

The settlers found the forests growing to the very edge of the shore, and the combination of cheap timber and excellent harbors offered an inviting outlook for shipbuilding. This industry gained an early start in New England. During the reign of Charles II, under the protection of the navigation acts, it became of prime importance. It has been said that in the history of the region, "one seems never to get away from the sound of the shipbuilder's hammer, and the rush of the launching vessel." Labor in New England, as in all the colonies, was much dearer than in Europe, but the readiness with which masts, timber and pitch could be had made it pos-

sible for the shipwrights of Ipswich or Salem to undersell
their rivals of the mother country.

In the Middle colonies the wider plain presented a
more inviting prospect for agriculture than in New England. The area of arable land was larger, there were
fewer stones, the fertility was greater. In certain parts
of south Jersey the soil was sterile, and this region remains today almost a wilderness, but elsewhere intelligent cultivation yielded an excellent return. The Middle colonies found no staple comparable to tobacco or
sugar, but they produced wheat, rye, barley and oats in
considerable quantities. Fruit trees bore well, while cattle and sheep throve on the native grasses.

The rivers, although less numerous, were wider and
deeper, and led further inland. The Hudson was navigable to Albany, the Raritan to New Brunswick, the
Delaware to Trenton, while small boats could use the
upper reaches miles above the fall line. For western
Pennsylvania the Susquehanna, despite its shallow waters
and its rapids, was a commercial highway of prime importance. On the other hand, the long unbroken expanse of the Jersey Coast from Sandy Hook to Cape
May, in contrast to the jagged New England shore,
tended to keep the people of the region from turning to
the sea. The Middle colonies were destined in the main
to become an agricultural rather than a commercial section.

South of Pennsylvania, where the coastal plain widens,
the summers are hot and the period of cultivation long,
it was inevitable that extensive farming should absorb
the attention of the settlers. The region around Chesapeake Bay proved especially suited to the cultivation of
tobacco, and this plant became the staple, almost the

only, product.   Natural facilities for other things were
not lacking.   Wheat, barley, oats, Indian corn and many
kinds of fruits grew in abundance; the timber was suitable both for shipbuilding and for smelting; the harbors
afforded ample facilities for commerce.   But in all these
concerns Maryland and Virginia would have faced the
sharpest competition, whereas in tobacco they could undersell the world.   For a century and a half the history
of the tidewater region from the mouth of the Susquehanna to Albemarle Sound was shaped by the needs of
the Indian plant.

Since tobacco was a product which sought, almost demanded, a world market, it was fortunate that facilities
for transportation were excellent.   Chesapeake Bay
stretched north and south like a vast natural boulevard,
while to the westward were a number of connecting rivers
that served as cross streets.   Each river in turn was fed
by many navigable creeks, so that the entire region assumed the aspect of a "sylvan Venice."   Until the growing population pushed the settlements far inland above
the fall line, almost every planter shipped his crop from
his own wharf.

England, when she secured a foothold in America, was
far from understanding the irresistible force exercised by
geography and climate upon the life of the inhabitants.
She was intent on securing one great natural resource—
the resource which she herself lacked and which she considered vital to her industrial life.   This was wood.
Three centuries ago the forests played a rôle in industrial
life comparable with that of iron and coal today.   For
England wood was necessary for three great industries:
shipbuilding, smelting and the manufacture of woolens.
The first it supplied not only with timber for frames,

planking and masts but with the pitch, tar and resin essential for making vessels watertight; for the second it served as fuel for the iron, copper and glass furnaces; for the third it yielded potash and dyes. Wood was a considerable element in the early cargoes sent back to England. A London poet wrote of the *Blessing* and the *Hercules* in 1610: in these

Two ships, are these commodities, furres, sturgeon, caviare,
Black walnut-tree, and some deale boards, with such they
        laden are;
Some pearle, some wainscot and clapbords, with some sassa-
        fras wood,
And iron promist, for tis true their mynes are very good.[1]

With the growth of population in England and the consequent encroachment upon the forests, prosperity declined and unemployment became widespread. By the end of the Tudor period the country was face to face with the alternative of securing new territory in which woodland abounded or of sinking into a position of economic dependence. "When therefore our mils of Iron, and excesse of building, have already turned our greatest woods into pasture and champion, within these few years," says one writer, "neither the scattered Forrests of England, nor the diminished Groves of Ireland will supply the defect of our Navy." [2]

[1] R. Rich, *Newes from Virginia* [1610] (J. O. Halliwell, ed., London, 1865). The first iron was mined at Falling Creek, Va., about 1622; see J. A. Mathews, *Economic and Metallurgical Aspects of Iron in Colonial Days* (Pittsburgh, 1923), 6.
[2] Anon., "A True Declaration of the Estate of the Colonie in Virginia [1610]," Peter Force, ed., *Tracts and Other Papers Relating Principally to the Origin, Settlement, and Progress of the Colonies in North America* (Wash., 1836-1846), III, no. 1, 25.

At first England sought relief by foreign importation. In the Baltic countries—Germany, Poland, Russia and Sweden—the forests were still vast in size and could supply her with the needed products. So an extensive trade sprang up with this region, the woolens and other manufactured goods of England passing through the Cattegat in exchange for pitch, tar, potash, cordage, timber, glass, iron and copper.

But England had good reason to be dissatisfied with this solution of her problem. It deprived her of economic independence and placed her chief industries at the mercy of foreign powers. At any moment a war in the Baltic might cut off her supply of basic materials and bring disaster to her working population. Moreover, the journey to Russia or Sweden was long and hazardous, while the northern ports were choked with ice during the winter months. Supplies, especially of the bulky commodities needed for shipbuilding, were often inadequate. The decay of English shipping was everywhere manifest. Many English mariners were forced to seek employment abroad.[1] One writer complained that there were not more than two ships of a hundred tons' burden belonging to the city of Bristol, and few or none along either side of the Severn.[2]

No wonder farsighted Englishmen began to cast longing eyes upon America. Many navigators of the time of Queen Elizabeth had already crossed the Atlantic, returning with stories of the amazing expanse of forest land

[1] R. I. (*pseud.*), "Nova Britannia: Offering Most Excellent Fruites by Planting in Virginia [1609]," Force, *Tracts and Other Papers*, I, no. 6, 21-22.
[2] Richard Hakluyt, "A Discourse on Western Planting [1584]," Charles Deane, ed., *Doc. Hist. of the State of Maine* (Cambridge, Mass., 1877), II, 89-90.

which lined every shore and extended far into the interior. In some regions long before the sailors sighted land they could detect the odor of the pine trees wafted out by the wind. In 1584 Hakluyt pointed out that America could produce ship stores and potash enough for all England, while Carleill pleaded with the Muscovy Company to divert at least a part of its energies from Russia to the northwest Atlantic. Thus, years before the London Company received its charter from James I, Englishmen had learned to regard America as the land of promise which was to put new vigor into their drooping industrial life.

The settlements of Virginia and New England were mere incidents in the story of English expansion, an expansion impelled chiefly by economic necessity. The London Company, among whose stockholders were some of the greatest noblemen and richest merchants of the kingdom, was national in its character and its aims; the Pilgrim Fathers and those who followed them would never have gained permission to found their Bible commonwealths had it not been anticipated that they would produce the raw stuffs needed at home. There were other motives in the English settlement of America—the desire to check the power of the king of Spain, the prospect of discovering a new route to the Orient, the hope of converting the Indians. But one need only read the letters and broadsides of the statesmen and economists of the day to realize that their minds dwelt long and hopefully upon the economic phases of the great undertaking. "The staple and certain commodities we have are Soapashes, pitch, tar, dyes of sundry sorts and rich values," wrote the council of the London Company, in February, 1608, "timber for all uses, fishing for sturgeon and divers

Sir Walter Raleigh.
after the painting by Federigo Zuccaro

other sorts . . . making of Glass and Iron, and no improbable hope of richer mines." [1]

The same expectation was an impelling motive in the settlement of New England. "How serviceable this Country must needs be for provisions for shipping, is sufficiently knowne already," said John White in *The Planters Plea*. "At present it may yield Planks, Masts, Oares, Pitch, Tarre and Iron, and hereafter (by the aptnesse of the Soyle for Hempe) if the Colonie increase, Sailes and Cordage." This pamphlet, written in 1630, at the moment when the great Puritan exodus was beginning, suggests that there were other than religious motives for that movement. Fourteen years earlier, Captain John Smith, after his voyage to New England in 1614, had pointed out that the "Pitch, Tar, Masts and Yardes" which England imported from Norway and Poland, the "Iron and Ropes" from Sweden and Russia, and the "Canvas, Wine, Steele, Iron and Oyle" from France and Spain, could easily be produced in that region.[2] In 1622 the council for New England reiterated that there was every reason to expect fish, furs, hemp, silk, naval stores and timber, "in a word, there comes no commodity out of France, Germany, or the Sound but may be had there, with reasonable labour and industry." [3] A decade later Thomas Morton emphasized the benefits to England which should accrue from the forests of New England: "Of these may be made rosin, pitch,

[1] Alexander Brown, ed., *The Genesis of the United States* (Boston, 1891), I, 239.
[2] John Smith, *Works* (Edward Arber, ed., Birmingham, 1884), II, 712.
[3] "A Briefe Relation of the Discovery and Plantation of New England," J. P. Baxter, ed., *Sir Ferdinando Gorges and His Province of Maine* (Prince Soc., *Publs.*, I), 231.

and tarre, which are such useful commodities, that if wee had them not from other Countries in Amity with England, our Navigation would decline. Then how great the commodity of it will be to our Nation, to have it our owne, let any man judge." [1]

We are left in no doubt, then, as to what England expected of her colonies. British America was not to be a mercantile country in a general sense, or an agricultural country. It must not compete with England herself, must not duplicate her manufactures—her cloth and clothes, her household utensils, her metal ware, her furniture. But it was to produce—indeed it was founded chiefly for the purpose of producing—the raw materials which the mother country sorely needed. Had the original wishes of England been fulfilled, the Chesapeake Bay colonies would never have been covered with tobacco plantations, and New England would not have turned to farming, shipbuilding, fishing and trading. She had expected to people the forests of the New World with smelters of iron and copper, with glass makers, with workers in potash, pitch and tar, with rope makers.

Nor was she lacking in persistence in her attempts to carry out this purpose. No sooner had the settlement at Jamestown been made than the London Company sent over a number of Dutchmen and Poles to begin the production of pitch, tar, turpentine and potash. Immediately after came machinery for the smelting and manufacture of iron. Later iron works were set up at Falling Creek, on the James River, so ambitious in size that the total cost to the company was between £4000 and £5000. So early as 1608 a glass furnace was built at

[1] Thomas Morton, "New English Canaan [1632]," Force, *Tracts and Other Papers*, II, no. 5, 44.

Jamestown, while thirteen years later Captain William Norton arrived with skilled Italians to continue the manufacture of glass ware.   In these first permanent English colonies on the mainland, Virginia and Plymouth, the colonists were regarded as servants of the English traders; for a time they worked under company direction and piled up their products in company storehouses, not their own.   The colony existed for the benefit of the mother country, not for the benefit of the colonists.

There is no more interesting experiment in the history of colonization than this attempt by England to establish a prearranged economic system in her new possessions.   Had she succeeded and the British America of her plans become the British America of reality, the course of events through succeeding centuries would have been entirely different.   Slavery would probably not have been fixed upon the South; there might have been no Civil War.   But the experiment was foredoomed to failure.   It was the geography of the region selected for settlement which was destined to shape its economic life, not the designs of the London Company, nor even the efforts of the British nation.   The glass furnaces at Jamestown proved a failure, the potash workers deserted, the iron furnaces were destroyed by the Indians.   Before the end of the third decade of the seventeenth century Virginia had given up all immediate hopes of producing the commodities England needed, and had turned her energies into the cultivation of tobacco.

Hakluyt and his fellow publicists had failed to realize that the infant colonies could not hope to compete with the long-established industries of other countries unless possessed of some outstanding advantage in soil or other resources. Virginia lacked skilled labor, especially such as would work at a reasonable wage. It had been expected that the colony would avail itself of the surplus population of England to supply her needs; in this way idle hands could be set to work producing the raw materials, the lack of which was chiefly responsible for unemployment in England. But the man who was classed as cheap labor in England, the moment he set foot on the soil of Virginia became dear labor. The voyage across the Atlantic was long and expensive, and the colonies at no time were able to secure workers enough for their needs. Virginia found that she could not compete with the Baltic nations in producing ship stores, potash and iron, and was forced to devote herself almost exclusively to tobacco for which her soil and climate were so wonderfully suited.

The results in New England were even more disappointing. The Massachusetts Bay Company, especially after the transfer of the charter to America, was less national in character than the Virginia Company. It concerned itself with the prosperity of Massachusetts rather than with that of England. It would have been glad to produce the materials needed by the old country, had it been profitable to do so, but it had no idea of repeating the costly experiments which had been made on the James. The first concern of the Puritan settlers was to insure an ample food supply, and for a number of years agriculture absorbed much of their interest. In after years, when they actually turned to the production of masts, timber, pitch and cordage, it was more to supply their own shipbuilders than those of England. New England never assumed the place intended for her in the British colonial system, and so far from supplementing and aiding English industries, to a large degree paralleled and competed with them.

Though the ambition of England to plant colonies in North America was gratified, though the foundations of her empire were securely laid, she failed in her chief end. The colonies eventually proved for her a means to prosperity and wealth—they absorbed her manufactured goods, stimulated her carrying trade, aided the royal revenue and supplied her with articles for foreign export— but for many decades they failed to furnish the raw stuffs she needed to free her from dependence upon foreign imports. As for the economic and social structures of the various colonies, so far from following the plans mapped out for them in advance of their settlement, they were shaped by their own peculiar conditions of climate, soil and geography.

CHAPTER II

LAND AND LABOR IN THE TOBACCO COLONIES

THE settlers in Virginia, as we have seen, were not long in discovering that their soil was peculiarly suited for the cultivation of tobacco. When Captain Newport first sailed up the James the English, who were accustomed to the product of the Spanish West Indies, considered the native leaf "poor and weake and not of the best kynde." [1]   But in 1612 Captain John Rolfe, the future husband of Pocahontas, by setting out a small crop and curing it according to the best methods, produced tobacco which Ralph Hamor considered as "strong, sweet and pleasant as any under the sun."   Immediately the colonists turned to the cultivation of the plant, almost to the exclusion of all else, and at one time tobacco was seen growing in the very streets of Jamestown.   The planter calculated he could do six times as well with this crop as with any other.[2] .   By 1627 the exports of leaf amounted to half a million pounds.   The English kings and the board of trade made repeated efforts to turn the colony away from the all-absorbing culture of this one product, but in vain.   Throughout the colonial period it remained the staple crop of the region surrounding the

[1] William Strachey, *The Historie of Travaile into Virginia Britannia* (R. H. Major, ed., London, 1849), 126.
[2] A. O. Craven, *Soil Exhaustion as a Factor in the Agricultural History of Virginia and Maryland, 1606-1860* (Univ. of Ill., *Studies*, XIII, no. 1), 30.

Chesapeake Bay and almost its sole export. It was inevitable, then, that tobacco should prove of prime importance in molding the economic and social life of Virginia and Maryland, and to a less extent, of North Carolina. The requirements of the plant determined the character of immigration, the labor system, the apportionment of land, the daily life of the planter.

The greatest need of the tobacco colonies was for cheap labor. Tobacco requires not skilled hands, but many hands. With land to be had almost for the asking, the only impediment to the rapid accumulation of wealth was the difficulty of securing adequate help in the tobacco fields. Had the English during the early years of the seventeenth century shared in the African slave trade, there can be little doubt that Virginia and Maryland would have been from the first inundated with black workers and the entire region divided up into large estates. But at this time slaves in large numbers were not to be had. The Dutch, the Spaniards and the Portuguese monopolized the trade, and woe to the English ship which ventured too near their stations on the Guinea Coast. A few enterprising planters succeeded in stocking their estates with slaves, even before the middle of the century, and by so doing laid the foundations of large fortunes; but for a hundred years the number of Negroes was insignificant. Virginia and Maryland had to solve their labor problem in some other way.

Naturally they turned their eyes to the unemployed of the mother country. At this time England was overflowing with indigent persons who worked for meager wages, if indeed they could find work at all. In 1622 a distinguished minister declared that often the ablest London workers complained to him that though they and their families wore away their flesh with long and excessive labor, they could hardly keep breath in their bodies. In 1610 Rutland County fixed the annual wages of a plowman at fifty shillings, of an ordinary workingman at forty shillings, of a skilled woman worker at twenty-six shillings and eight pence, of a female drudge at sixteen shillings.[1] Had the Virginia planters been able to secure labor at such prices, they would have flooded the world with tobacco and reaped a tremendous profit.

But it was no easy matter to transport thousands of laborers from the farms and towns of England to the planters on the James and the Potomac. The fare was from six to ten pounds sterling, sums so far above the means of the poor English laborer as to make the voyage impossible for him unless some scheme were devised to advance him credit. This scheme took the form of the indenture. The planters and their agents agreed to pay the immigrant's passage to America, and he in turn bound himself to make good the sum by working after reaching the colony. In this way, the indentured—or indented—servant, as he was called, sold his labor in the better market. It would have required a lifetime for him to save enough from his wages in England to pay his fare, but in Virginia the work of four or five years was sufficient. True, he had to surrender for this period the liberty so dear to every Englishman, but the compensa-

[1] "When food was not provided by the employer, the amount of these wages was in each instance doubled. . . ., It was estimated that the smallest sum upon which a family could be maintained during a period of twelve months was twenty pounds and eleven shillings, including the cost of renting a cottage and the price of the necessary amount of bread, meat, fuel and clothing." P. A. Bruce, *Economic History of Virginia in the Seventeenth Century* (N. Y., 1896), I, 578-579.

tions were great. When his service was completed he found himself a freeman in a new country where land was cheap, wages high and advancement rapid.

This system of immigration was the foundation of the economic life of the tobacco colonies for almost a century. The English manufactured goods, which were the chief imports of Virginia and Maryland, were far less bulky than their exports of tobacco, so that on every vessel which left England for the Chesapeake there was space available for passengers. The indentured servant became a regular part of the cargo, and the incoming fleet never failed to bring its annual supply. Not until the influx of Negro slaves at the end of the century finally satisfied the need of the planters for cheap labor did this tide of immigration cease. To Virginia alone there came annually from fifteen hundred to two thousand in the years from 1635 to 1705, making a total for these seven decades of from 100,000 to 140,000.[1] The men and women who availed themselves of the indenture to better their fortunes in the New World were, for the most part, neither menials nor criminals. A certain proportion of undesirable persons joined the movement, but the bulk were poor laborers who were no longer content to work in misery and rags in England while opportunity beckoned from across the Atlantic. Among them were men of sturdy mind and sturdy body, eager to aid in the upbuilding of a new country.

The fact that the term of service for indentured immigrants was short was of the utmost importance to the economic and social life of the tobacco colonies. If we assume that in both Maryland and Virginia the average

[1] Virginia Land Patents (Register of Land Office, Va. State Capitol).

was four years (and the records prove that this is approximately correct) and the annual number of newcomers twenty-five hundred, there might be working in these two colonies at any one time ten thousand servants.[1] As the mortality was very heavy, however, and as a certain proportion escaped, the actual number was probably smaller. Sir William Berkeley estimated the number of servants in Virginia in 1671 at six thousand. Since at the same time he placed the number of slaves at two thousand, there were then in Virginia about eight thousand workers, other than freemen, to serve the needs of a population of about forty-five thousand.[2] In other words, more than eighty-two per cent of the people were free, about thirteen per cent were under indenture and about five per cent were slaves.

Under these circumstances, even the cheapness of land and the fertility of the soil were not sufficient to build up a large group of wealthy planters. It would have been easy for the well-to-do to accumulate large tracts of land, but there was no object in doing so when it was impossible to secure the labor to put them under cultivation. A few men, possessed of larger capital or greater business acumen than their neighbors, succeeded in overcoming these difficulties and in laying the foundations of fortunes of considerable size. During the last decades of the century the powerful clique which centered in the council of state was made up chiefly of planters owning several plantations and many servants and slaves. Typical of this group were the elder Nathaniel Bacon, Lewis Bur-

---

[1] T. J. Wertenbaker, *The Planters of Colonial Virginia* (Princeton, 1922), 41-42.
[2] Berkeley to the Board of Trade, C. O. 1: 26-77 (Brit. Pub. Rec. Office).

well, William Fitzhugh, William Byrd II and Robert Carter. "In every river there are from ten to thirty men who by trade and industry have gotten very competent estates," wrote Colonel Robert Quary in a report to the board of trade in 1703.[1] It must be understood that these large planters were possessed of influence in the colony out of proportion to their numbers. "The Council have vanity enough to think themselves almost upon equal terms with the House of Lords," it was stated, and more than one governor found himself little better than a puppet in their hands. The poorer planters both respected and feared them.

Nothing can be further from the truth, however, than the common belief that in the tobacco colonies during the seventeenth century the average plantation was five thousand acres or more in extent. It is true that the proprietor of Maryland, with the purpose of imitating the old manorial system of England, made many large grants in the first years of that colony.[2] In a few cases the holders of these tracts succeeded in getting a certain proportion of tenants and actually established leet courts. But Lord Baltimore soon discovered that it was impracticable to initiate in the wilderness of America a system peculiar to medieval Europe.[3] With land to be had almost for the asking, there was no reason why a man with the ability to shift for himself should voluntarily become a manorial tenant. It became obvious that if Maryland were to attract settlers, land must be granted in fee simple to all comers, and soon after 1640 patents

[1] C. O. 5: 1314, Doc. 63 (Brit. Pub. Rec. Office).
[2] "The First Land Grants in Maryland," *Md. Hist. Mag.*, III, 158-169.
[3] See John Johnson, *Old Maryland Manors with the Records of a Court Leet and a Court Baron* (Johns Hopkins Univ., *Studies*, I, no. 7), for records of St. Clement's and St. Gabriel's manors.

were issued in large numbers to small holders. As for the manors themselves, some of them held together until the influx of slaves made it possible to cultivate them profitably; others began to disintegrate immediately.

Most of the indentured servants who came to Virginia and Maryland did so with the intention of becoming freeholders upon the expiration of their terms. The prospect of owning land was held up to them as a principal inducement for leaving England, and in certain cases the indentures stipulated that they were to receive fifty or more acres. In 1648 the council of Maryland issued an order that "every man servant of British or Irish descent . . . shall at the Expiration of the Time of their Service . . . be accompted a Planter within the said Province and shall have . . . Land Granted unto him." [1] In Virginia the servant could claim no such right, but this was not a matter of great importance for a very small sum would purchase all the land he could put under cultivation. George Alsop, who himself came to Maryland under terms of indenture, pictures the life and prospects of the servant in a most favorable light. They are no sooner free, he says, "but they are ready to set up for themselves, and when once entered, they live surprisingly well." [2]

Each year hundreds of men and women graduated from the class of indentured servants and, as freemen, began the work of establishing for themselves a place in

[1] "The servants . . . could, on the expiration of their term, readily obtain land, and need only procure laborers to become planters themselves. . . . These servants either became land-owners, or squatted on unpatented or unused land. . . ." Basil Sollers, "Transported Convict Laborers in Maryland during the Colonial Period," Md. Hist. Mag., II, 17.

[2] George Alsop, A Character of the Province of Mary-land (London, 1666), 59.

colonial life. Despite the heavy mortality among the newcomers it seems certain that not less than one hundred thousand persons completed their terms and became freedmen in the tobacco colonies in the seventeenth century. The freedman, then, rather than the servant became the most important factor in the industrial structure of this region.

Just how many of those who came over as servants succeeded in accumulating capital, purchasing land and entering the planter class, it is impossible to say. That thousands did so is amply proved by the records of both Maryland and Virginia. When once established, there was no reason in the period prior to the introduction of slavery why the poor man should not compete successfully with his wealthy neighbor. In some cases the freedman, especially in Maryland, became a tenant; in some cases he worked for wages; but of those who were possessed of ability and ambition, the larger part purchased small tracts of land and became freeholders. Virginia and Maryland, so far from being the region of huge plantations worked by scores of servants and slaves, were in large part divided up into comparatively small farms tended solely by their owners. The most important factor in the life of these colonies during the seventeenth century was the sturdy yeomanry whose little plantations covered the face of the country.

It has often been assumed that the Virginia land grants preserved in the register's office prove that the average plantation in that colony was of considerable extent. One historian has worked out the averages from many thousands of patents: during the period from 1634 to 1650 inclusive the size of the average patent was four hundred and forty-six acres; from 1651 to 1700 inclu-

sive it was six hundred and seventy-four acres.[1]   But
the size of these grants did not coincide with the size of
the average cultivated plantation.   In both Virginia and
Maryland the patents were granted almost exclusively as
a reward for bringing immigrants into the colonies, and
any person who paid for the transportation either of
himself or of another could claim his portion of acres.
If it proved economical to bring in servants in small
groups the grants would be small; if they came in large
batches the grants would be large.   In Virginia the
patents ran all the way from fifty acres to ten thousand.

It is clear that if economic conditions were unfavorable to large plantations, if labor was scarce and dear, the
traders in servants would be compelled to sell their land-
holdings to small proprietors.   That this is what actually
occurred the records show clearly enough.   Over and
over again, both in Maryland and in Virginia, in the
transfers of small holdings it is stated that the property
in question had belonged to a more extensive tract.   In
some cases we can trace the disintegration step by step.[2]
Governor Nicholson's rent roll of 1704 throws a flood
of light upon the yeomanry of Virginia.   This docu-
ment gives the name of every freeholder in the colony,
exclusive of the few counties lying between the Potomac
and the Rappahannock, together with the number of
acres they possessed.   It shows that Virginia was divided
into hundreds of small farms, varying in extent from
fifty to six hundred acres, with here and there a plantation of from six hundred to five thousand acres.   But
the most striking revelation is not so much the size of

---

[1] Bruce, *Economic History of Virginia*, I, 529-532.
[2] Wertenbaker, *Planters of Colonial Virginia*, 49-50.

the farms as their number.[1] In the region embraced by the rent roll there were no less than five thousand five hundred holdings.[2] If we estimate the plantations in the Northern Neck at five hundred, we find that the total number in all Virginia was about six thousand. At this time the population of the colony was still small. In 1697 it was estimated at seventy thousand,[3] but in 1698 Governor Francis Nicholson, in a report to the board of trade, placed it at 58,040, and in 1701 at 54,934,[4] while Robert Beverley gives sixty thousand as the number. If we accept sixty-five thousand as approximately correct, we find that there were on the average about eleven people to each plantation. This was not greatly in excess of the normal family of that day.

The tax lists in both Maryland and Virginia give ample confirmation to the size and importance of the yeoman class. In Baltimore County in 1699 there were six hundred and forty-seven tithable persons, of whom only twenty-one were servants and ninety-eight slaves. Timothy Connell, who possessed twelve slaves and six servants, was the only planter listed who could possibly have had under cultivation an extensive tract of land. In Surry County, Virginia, the lists for 1675 show two hundred and forty-five taxpayers and one hundred and ninety-eight persons, whether servants, slaves or the planters' sons, whose taxes were paid by others. In all Virginia south of the Rappahannock the tithables, which

[1] "A planter's income was not in proportion to the number of acres owned by him, but in proportion to the number and efficiency of the laborers he could obtain." Basil Sollers, "Convict Laborers," *Md. Hist. Mag.*, II, 17.

[2] C. O. 5: 1314, Doc. 63, VIII (Brit. Pub. Rec. Office).

[3] C. O. 5: 1359, 119 (Brit. Pub. Rec. Office).

[4] C. O. 5: 1409, 457 (Brit. Pub. Rec. Office).

included free males over sixteen, all servants over fourteen, female servants who worked in the fields and all
slaves over sixteen, amounted in 1702 to 19,715. After
deducting all male freeholders listed in the rent roll, there
are left only 14,700 persons to make up the total of
servants, slaves, wage-earners, professional men and male
minors over sixteen.[1]

As for the distribution of servants and slaves, a study
of wills, inventories and tax lists, both in Virginia and
Maryland, shows that by far the larger part of the freeholders owned none, that a fair number had from one
to five, and that a few wealthy planters had gathered
around them from ten to one hundred. In Surry
County, in the years from 1671 to 1686, we find listed
the estates of fifty-nine persons. Of these no less than
fifty-two are accompanied by no mention of servants
or slaves.[2] Other county records yield similar results.
A conservative estimate would place the proportion of
freeholders who owned no slaves or servants and cultivated their plantations with their own hands at sixty-
five per cent.

It is possible to follow the careers of many immigrants through the successive stages of servant, freedman, landowner and, in a few cases, member of the
house of burgesses. The author of *Virginia's Cure*, published in 1662, makes the statement that most of the
burgesses came to the colony under terms of indenture,[3]

[1] "Public Offices in Virginia, 1702, 1714," *Va. Mag. of Hist. and Biog.*, I, 364-373.
[2] Surry County Wills, Deeds, etc., 1671-1684, 1684-1686 (Va. State Library).
[3] R. G. (*pseud.*), "Virginia's Cure: or an Advisive Narrative Concerning Virginia [1662]," Peter Force, ed., *Tracts and Other Papers* (Wash.,
1836-1846), III, no. xv, 16.

and though this unquestionably is an exaggeration, it is true that a goodly proportion of the members of the earlier assemblies are to be found on the patent rolls as "headrights," or persons whose passage was paid for them.   Of the forty-four burgesses in the assembly of 1629, seven were listed as servants in the muster roll of 1624; in the assembly of 1632, there were at least six former servants.

Prior to the passage of the navigation acts at the beginning of the reign of Charles II, Virginia and Maryland were the lands of opportunity for the poor immigrant.   With land abundant, fertile and cheap, with the price of tobacco high enough to yield an excellent return, with food plentiful and taxes low, the future of every freedman depended only upon his own industry. Hundreds took up land, accumulated property and won for themselves positions of respect, if not of prominence.

By no means all the yeomen were recruited from the ranks of the freedmen.   Many came from England not bound by indenture, paying their own fare and that of their wives and children.   The patent rolls, both of Virginia and Maryland, contain innumerable cases of this kind.   Typical of this class of immigrants are John Gresham, of Isle of Kent, who received one hundred acres "for transporting himself into the Province" of Maryland, and Roger Symonds who had one hundred acres in Charles City County, "due him for the transportation of his wife, Alice, and one servant, Richard Key."   It has been estimated that of the 2675 persons listed on the rolls of Virginia during the years from 1623 to July 14, 1637, six hundred and seventy-five came to the colony as freemen.[1]

[1] *Va. Mag. of Hist. and Biog.*, III, 441.

Thus from these two sources, from the servants who had completed their terms, and from the free immigrants of small means, there was built up in Virginia and Maryland a yeomanry which constituted the main strength of those colonies. Almost entirely Anglo-Saxon in blood, they promised for the future a homogeneous community, sound socially, economically and politically.[1]   There exists an essential difference between the seventeenth and eighteenth centuries in Virginia and Maryland.   In the seventeenth century the economic system of these colonies was based chiefly upon the labor of free citizens who tilled their own soil with their own hands; that of the eighteenth century was based almost entirely upon the toil of Negro slaves.   The importation of Negroes in large numbers did not destroy the class of small farmers, but it transformed their economic and social life by making them slaveholders.   The indentured servant, by the nature of his agreement, could not play the rôle afterward taken by the slave.   At no time were there enough to make possible the building up of numerous large estates, while their early translation into freemen constantly swelled the ranks of the small proprietors.   Nor was the seventeenth century the eighteenth in embryo.   Although an inkling of what was to happen in the latter period is found in the limited number of large estates in the earlier, the two are separated by an important social and economic revolution, caused by the introduction of thousands of African slaves.

In the seventeenth century, the small group of well-to-do planters exercised an influence out of proportion to their numbers.   But this so-called gentry did not, as has often been said, fill the courts, the vestries, the clerkships

[1] J. T. Scharf, *History of Maryland* (*Balt.*, 1879), II, 12.

and every other public office of influence, make up the membership of the Long Assembly, and take the lead in opposing the encroachments of the crown upon the political rights of the people.

It must be remembered that there was no caste in colonial Virginia, no sharp line of demarkation between the classes. The small planter of today might be the large planter of tomorrow. Governor William Berkeley, in an address before the assembly, stated that hundreds of examples testified to the fact that no man in Virginia was denied the opportunity to rise and to acquire both property and honor. If the yeomanry of the colony, unlike the yeomanry of ancient Rome, produced few leaders, it was because the men who had the ability and force for political and social leadership soon graduated from the yeoman class. The very qualities which won them a seat in the county court or sent them to the house of burgesses made them successful above their fellows in accumulating property.

It is true that the Virginia yeomen usually elected to posts of importance in each county those men who by education and training were best qualified to fill them creditably. Nathaniel Bacon, in his indictment of Governor Berkeley, complains that he had corrupted the larger part of the men of parts and estates, "out of which it was necessary our representatives and Burgesses should be elected." But a large part of the burgesses were self-made men. This becomes evident when we compare the list of members of the famous Long Assembly with the headrights preserved in the register's office. Of the thirty men who held seats in the house of burgesses in 1663, no less than thirteen, or forty-three per cent, seem to have had their passage to Virginia paid by some person other than themselves. This does not furnish conclusive evidence that they had been indentured servants, but the presumption is that they had been. If they may properly be classed as "gentry," it is only because they had forged ahead and won for themselves a position of prominence. Nor can it be said that the house of burgesses did not represent fairly the yeoman class. Over and over again the burgesses are spoken of as the commons of Virginia, and seldom did they betray the interests of the men who elected them. The franchise in Virginia was exercised by freeholders, while at times it included even freemen who owned no real property; and it was this rather than the personal complexion of the assembly which gives us the key to the political history of the colony in the seventeenth century. The constituents controlled their legislature.

Nor must we exaggerate the part played by the gentry in opposing the encroachments of the crown. If it was the council of state which took the lead in expelling Governor Harvey in 1636, the councilors were careful to secure the support of the commons before venturing upon this bold step. One of the chief grievances against Harvey was his refusal to send to the king a petition of the burgesses which he called a "popular business, by subscribing a multitude of hands thereto." [1] During the Commonwealth period of Virginia history the yeoman class ruled the colony, making of it a veritable little republic, and after the Restoration upon their shoulders fell the real burden of resisting despotic governors and still more despotic kings. That in the struggles of the next few decades, in the legislative hall and on the battle-

[1] C. O. 5: 8 (Brit. Pub. Rec. Office).

field, they were fortunate enough to secure able leaders from the class of the well-to-do derogates nothing from their credit. In the rebellion of 1676, Bacon's army was made up almost entirely of small planters, while most of the wealthy grouped themselves around Berkeley's standard. Later, when Charles II, flushed with his victories over the English Whigs and elated at the power which the gold of Louis XIV gave him, began his assaults on the constitutional rights of Virginia, it was again the yeomanry which blocked his efforts until the Glorious Revolution ended the peril. They were led by two prominent planters, Philip Ludwell and Robert Beverley, both of whom had fought under Berkeley's standard in 1676, but later had found themselves in the position of political outcasts because of their quarrels with his successors. These men did noble work for the cause of colonial liberty, but we miss the meaning of their careers if we fail to see behind them in all their bitter contests the votes of thousands of small landholders.

The cheapness of land and the unscientific methods of cultivation then in vogue made it advisable for the small planter to secure a much larger tract than he could put under cultivation. Tobacco quickly exhausted the soil, and there were no precautions taken to preserve its fertility by a rotation of crops or by the use of manures. The planter sowed the same crop year after year in the same spot until the diminishing yield warned him that the time had come to clear new fields. A plantation of five hundred or six hundred acres usually consisted of a goodly expanse of virgin forest, a restricted area of cultivated land, and perhaps one or two abandoned fields. A freehold which in England, or even in the Northern colonies, would have been considered a large estate, in

Virginia or Maryland supported but one family of yeomen.[1]

When the planter first settled upon his land, his severest task was the clearing of a space in the woods for his crop. This he did in the crudest way, often cutting down the trees, but usually girdling the trunks and leaving the trees to die, and cultivating between the stumps. Consequently he found it difficult to make use of the plow and had to break the ground with the spade and the hoe. Even in the eighteenth century, we learn from Hugh Jones, cultivation consisted of "hoeing up the ground and throwing seed upon it and harrowing it in." [2] The plow—a clumsy wooden hulk with iron tip and share—was not unknown, but its use in the first half century was very restricted. In 1649 the entire number of plows in Virginia was about one hundred and fifty.[3] Even in later years, when references to this implement are more numerous, the yeoman still clung to his spade and his hoe.

The chief crop of every planter, large and small, was tobacco. The plants were set out in the spring in little mounds placed about four feet apart. Care was taken to keep them free of weeds, and when a certain number of leaves had appeared, the stalk at the top was broken off. As the tobacco became ripe it was cut down and carried to the barn to be cured. After this process had been completed the leaves were stripped from the stalk, assorted and packed in hogsheads for shipment. Some of the small planters possessed private wharves capable

---

[1] Craven, *Soil Exhaustion*, chap. ii.
[2] Hugh Jones, *Present State of Virginia* (London, 1724), 124.
[3] Anon., "A Perfect Description of Virginia [1649]," Force, *Tracts and Other Papers*, II, no. viii, 14.

John Rolfe describes the legislation on tobacco, 1616.

Nathaniel Bacon's Castle, Surry County, Virginia, built before 1676.

The Tobacco Country.

of receiving ocean-going vessels, but it was more usual for them to make use of those of their well-to-do neighbors. In return for his tobacco the planter received from the English merchant all the articles which he found it impossible or uneconomic to make for himself—clothing, shoes, farm implements, household furniture, table ware, linen, fire arms, tools. His welfare was bound up in foreign trade, and he had little of the economic independence which usually attends frontier life. A decline in the price of tobacco, whether occasioned by legislation in England or by a war in the Baltic, brought him hardship, if not suffering. With business transacted in terms of tobacco, a note of hand given in one year for so many pounds might be worth twice as much or half as much the next year with a turn in the price.

But nothing could deprive even the poorest planter of an adequate supply of food. The abundance of land and the mild climate made the raising of cattle easy and lucrative. In 1649 there were in Virginia alone "of Kine, Oxen, Bulls, Calves, twenty thousand, large and good," [1] while fifteen years later the number had increased to a hundred thousand. The inventories of the smaller estates usually show from one to ten cattle. Typical is that of John Gray. Although this planter possessed goods totaling only 9340 pounds of tobacco, he left six cows, six calves, two steers and one heifer. In both Maryland and Virginia innumerable hogs ran loose in the woods, feeding upon acorns and roots. On the other hand, the scarcity of pasture land made it impossible for sheep to multiply. [2]

[1] Anon., "A Perfect Description of Virginia," 3.

[2] Little care was taken of the livestock; thus, 25,429 cattle and 62,377 hogs perished in Maryland during the winter of 1694-1695. Craven, *Soil Exhaustion*, 33.

Game existed in lavish abundance. In Kent County, Maryland, the wild ducks are said to have existed in such great numbers that the water was often black with them; and "when they flew up there was a rushing and vibration of the air like a great storm coming through the trees." Hammond in his *Leah and Rachel* declares that "deer are all over the country, and in places so many that venison is accounted a tiresome meat, wild turkeys are frequent, and so large that I have seen some weigh near three-score pounds." From his garden the planter secured a variety of vegetables, from his orchard fruit in abundance. "The country is full of gallant orchards," says Hammond, "and the fruit generally more luscious and delightful than here, witness the peach and quince." [1] The planters cultivated wheat and Indian corn, potatoes, asparagus, carrots, turnips, parsnips, apples, strawberries, pears and raspberries.

The inventories of the poorer class of freeholders give an excellent idea of the conditions of their daily life. The yeoman's spinning wheel shows that the making of homespun was not unusual; the earthenware, the pewter utensils, the scarcity of furniture and the high value placed on beds and bolsters all picture the crudeness of his domestic economy; the gun reveals him as a hunter; from his pots, pestle and frying pans we gather the details of his primitive methods of cooking.

Christopher Pearson, who died in 1698, left two feather beds, four blankets, two bolsters, two pillows, a curtain and valance, in all worth £7; a pair of sheets, some old table linen, valued at 18s.; plates and other

---

[1] John Hammond, "Leah and Rachel, or, the Two Fruitful Sisters Virginia, and Mary-land [1656]," Force, *Tracts and Other Papers*, III. no. xiv, 13.

pewter worth £1 18s.; an old warming pan and other brass articles, placed at 6s.; wooden ware at £4.13.6 comprising three chairs and one table, a couch, four old chests, a cask, two ten-gallon rundlets, a cheese press, a box of drawers, an old table, three pails, a spinning wheel with cards, two sifting trays, a corn barrel, three bedsteads, four sieves and a funnel; ironware worth £2.1.0, including three pots, two pot rocks, a pestle, a frying pan, a looking glass; three cows appraised at £6.5.0, a yearling at 10s., a colt at £2 sterling. The entire estate was valued at £25.19.6.[1] John Splitimber, who died in 1677, was possessed of one feather bed, one bolster, one red rug, one pillow, two blankets, one turned bedstead, one old mattress, eight cows, six calves, one bull, four mares, thirty-five hogs, two horses, a long gun and a short gun, fifty-six pounds of old pewter, one old flock bed, one old rug, a long table and form, three chests, an old couch, two old boxes, two iron pots, two small brass kettles, one pair of steelyards, spitfire shovel and tongs, two smoothing irons, two old weed hoes, two old axes, a few carpenter's tools, one iron pestle, a saddle and bridle, a frying pan, a butter pat, a jar, a looking glass, two milk pans, one tablecloth, nine spoons, a churn and a Bible.[2]

The yeoman class of Virginia and Maryland was formed and attained its greatest prosperity in the period preceding the restoration of the Stuarts. During the Civil War and under the Commonwealth England had no opportunity to perfect her colonial policy. While Cavalier was fighting Roundhead or while Cromwell was busy with his wars, the Chesapeake Bay colonies were

[1] York County Records, 1694-1702 (Va. State Library).
[2] Surry County Wills, Deeds, etc., 1671-1684 (Va. State Library).

enjoying a large degree of freedom from political and economic control. This freedom they made use of to build up their exports of tobacco to foreign markets, which passed chiefly through the hands of Dutch merchants. Before the end of the sixth decade of the century Virginia and Maryland enjoyed a world market for their staple, the price of tobacco was high, and the margin of profit for every planter excellent.

With the accession of Charles II Parliament enacted the navigation acts, designed to make the British Empire a compact economic unit. The planters were forbidden to ship their tobacco to foreign countries, the colonial market was reserved in large part for English exports and the colonial carrying trade monopolized by English and colonial masters. At the same time the government placed a duty upon colonial tobacco consumed in England varying from two hundred per cent in 1660 to six hundred per cent in 1705. To prevent these huge tariffs from stimulating the otherwise unprofitable culture of tobacco in England and so cutting down the revenue, the law forbade anyone to grow it there. Despite this favorable feature the navigation acts seriously injured the people of the Chesapeake Bay region, for they increased both freight rates and the price of imported goods, and by limiting the market for their staple reduced the price received for it.[1] The small farmer, who formerly had lived in plenty, now found himself living in straitened circumstances. The margin of profit from his little crop was either entirely wiped out, or so reduced that he found it difficult to make ends meet.

"Twelve hundred pounds of tobacco is the medium of

[1] Thomas Ludwell to Lord John Berkeley, C. O. 1: 21 (Brit. Pub. Rec. Office).

men's crops," stated Secretary Thomas Ludwell in 1667,
"and half a penny per pound is certainly the full medium
of the price given for it, which is fifty shillings out of
which when the taxes . . . shall be deducted, is very little to a poor man who hath perhaps a wife and children
to cloath and other necessities to buy.   Truly so much
too little that I can attribute it to nothing but the great
mercy of God . . . that keeps them from mutiny and
confusion." [1]   Nine years later when Bacon's ragged
men swept Governor Berkeley from his capital and took
possession of all Virginia west of Chesapeake Bay, these
fears were fully realized.   This long period of hardship
did not destroy the yeomanry of Virginia and Maryland,
but it greatly retarded its growth.   The small proprietor
who had bought his plantation prior to the navigation
acts usually managed to keep it, even though he and his
family were in rags.   But the indentured servants who
completed their terms after 1660 found it very difficult
to establish themselves as independent planters.   Consequently it became usual for them to move away to the
frontiers, or, in the later years of the century, to Pennsylvania, Delaware and New Jersey, where there was a
better chance for advancement.

This movement was accelerated by the great increase
in the importation of slaves which began about 1680.
The poor white man, already struggling against adverse
economic conditions, now had to face the competition of
slave labor.   The savage blacks were the crudest of
workers; but under careful supervision they proved capable of tending the lower grades of tobacco, and, in
time, learned to produce even the best Sweetscented.

[1] Wertenbaker, *Planters of Colonial Virginia*, 87-88, 115-118.

The tobacco which the small planter raised with his own hands he had to sell in the same market with that made by the Negroes.   It sold, therefore, for a price so low that the white man could hardly live on the returns.   For a full half century the tobacco colonies were subjected to a double movement, the influx of African slaves, and the flight before them of poor whites.   This development, however favorable to the economic output of the region, eventually proved calamitous.   It deprived Maryland and Virginia of their homogeneity of race, it placed their economic life upon an unsound basis, it robbed them of thousands of intelligent workers.   Of the small planters who remained, some themselves purchased slaves and so were able to turn to advantage the very movement which had threatened their destruction; others gradually sank to a state of poverty and misery.

The life upon the plantations of the well-to-do differed widely from that of the yeoman.   The possession of capital and the employment of servants and slaves made it possible for the large planter to enjoy a degree of economic independence impossible for his smaller neighbor.   The case of Captain Samuel Matthews, prominent in the first half of the seventeenth century, is typical.   "He hath a fine house," we learn from a contemporary, "and all things answerable to it; he sowes yearly store of Hempe and Flax, and causes it to be spun; he keeps Weavers, and hath a Tan-house, causes Leather to be dressed, hath eight Shoemakers employed in their trade, hath forty negroe servants, brings them up to Trades in his house: He yeerly sowes abundance of Wheat, Barley, &c.   The Wheat he selleth at four shillings the bushell, kills store of Beeves, and sells them to victuall the ships when they come thither: hath abundance of Kine, a brave Dairy, Swine great store, and Poltery." [1]

The example of Captain Matthews in instituting plantation manufacture was followed by the large landholders of later decades. The will of Colonel Robert Carter shows that on one of his farms were two house carpenters, a ship carpenter, a glazier, two tailors, a gardener, a blacksmith, two brickmakers and two sailors, all indentured servants. The inventory of Ralph Wormeley, who died in 1691, mentions at the main residence eight English servants, among them a shoemaker, a tailor and a miller. Attempts were made to train the Negro slaves to various trades, but as Hugh Jones tells us they proved to be "none of the aptest or nicest."

Thus the large plantation was a little community to itself, bustling with activity and depending upon its own exertions for many of the necessities of life. One might see at work, in addition to the field hands, carpenters, coopers, sawyers, blacksmiths, tanners, curriers, shoemakers, spinners, weavers and distillers. The woods furnished plank for the erection of the outhouses and charcoal for the blacksmith; the cattle supplied skins for the tanners and shoemakers; the sheep gave wool and the fields cotton and flax for the weavers; the orchard produced the fruit used by the distillers. The coopers made the hogsheads in which the tobacco was shipped, and the casks for wine and cider. The blacksmith repaired plows, harrows, chains and hinges; the shoemaker made shoes for the Negro slaves, the spinners and weavers the cloth for their clothes.

We secure an intimate picture of the life and condition

[1] Anon., "A Perfect Description of Virginia [1649]," Force, *Tracts and Other Papers*, II, no. viii, 15.

of the wealthy planters of Virginia and Maryland at the end of the century from a letter from William Fitzhugh to Dr. Ralph Smith, written April 22, 1686. "The plantation where I now live contains one thousand acres at least," he said,

> seven hundred acres of which are a rich thicket, the remainder good hearty plantable land without any waste . . . and upon it, there are three quarters well furnished with all necessary houses, grounds and fencing, together with a choice crew of negroes at each plantation, most of them this country born, the remainder as likely as most in Virginia, there being twenty-nine in all with stocks of cattle and hogs in each quarter. Upon the same land is my own dwelling house furnished with all accommodations for a comfortable and gentle living, with rooms in it, four of the best of them hung, nine of them plentifully furnished with all things necessary and convenient, and all houses for use furnished with brick chimneys, four good cellars, a dairy, dove cot, stable, barn, henhouse, kitchen and all other convenienceys, and all in a manner new, a large orchard of about 2500 apple trees, most grafted, well fenced with a locust fence, which is as durable as most brick walls, a garden a hundred foot square well paled in, a yard wherein is most of the foresaid necessary houses pallisadoed in with locust puncheons, which is as good as if it were walled in, and more lasting than any of our bricks, together with a good stock of cattle, hogs, horses, mares, sheep, necessary servants belonging to it for the supply and support thereof.

He declared his annual surplus reached 60,000 lbs. of tobacco, which at the rate current that year—one pound sterling for two hundred pounds of the "weed"— meant £300 profit from his plantation, besides his in-

crease in Negroes and in cleared land.   But he was also
a trader and a miller.

> About a mile and a half distant [is] a good water grist
> mill, whose tole I find sufficient to find my own family
> with wheat and Indian corn for our necessities and
> occasions.   Up the river in this county, three tracts of
> land more, one of them contains 21,996 acres, another
> 500 and one other 1000 acres, all good convenient and
> commodious seats and which in a few years will yield a
> considerable annual income.   A stock of tobacco with
> the crops and good debts lying out of about 250,000
> lbs., besides sufficient of almost all sorts of goods to
> supply the familys and the quarters occasion for two or
> three years.[1]

Though the skilled English servant was useful in this
system of plantation manufacture, the existence of the
large estates themselves was dependent from the first upon
slave labor.   The indentured worker was too expensive,
his term of service too short to permit of a large margin
of profit from his work.   But when the planter was farsighted enough or fortunate enough to secure a supply
of blacks, his fortune was as good as made.   An examination of the patent rolls, inventories and wills shows that
the slaves were almost exclusively brought in by wealthy
planters, or purchased by them when imported by slave
dealers.   Among the Virginians who had slaves in the
first half of the century were Ralph Wormeley, George
Menifie, Samuel Matthews, Richard Kemp, Francis Epes,
John Banister, John Robbins and Christopher Wormeley, all of them leaders in the life of the colony.   Con-
spicuous for the number of their slaves in the later decades were Ralph Wormeley, who had ninety-one; Robert

[1] Letter of William Fitzhugh quoted in Bruce, *Economic History of
Virginia in the Seventeenth Century*, II, 243-244 n.

Beverley, with forty-two; Mrs. Elizabeth Digges, with one hundred and eight; the elder Nathaniel Bacon, with forty; John Carter, with one hundred and six; William Fitzhugh and the first William Byrd.[1] When we consider that there were but two thousand slaves in Virginia in 1671 and probably not more than four thousand in 1690, these figures throw fresh light upon the size of this select group. Had all the slaves in the colony in 1671 been distributed among the large planters in holdings of fifty each, there would have been enough for forty estates only.

With the influx of Negroes which followed England's successful intrusion upon the slave trade in the latter part of the seventeenth century, the class of large slaveholders in Virginia and Maryland was widely expanded. It is probable that at the time of the American Revolution Dinwiddie County alone could boast of more planters who owned twenty or more slaves than all Virginia a hundred years earlier. The study of the history of these colonies in the seventeenth century has proceeded so far that we can no longer accept the small group of wealthy men as typical of all the planters, and so ignore the thousands of small freeholders who owned the bulk of all the cultivated land, produced the bulk of the exports, controlled through their votes the lower houses of the assemblies and struggled manfully to maintain their liberties against the encroachments, on the one hand, of the Stuart monarchs, and, on the other, of the aristocratic clique whose influence centered in the council of state.

[1] Bruce, *Economic History*, II, 88 *n.*

CHAPTER III

THE NEW ENGLAND TOWN AND ITS PEOPLE

THE hope of the English economists that the New England forests would afford the mother country a large measure of economic independence was, as we have seen, destined to disappointment. To a less degree the hopes of the settlers themselves also proved illusory. The Puritans who swarmed into the region in the fourth decade of the seventeenth century came not only with the purpose of working out their religious ideals secure from the dangers and heresies of the Old World, but also with the firm intention of pursuing their hereditary occupation as cultivators of the soil. But these two things they found it difficult if not impossible to reconcile. Land they secured in abundance, and though not very fertile, yet it yielded to well-directed effort an abundant food supply. Isolation, however, could be had only with economic independence, and for that, agriculture alone was not sufficient. Either the colonists had to produce some staple agricultural product which could be exchanged in the markets of the world for manufactured articles, or develop other forms of industry. Since the soil was not adapted to tobacco, sugar or indigo, a part of the settlers had to lay aside the hoe for the fisherman's net or the shipwright's hammer and saw. Hard work and intelligence did make it possible for the New England farmer to produce a surplus above local needs, and agricultural products constituted an important item in exports; but they were at all times insufficient in quantity to balance the essential imports.

When Captain John Smith visited New England and Newfoundland, he predicted that the cod fisheries would be invaluable to those regions. "Let not the meannesse of the word Fish distaste you," he said, "for it will afford as good gold as the mines of Guiana and Potassie with less hazard and charge, and more certaintie and facility." [1] Captain Smith was right. The myriads of cod and herring which used for feeding grounds the icy waters from Cape Cod to Newfoundland constituted an almost inexhaustible source of wealth to New England. The Pilgrims early sought to take advantage of this opportunity and sent a vessel under a Captain Baker to catch fish at Cape Ann. With the wave of immigration under the Massachusetts Bay Company, the industry grew rapidly. The king, in the charter, guaranteed that nothing should "hinder our loving subjects whatsoever to use and exercise the trade of fishing upon that coast of New England" or set up "wharfes stages and worke houses as shalbe necessarie for the salting, drying and packing their fish."

Dorchester was "the first that set upon the trade of fishing in the bay," but other towns were quick to follow. Before the lapse of a decade, the fishermen were not only supplying the needs of New England, but were exporting dry fish in large quantities. In 1641 the number sent to foreign markets was three hundred thousand, while in 1647 the Marblehead catch alone brought four thousand pounds. In 1664 it was reported that thirteen

[1] John Smith, "The Present State of New-Plimoth," *Works* (Edward Arber, ed., Birmingham, 1884), 784.

hundred boats were engaged in fishing, while the exports had become of the first importance. Salem, Ipswich and Charlestown became centers of the cod and mackerel industries; the Isles of Shoals employed no less than fifteen hundred men. The best grade of fish was sent to Malaga and the Canaries, the second grade to the Portuguese islands, and the worst to Barbados as food for the Negro slaves. Before 1690 the New Englanders were competing with English fishing; in their balance of trade fish weighed heavily. Of the Puritans who followed their ministers into the wilderness thousands turned from agriculture to this dangerous but lucrative occupation. It has been said that in colonial New England one cannot get far from the smell of brimstone and fish.

For catching cod and exporting it to far-off countries vessels were essential; and New Englanders had neither the means nor the inclination to purchase them from English builders. But they soon learned to supply their own needs: their forests which grew close to the shore in many places yielded timber, masts, pitch and tar, while their coast abounded in harbors and rivers suitable for shipyards. On July 4, 1631, John Winthrop launched at Mystic a vessel of sixty tons burden which he named the *Blessing of the Bay*. The construction of this ship, the first sea-going craft built in New England, may rightly be regarded as the beginning of the American merchant marine.[1]

Five years later the *Desire*, a ship of one hundred and twenty tons, was under construction at Marblehead. In 1643 vessels were laid down at Boston, Salem, Dor-

---

[1] W. B. Weeden, *Economic and Social History of New England, 1620-1789* (Boston, 1890), I, 123-124.

chester, Gloucester and other towns. In 1647 Edward Johnson reported that the building of ships was "going on gallantly," and two years later the industry had extended to the Connecticut River. Salem showed that the New England builders were capable of turning out the larger type of ships by launching the *Trial*, a vessel of three hundred tons financed by the united endeavors of the town. But this was unusual, and a merchantman constructed at Gloucester by William Stevens is more typical of the early New England ships. She was 91.2 feet long in the hold under the beam, 23 feet broad, and had "two decks, fore castle, quarter deck." The price of construction was £3 5s. per ton.[1] Before the end of the century shipbuilding had become one of the vital industries of New England, giving employment to thousands of men, bringing rich returns and, therefore, a store of capital.

Although the master builders of Salem and Boston occasionally sold their vessels to English merchants, most of them remained in the hands of New Englanders to meet the needs of the expanding commerce of the region.[2] In the South the profits derived from tobacco tempted many an English trader to desert the sea for a plantation on the James or the Potomac. In New England where the soil was poor and the advantages for trade unsurpassed, the farmer often sold his holdings in order to purchase shares in a merchantman. From the early days

[1] Weeden, *Economic and Social History*, I, 143-144, 167.
[2] New England was becoming maritime. "And I am confident," said Samuel Maverick in 1660, "there hath not in any place out of so small a number of People been raised so many able Seamen and Commanders as there hath been." Samuel Maverick, *A Briefe Description of New England and the Severall Townes Therein together with the Present Government Therein* (Boston, 1885), 27.

foreign commerce became an integral part of New England life and its importance grew with the years.

The Massachusetts traders found their way to New Amsterdam, to Chesapeake Bay, to England and to the West Indies. At first, however, they had little to offer which could tempt the Dutch settlers on the Hudson, the Virginia planters, or even the merchants of the mother country. Their chief exports were fish, furs and food stuffs. Furs the English purchased readily, but they stood in no need of provisions; their own fishermen supplied them with cod and herring in abundance. The industries of New England competed with, rather than supplemented, those of the old country, and the interchange of goods was unimportant.[1] A limited amount of linen, woolens, shoes, stockings, firearms, implements and other wares were imported from England, but in the early days three or four ships seem to have been adequate for the entire trade. To export beaver skins to New Amsterdam or corn and lumber to Virginia would have been like taking coals to Newcastle. It dawned upon the New Englanders that, to trade with these places, they must supply them with the commodities which they needed; and these could be had only in foreign lands. They had to become world merchants, not merely the carriers of goods to and from New England.

They found their greatest opportunity in the West Indies. The sugar planters welcomed the New England products, and gave in exchange commodities needed for the trade with England or the colonies on the American

[1] E. R. Johnson and others, *History of Domestic and Foreign Commerce of the United States* (Carnegie Inst., *Contribs. to Am. Econ. Hist.*, Wash., 1915), I, 31-32.

continent. The fish, provisions, lumber and horses of
Massachusetts and Rhode Island went in large consign-
ments to Barbados and Jamaica, to be traded for sugar,
molasses, indigo and cotton. In turn these goods were
often taken into Chesapeake Bay or to New Amsterdam,
and exchanged at a good profit for the fragrant Orinoco
or the pelts brought down by the Indians. The tobacco
and furs proved invaluable in stimulating the trade with
England and in bringing to New England the manufactured goods of the old country.

At the same time the Azores and the Catholic countries
of southern Europe offered a tempting market for fish.
Hundreds of thousands of dried cod and herring were
sent across the Atlantic each year in exchange for wines.
The voyage of the *Trial*, in 1642, is typical of the
course followed by many a Yankee merchantman. Taking on a cargo of fish and pipe staves, her commander,
Thomas Coytmore, made for Fayal in the Azores. Here
he found an "extraordinary good market," and had soon
disposed of his northern products for wine and sugar.
Turning his prow in the direction of the West Indies,
he arrived in good season at St. Christopher's, where he
traded part of his wine for cotton and tobacco and for
iron saved by the natives from wrecked vessels. Upon
returning to Boston he sold a part of his cargo for good
hard cash, reaping a rich reward "through the Lord's
blessing" and making wine, sugar and cotton "very
plentiful and cheap" in the thriving little port.[1]

So important had the West India trade become at
the time of the Restoration that Secretary Nicholas
stated that the New Englanders "maintain and supply
the plantations of Barbadoes and Jamaica." Vessels

[1] Weeden, *Economic and Social History*, I, 143-144.

sailed regularly from Boston, Salem, Ipswich, Newport, New London, New Haven and Windsor, making usually two voyages a year. Fish, pipe staves, lumber, provisions and horses were still the chief exports, while sugar, molasses, indigo and cotton were purchased in exchange. The trade was bringing riches to many a Yankee merchant and prosperity to New England. It was recognized that the trader was indispensable to the region; without him the shipbuilders would have lacked employment, the fishermen would have lacked a market. As for the farmers along the shore, they too were well aware of their dependence upon foreign commerce. "If the merchant trade be not kept on foot," it was said, "they fear greatly their corne and cattel will lye in their hands."[1]

Agriculture in New England, for a new country where land was plentiful, was intensive in character, following somewhat the custom of the English manor, though with no vestige of a manor lord's monarchical control. In fact the land system of the New England towns affected their life profoundly, the agrarian bond rivaling the ecclesiastical in holding the community together. First, a company of applicants to the legislature, perhaps a fragment of a church congregation, was granted a "plantation right," which authorized a settlement in a designated region just beyond the existing frontier line. If, in the passing of a year or two, the experiment proved successful, they were given a "town right," allowing them not only full representation in the general court but the common proprietorship of the land, which was at this time precisely bounded.

Through selected representatives the group then as-

[1] Weeden, *Economic and Social History*, I, 157.

signed the holdings to the individuals, small plots which they could till with their own hands: the home lot, varying in size from a little yard to some thirty acres, where the farmer had his dwelling, his cowshed and his garden, and the share of long strips scattered through the arable upland, where he might plant his Indian corn or rye. These he held in severalty; but the outlying meadows and pasture land, including woods and waste, were held in common and regulated by town ordinances. The allotments were made according to each family's ability or need, and in some towns the "planters," or "commoners," were classified into groups according to their wealth. At any rate the magistrate and the minister were given larger plots, oftentimes near the meeting house and green, and corresponding holdings in the arable land.[1] An industrious man with an unusually large family might find himself similarly favored with more acreage.

Thus, when the division of land was made in Salem in 1634, it was ordered that "the least family shall have 10 acres, but greater families may have more according to their number." In Dorchester every settler received "a great lot" of from sixteen to twenty acres. The first Watertown "dividént," containing about one thousand and ninety acres, was parceled out among thirty-one men in lots ranging from twenty to seventy acres; in both the second and third divisions the average

[1] Professor Krapp, working through seventeenth-century town records in preparation for his two volumes on The English Language in America, found certain words then apparently in common use but now obsolete: spong, spang or spung meant a meadow strip; rubbish meant land overgrown with brush; doak meant valley; folly probably meant a clump of trees; homestall was sometimes used for homestead; haysill for the haying season; and jade for a horse, whether good or bad. G. P. Krapp, The English Language in America (N. Y., 1925), I, 79-93, passim.

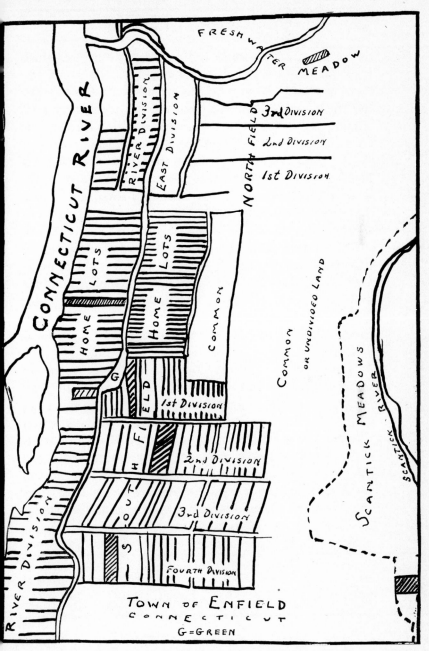

Land Division in a New England Town.

grant was about thirty-five acres; while in the fourth the lots varied from twenty to sixty acres. The typical holdings of one man in this place consisted of "a homestead of six acres, one acre and a half of planting ground, one acre of plowland in the further plain and nine acres of upland beyond the further plain." The holdings at Dorchester may be judged by a purchase made by David Sellecke, a "soape boyler," of William Hutchinson of Aquidneck and Edward Hutchinson of Boston. For the sum of eighty pounds the purchaser received "one Dwelling house situate in Dorchester," and "all outhouses and one garden or home lott thereunto belonging and sixteen acres of wood ground," together with an interest in some three acres of land on Dorchester Neck. The holdings were seldom more than a hundred acres in extent and usually much smaller.

The "arable" was generally divided into great fields, at least the north and the south, and the commoners within such limits might carry on their operations jointly, if they could come to an agreement as to what and when to plant. In such cases they were responsible as a group for keeping up the fence. But these attempts at coöperation were so unsatisfactory that in most towns the individual plots were soon enclosed, and the farmer went out each morning over an intricate system of paths and rights of way to till one or another of his little parcels.

Since little or nothing was known of the rotation of crops, about half the great fields were lying fallow at any one time, usually for several years, while grazing cattle waged hopeless contest with the thrifty weeds and underbrush. The cattle were herded by a town functionary, appointed for the purpose by the selectmen, and the milch cows were driven back and forth, morning and night, between the home plots and the pasture. Since they all ranged together on the common land—which in shore towns often included peninsulas especially convenient for preventing strays—no farmer could improve his stock by careful breeding or, probably, even keep it from deterioration. The first cattle brought into New England were Devonshires, but with neglect, hardship and miscellaneous crossings the breed deteriorated and, big-boned, rangy and tough, were known as the "red" or "native" stock.[1]

The tools, handmade of course, were of the rudest kind, chiefly broad hoes, mattocks and forks. The Pilgrims had no plow for twelve years, and they were scarce throughout the century. To the modern farmer they would seem of little use—great clumsy wooden contrivances with which four or six oxen and two men scratched the topsoil to a depth of three inches over an acre of land in a day. But in those needy days they were an asset indeed, and some towns paid a bounty to any resident who would thus equip himself and sell his services now and then to others. Oftentimes maize fields were not replowed for many years, the farmer poking the seed, along with a herring for fertilizer, into the side of the old hill. It is not surprising that the crops, according to our modern standard, were meager and uncertain.[2]

[1] William Wood in "New-England's Prospect [1634]," Prince Soc., Publs., I, 52, says that the four thousand people in 1634 had fifteen hundred cattle!

[2] On the New England farming and town system, see Thomas Lechford, "Note-Book," Am. Antiq. Soc., Trans., VII, 101; H. L. Osgood, The American Colonies in the Seventeenth Century (N. Y., 1904), I, chap. xi; Anne B. Maclear, Early New England Towns (Columbia Univ., Studies, XXIX, no. 1), chap. i; C. M. Andrews, River Towns of Con-

Yet the Northern farmer played a major part in the making of America. Upon his little parcels he expended his labor, seeking by intelligent management and hard work to compensate for the stubbornness of the glaciated soil and the shortness of the summer. It is safe to say that there was nothing in New England or in the Middle colonies quite comparable to the wasteful system in vogue in Maryland, Virginia and parts of the Carolinas. The Northern farming was not intensive when measured by European standards, for there was no need as yet to husband every tiny bit of soil; but it was farming which did require diligence and care, the kind of care which only the owner himself could give. The New England town system, under which land was granted to the town as a corporation, and by it conveyed to members for personal improvement, took that commodity largely out of the domain of speculation and prevented, at least during the seventeenth century, the building up of large land fortunes such as characterized New York.[1] It also made for a comparatively solid settlement and a definite frontier. Common possession of land and the problems involved in it gave the New England townsman a certain political training that was recognized as important in

necticut (Johns Hopkins Univ., *Studies*, VII, nos. 7-9), 5; P. W. Bidwell and J. I. Falconer, *History of Agriculture in the Northern United States, 1620-1860* (Carnegie Inst., *Contribs. to Am. Econ. Hist.*, Wash., 1925), 24, 35, 49-58, 107.

[1] The Jersey proprietors and William Penn, however, showed that it was possible to develop a colony with small holders by direct sale. See A. C. Myers, ed., *Narratives of Early Pennsylvania, West Jersey and Delaware, 1630-1707* (J. F. Jameson, ed., *Original Narratives of Early American History*, N. Y., 1906-), 219; and Samuel Smith, *History of the Colony of New Jersey* (Burlington, N. J., 1765), 512. The New England system itself was extended by settlers from that region to Long Island and part of Westchester County, New York, and to certain counties in New Jersey.

Revolutionary days. Land was a community concern, which made the records of transfer particularly important; to insure that it was held by proper citizens provision was early made that anyone desiring to sell his plots or his "undivided rights" must first offer them to the town and that no stranger should buy without the town's consent.[1]

The New England town strove to attain to some degree of economic independence and imported nothing which it could make for itself. The village shoemaker, the blacksmith, the currier, the carpenter, the cooper, the miller, the tanner, the weaver, the bricklayer, the mason, the wheelwright, the tailor, the glazier—all played important parts in the economy of the little community. It is interesting to note the extent to which the division of labor was carried, the town records disclosing such specialists as the "set work cooper" and the "clapboard-dryver." Many times an artisan was also a farmer; but in most cases, versatile though he might be, he gave most of his attention to his trade. So important to the town were these workers that the authorities often sought them out and offered them special inducements to settle in their midst. In 1658 Haverhill presented a house and land valued at twenty pounds to a blacksmith, John Johnson, in return for his promise to follow his trade there for seven years. In 1655, Windsor, Connecticut, gave a currier a house, land, and "something for a shop, to be to him and his heirs, if he lives and dies with us, and affords us the use of his trade." [2]

The industry of the seventeenth century is remarkable

[1] J. H. Beale, jr., *The Origin of the System of Recording Deeds in America* (Boston, 1907), 7.

[2] Weeden, *Economic and Social History*, I, 81.

for two things: its diversification and the high type of labor which it required. The region never became dependent upon one staple crop or upon one all-important industry. Virginia was the land of tobacco planters, where the bricklayer laid down his trowel and the shipbuilder his saw to devote themselves to the needs of the Indian plant. In New England, living side by side were men of widely divergent occupations—merchants, fishermen, farmers, shipbuilders, artisans, sailors. Upon the Hingham board of selectmen we find Daniel Lincoln, "seaman;" James Hersey, "husbandman;" William Hersey, "farmer;" John Fearing, "weaver;" Matthew Cushing, "wheelwright;" Jeremiah Beal, "blacksmith." [1] New England was by no means cut off from the rest of the world—it did not enjoy complete economic independence, for her ships and her products found their way into many distant lands; but the diversification of industry added strength to the economic system and made for a vigorous, wholesome society.

Even more important was the fact that in all these various industries the fundamental need was for skilled, not for unskilled labor. In the tobacco fields the African slave, when he could be secured, answered every requirement; in New England he proved unfit for any save a few unessential tasks. Massachusetts and Rhode Island had a better opportunity to secure Negro slaves than the Chesapeake Bay colonies, for their own traders were not slow to take advantage of the opening afforded to independent merchants by the activities of the Royal African Company. So early as 1676 we find them starting out for Guinea and Madagascar with masts and yards and

[1] George Lincoln and others, *History of the Town of Hingham* (Hingham, 1893).

returning with cargoes of slaves. But there were Negroes in New England many years prior to this date. Mr. Chester of Hartford died in 1650, leaving "a neager Maide," valued at £25. The inventory of the estate of Robert Keayne, filed in 1657, mentions "2 negros and a negro child" worth £30; while in 1661 John Hanniford left a Negro boy, valued at £20. The farmers failed to turn the Negroes into "handy men," and slavery never secured a firm foothold in New England. It proved quite practicable to teach the savage African the one task which was required of him in the Southern colonies, that of tending the sugar or the tobacco crops; but for the hundred and one things that the New England farm hand had to do, he was entirely inadequate.

Nor could the slave traders find purchasers among the shipbuilders. The construction of sailing vessels was then, as it is now, a matter of the strictest nicety. The artisans who laid down the keels of the New England merchantmen, who fashioned their sides and fitted them with masts and sails, had of necessity to be the very highest type of workmen. As for the men who made their living by catching fish, they too had nothing to fear from the competition of the blacks. The native African, fresh from his tropical home, was unable to withstand the hardships of this occupation. Even as a sailor he failed. In rare cases the ship captains did make use of Negroes, but only for the simpler tasks. The New England sailor, who had to know every brace and stay, every spar and every sail of his vessel, could not be discarded in favor of this dusky barbarian. In other words, the industry of New England, tap it where you would, was too sound to gain by a transfer from the basis of free, intelligent labor to a basis of unintelligent, slave labor. There existed in the region no especial prejudice against slavery, and in the closing decades of the seventeenth century slaves were available in numbers; but the institution gained no headway.

Nor could the custom of bringing poor persons from England and binding them to work out their passage supply New England with the needed labor. Indentured servants, although not uncommon, were far less numerous than in Virginia and Maryland. One could kidnap a man at random in the alleys of London and be sure of a ready sale for him in the South, no matter how untrained, or whatever his antecedents. But in New England the case was different. The newcomer had to have some experience as a seaman before he could be disposed of to a shipowner; unless he was a skilled ship carpenter, the master builders would not want him; unless a blacksmith or shoemaker or cooper or weaver or bricklayer, he would not be desirable as a helper to any of these artisans.

Skilled men, even in England, were by no means financially helpless. They usually could pay their own fare across the ocean and so start life in the New World as freemen. Despite this fact we know that many youths were brought to New England to become apprentices. Lechford cites a case in which a worker "did retayne one Servant Ambrose Sutton to serve in the trade of Carpentry" for the space of five years. Among the lists of runaway servants we find tailors, clothiers, house carpenters and other skilled workers. In September, 1639, John Bourne offered to bind himself to Nehemiah Bourne "for 6 yeares if he will undertake his coming from England to instruct him in the trade of shipwright." In the same year Richard Gridley turned over

his servant William Boreman to William Townsend
of Boston, to be "Apprentice of the crafte of thatcher."

On the other hand, in securing promising apprentices
it was not necessary for artisans to look all the way across
the Atlantic. If the weaver, mason or wheelwright had
no son of his own to succeed him in his trade, he could
easily secure a youth from among the neighboring families. John Chandler, a Boston shoemaker, placed his
son John as "Apprentice unto William Webb, of Rox-
berry," for seven years, "to be instructed in the trade of
Baker and to have meate & clothes, washing and wring-
ing, and in the end of the term double apparell & 20s."
We find John Crabtree, a Boston joiner, agreeing to take
John Greene, the son of Solomon Greene of Hadley, as
his apprentice for seven years, after which he was to
become his journeyman for a year at a salary of eight
pounds. Samuel Cole of Boston placed his grandchild,
John Cole, as apprentice for seven years to John Mylam,
a cooper.

It was more usual, however, for the son to follow in
his father's steps. There are innumerable cases in colonial New England in which one trade persisted in the
same family for generations. When there were several
sons in one family, the father, after taking one as his own
assistant, usually put the others out as apprentices.
Among the sons of Samuel Lincoln of Hingham were
Samuel, the carpenter; Daniel, the planter; Mordecai, the
blacksmith; and Thomas, the tailor. John Tower, of
Hingham, had five sons who attained to maturity, of
whom John probably became a farmer, Ibrook and
Samuel were coopers, while Jeremiah and Benjamin were
weavers. When parents neglected to teach their children
to read, public officers bound them out as apprentices

so that they might receive the rudiments of an education. The officers also found places for the children of the poor.[1]

The limited scope of the trade between New England and the mother country also retarded the immigration of indentured servants. Moreover, most of the people who came to Massachusetts under terms of indenture seem to have been used as domestics. We know that the early settlers brought household servants with them, and the demand for this kind of labor was constant throughout the period. John Josselyn, in the account of his second voyage to New England, declared that the people were "well accommodated with Servants," of whom some were English, others Negroes. On the other hand, a correspondent writing in 1660 advises well-to-do persons who expected to migrate to New England to bring their own servants, as there were few available there and not to be hired for any length of time. The shortness of the term of indenture, together with the prevailing high cost of labor, tends to confirm the latter statement rather than the former. Even so prominent a man as Cotton Mather found the problem of securing domestics a difficult one, and made it "an Article of special Supplications before the Lord, that He would send a good Servant into" his family.[2] John Wheelwright sent all the way to County Glamorgan for a servant, and contracted to pay not only her passage but wages of three pounds sterling a year. John Beal, of Hingham, when he came to New England in 1638, brought two servants with him.

[1] R. F. Seybolt, *Apprenticeship and Apprenticeship Education in Colonial New England and New York* (Teachers Col., Columbia Univ., Contribs. to Educ., LXXXV), 34-41.

[2] Cotton Mather, *Diary* (Mass. Hist. Soc., *Colls.*, ser. 7, VII-VIII). II, 112.

In New England as elsewhere in America, a bright future opened to servants of ambition and industry. Two decades after the founding of Boston, Edward Johnson states that "there are many hundreds of laboring men who had not enough to bring them over, yet now worth scores, and some hundreds of pounds." John Winthrop was much annoyed because his former servant Richard, immediately after securing his freedom, took very high wages in ready money only, and in a little more than a year "had scraped together about £25, and then returned with his prey to England." Most of the freedmen remained to make the most of their opportunities for advancement, many becoming landowners and some winning positions of honor and influence. Although servants who had just finished their terms were excluded from participation in the divisions of land in some towns, in many others they shared equally with those who had come over as freemen. In 1662, Hadley granted three men, at least one of whom had been a servant, home lots and £40 allotments in the meadow.

The indentures usually specified that the master should furnish his servant, at the end of his service, with at least a meager equipment for starting life as a freeman. Clothing, provisions, guns and even domestic animals were among the articles usually demanded. Dermodt Matthew, a servant of George Strange, stated that his indenture called for wages of four pounds sterling a year, "a pigg to be payd at every years end and in the end of the term to have a Convenient lott," together with "thre suits of apparel & six shirts." William Boreman, for serving Richard Gridley of Boston, was to receive "meat, drink, lodging & apparell, & double apparell at the end of the term." Isaac Cullimore agreed to give his apprentice, besides his board and keep, a ewe kid at the end of four years and five at the end of his term, besides "double apperell." Often masters, out of a sense of duty or of kindliness, would give assistance to the servant beyond the specifications of the indenture. Benjamin Bates in his will, dated 1678, made especial provision for his "servant Nathaniel Wilson," while Joshua Beal left property to Ruth Gannett "that was formerly my servant."

Of the so-called criminal class of servants who were swept over to America in the seventeenth-century tide of migration, New England received her share. President Timothy Dwight, of Yale, went so far as to state that the early settlers brought with them "a collection of peasants and servants remarkable for their profligacy." Certain it is that some of the freedmen neglected their opportunities and fell into a life of crime and idleness. In 1657, Boston gave notice that every master must see to it that his servant, upon attaining freedom, secure employment and not, through idleness or other cause, become a burden upon the town. An examination of the criminal records in the various New England colonies reveals the fact that the servant class was responsible for a very large proportion of the worst offenses. A New England historian, after following the lives of many persons of this class, found proof that they provided most of the early criminals. "The fittest seemed to survive," he adds. "Others of the baser sort perished." [1]

The use of indentured labor on farms seems to have been the exception rather than the rule. The cost of servants was too high, the requirements of the task too exacting, the available supply too limited. Upon the

[1] W. DeL. Love, *The Colonial History of Hartford* (Hartford, 1914).

few larger estates, on the other hand, labor of some kind
had to be secured, or a part of the land would lie idle.
We find Edmund James, a planter of Watertown, paying
eight pounds sterling for the passage of a servant and
agreeing to furnish food, clothing and lodging, and to
give him at the end of seven years of work "double
apparell & five pounds in money." It is almost certain
that this man acted as a farm laborer. In 1639 a farmer
of Piscataqua was in search of Richard Price, his servant,
who had escaped while his term still had four years to
run. In 1640 Zaccheus Gould of Lynn complained to
the governor and assistants, on behalf of himself and
other husbandmen, that their servants were often
"drawne from their worke to trayne in seed time, hay
tyme & harvest," and petitioned that they might be excused from military service during these seasons.[1] On
the whole, however, the average New England farmer
must have depended entirely upon his own labor or that
of his sons.

New England industry, then, in all its various forms
was based, not on the work of slaves or servants, but
upon free labor. It was this all-important fact, even
more than the rigid moral code prescribed by the clergy,
which made the social fabric sound; it was this, even
more than the inherited ideals of liberty, which rendered
it democratic. The small farmer, the skilled artisan, the
fisherman and the sailor were the backbone of the region,
and in the end nothing could deprive them of the influence which came from that fact. The magistrates and
the clergy might extend the franchise to them sparingly,
they might withhold certain social privileges, but there

[1] Thomas Lechford, "Note-Book," Am. Antiq. Soc., *Trans.*, VII, 64,
322.

is obvious at all times a grudging recognition of their power.

At first the aristocracy were much alarmed at the excessive wages demanded by artisans, or the high prices which they charged for their products. If these men could earn a living hardly inferior to that of many gentlemen, there would be a general leveling of society. Over and over again the magistrates tried to set a maximum wage for all kinds of workers. In 1633 a Massachusetts statute limited master carpenters, sawyers, masons, bricklayers, tilers, mowers and other skilled workers to two shillings a day when "boarding themselves," or fourteen pence when "dyett" was provided. All were to work the whole day, with a reasonable time for "foode and rest," while idleness, so abhorrent to Calvinists, was sternly punished.[1] In 1635 several men were fined for accepting two shillings sixpence per day. But it was obviously impossible to enforce the law. There were too many opportunities for advancement in this new country, and the demand for labor was too great for the artisan to be held down by restrictive legislation. If the blacksmith were limited to two shillings a day, he would desert his bellows to become a farmer in some other town. The law of 1633 was repealed after two years, although individual towns were still permitted to fix wages. During the economic crisis of 1640 the general court attempted to make wages conform to the increased purchasing power of money; but they met with scant success. It was economic law that determined the wages of these workers, and economic law could not be upset by the Massachusetts legislators.

In fact the New England artisan attained a degree of

[1] Weeden, *Economic and Social History*, I, 83.

well-being unheard-of in England and rare in all ages. We find Christopher Stanley, a tailor, purchasing "one house & garden thereto belonging, lying in Boston betweene the houses of Richard Bellingham, Esqr., on the eastparte & the house of Thomas Buttolph on the west, for £50 in hand." [1]   Edward Wood, baker, could afford to buy a dwelling house in Charlestown for £39 10s.   Andrew Lane, hatter and farmer, left an estate appraised at £235 3s., which included dwelling house, barn, salt meadow and other lands, four oxen, four cows, two yearlings, etc. [2]   The property of John Tower, "boatman and weaver," was valued at £171 12s. 10d. [3] In the affairs of the town the farmer and the artisan were alike prominent.   We find them serving as selectmen, constables and as officers in the militia.   These men held a social rank next to that of the clergymen, squires, merchants and men of substance, a rank carrying privileges which they guarded with jealous solicitude.

As for the upper class, in the early days its bounds were narrow and clearly drawn.   To it belonged only the ministers and the small group of Puritan gentlemen who had been their backers in the pilgrimage to America and who coöperated with them fully after reaching New England.   These men opposed democracy in any form, for they believed that the state should be based upon an aristocracy of God's elect.   It was from this class almost exclusively that the early magistrates were drawn.   But with the beginnings of trade, merchants began to come to New England, men often not fully in sympathy with

[1] Thomas Lechford, "Note-Book," 147.
[2] Lincoln and others, *History of Hingham*, II, 411.
[3] *Ibid.*, III, 254.

the old order, yet whose wealth and influence could not be ignored. That the merchant class was forming even in the first decade after the Massachusetts Bay settlement we gather from Thomas Lechford's *Note-Book*. Among the traders were William Tyng,[1] John Cogan, Richard Parker and John Pollard. Soon after the founding of New Haven a number of wealthy and experienced merchants settled there and erected "fair and stately homes." To Rhode Island came several families of rich Jews from the Netherlands, bringing with them their goods and their unsurpassed mercantile skill. Typical of the early traders was John Holland, who settled at Dorchester. This man, through his various ventures in fitting out vessels for fishing and trading, accumulated a fortune estimated at his death in 1652 at £4,000.

Even more successful was John Hull, a pious man whose early training among the English goldsmiths gave him a knowledge of banking and finance which made him a commanding figure in New England. Capitalist and merchant, his ventures ran into thousands of pounds sterling, and were almost invariably profitable.[2] During the Restoration period the commerce of New England grew apace and the merchants prospered. When Edward Randolph visited the region in 1676 he reported that in Massachusetts alone there were about thirty merchants worth from £10,000 to £20,000. "Most have considerable estates and very great trade," he added.[3] That

[1] In 1639 Tyng purchased property from William Coddington worth £1,300. Thomas Lechford, "Note-Book," 164.

[2] It was he who set up the mint for Massachusetts in 1652 and coined pine-tree shillings—an example of the colony's arrogance. John Hull, "Diaries," Am. Antiq. Soc., *Trans.*, III, 141 ff., 145-146.

[3] Thomas Hutchinson, *Collection of Original Papers Relative to the History of Massachusetts Bay* (Boston, 1769), II, 219.

Randolph did not greatly exaggerate we know from the inventories that have come down to us. Both James Richards of Hartford and Thomas Brattle of Boston left estates valued at £8,000. Men of this type took their position as leaders in the community, even though the clergy might frown upon them or thunder against them from the pulpit.

Thus it will be seen that New England society in the seventeenth century was divided into several groups with clearly defined limits.[1] At the top was an ill-assorted aristocracy of religion, wealth and rank—an aristocracy which included the clergyman, whose power rested upon his moral influence and his control of the franchise; the gentleman, who brought his rank with him from England; and the merchant, who won recognition through the vitally important part he played in the economic upbuilding of the country. Next in rank were the skilled artisan and the freeholder, who did most of the work and were responsible for most of the economic output. Sturdy, intelligent, hard-working folk they were, priding themselves on the title of "Goodman" or "Goodwife" and jealous of the social distinctions due their rank. Constituting the greatest element of strength in New England society, not only did many of them enjoy the franchise but they furnished most of the town officials. Next beneath them was the unskilled laborer—the wage-earner or the journeyman—who not only had no title but who was usually addressed by his Christian name alone. The indentured servants formed a fourth

[1] The graduates of Harvard and Yale, far into the eighteenth century, were listed not in alphabetical order but according to their "dignities." F. B. Dexter, "On Some Social Distinctions at Harvard and Yale," Am. Antiq. Soc., *Proceeds*, IX, 50; and W. G. Brooks, "The Rank of Students in Harvard College," Mass. Hist. Soc., *Proceeds.*, IX, 252-254.

class, and the slaves, whether Indian or Negro, a fifth. Men of the three lowest classes were often admitted to the church society, but seldom to political citizenship, and the line of social distinction was sharply drawn in each case.

These various ranks by no means existed only as an arbitrary valuation set on men by their neighbors, but carried with them certain well-defined legal privileges. The gentleman was permitted to adorn himself with articles of dress forbidden to the goodman; the goodman wore others which were withheld from the day laborer or the servant. Lace, silver and gold thread, slashed sleeves, embroidered caps, "bands & rayles," gold and silver girdles, hat bands, belts, ruffs were forbidden to all save the upper class. In 1653 two women were presented at Newbury for wearing silk hoods and scarfs, but they were discharged upon presenting proof that their husbands in each case were worth £200. John Hutchins's wife, in a similar case, was discharged "upon testimony of her being brought up above the ordinary ranke." In 1676 Connecticut passed a law that any person wearing "gold or silver lace, or gold or silver buttons, silk ribbons or other superflous trimmings" was to be taxed as though in possession of property valued at £150. But the families of magistrates and commissioned officers in the militia were excepted, together with "such whose quality and estate have been above the ordinary degree though now decayed." Even before this date we find thirty women of various towns in Connecticut presented as "persons of small estate who used to wear silk." Again in 1676 thirty-eight women and thirty young men were called to account by the magistrates for "wearing silk, some for long hair and other extravagancies." [1]

These class distinctions were also carried into the allotment of pews in the church. In Dedham the elders assigned seats in accordance with the amount of taxes paid by the members; but in most towns it was rank as well as property which determined precedence. In New Haven no seats were assigned to any beneath the rank of goodman, while "four backer seats in the gallery" were set aside for young men.[2] At Saco, the people were divided into seven classes and were seated accordingly by a vote of the town. Woburn had a committee of five to assign seats to the congregation in respect to "estate, office and age," while the committeemen themselves were seated by another committee of two. Stamford voted to assign pews to its people according to "dignity, age and estate." Persons who ignored these allotments by intruding upon the pews of their neighbors were often heavily fined.[3]

An interesting illustration of the sentiment in favor of rigid class distinctions is furnished by Swansea. When the town was laid out in 1667 the committee appointed to carry out the work arbitrarily divided the inhabitants into three ranks. Not only did this action receive the sanction of the townsmen, but in after years committees were appointed to perpetuate these distinctions, or to promote and degrade persons from one rank to another.

[1] Weeden, *Economic and Social History*, I, 226-227, 288-289; *Mass. Col. Laws*, for 1651; Alice M. Earle, *Customs and Fashions in Old New England* (N. Y., 1893), 316-317.

[2] Weeden, *Economic and Social History*, I, 75.

[3] In addition to Weeden, who has many citations in I, 280, the reader should consult the interesting chapter on "Seating the Meeting," in Alice M. Earle, *The Sabbath in Puritan New England* (7th edn., N. Y., 1893).

The same spirit appears in the matter of punishments, it being a fairly well-fixed principle that all gentlemen should be exempt from corporal punishment. In 1631, when Mr. Josias Plaistowe was convicted of stealing corn from the Indians, the court merely imposed a fine and directed that thenceforth he "should be called by the name of Josias, and not Mr. as formerlie." On the other hand his servants who had assisted in the theft were severely flogged. Though the upper classes usually escaped the whipping post and the pillory, in the matter of fines they suffered more than their humbler neighbors. At Swansea, for certain offenses the first class had to pay £3 12s., the second £2 8s., and the third only £1 4s.

It must not be imagined from these distinctions that colonial New England was essentially aristocratic. The great contrasts in the life of the people, on the one hand a privileged class of wealth and power, on the other a fairly large group of servants, slaves and unskilled laborers, form but a part and not the most important part of the picture. Overshadowing all else was the great middle class, composed of small freeholders and skilled artisans. Upon this class the economic and social fabric was based. Sooner or later social distinctions disappear when they have no foundation in economic conditions, and colonial New England economically was democratic. Much has been said about the influence upon American life of the New England conscience, much concerning her contributions to political freedom, but her most valuable legacy has been overlooked or minimized—her essentially sound economic and social system, her democracy of labor.

The New Englander, unlike his cousins of Virginia and Maryland, was himself compelled to produce most of the manufactured articles essential to his daily life. The tobacco colonies found it profitable to devote their energies almost exclusively to their one great staple crop, receiving from England in exchange all kinds of fabricated goods. But since New England had little which the mother country desired, the people of that region could not make extensive purchases of English goods. Their export of furs, naval stores and fish oil gave them but a meager credit in London and Bristol upon which to draw for farm implements, clothing, glass, leather, gunpowder and other needed articles. And so, with characteristic energy and resourcefulness, they set to work to supply their own wants.

So early as 1640 both Massachusetts and Connecticut took steps to encourage the planting of flax and the manufacture of linen, and in the course of time many households in both colonies were actively engaged in this industry. The work was excessively tedious and difficult. After the seeds had been sown, and the graceful plants with their pretty drooping blue flowers had grown to full size, the stalks were pulled up by the roots, dried in the sun or by fires,[1] drawn through a heavy comb to break off the seed bolls, bundled, rotted in water, dried again, pounded in the ponderous flax break, scutched with the swingling block and knife, drawn through the hatchel, placed on the clock reel and spun into long, even threads, bleached in water, seethed, rinsed and dried. The yarn was now ready for the loom. Usually the weaving was done at home, in the attic or shed loft, but at times this part of the work was left to

[1] On a number of occasions houses were accidentally burned down during this operation. See John Winthrop, *History of New England* (J. K. Hosmer, ed., in J. F. Jameson, ed., *Original Narratives of Early American History*, N. Y., 1906-), II, 88.

professional weavers. Weaving was also a very complicated procedure, and there now followed the winding of the quill and bobbin, the "warping" and "beaming," then "drawing" or "entering." [1]

The Massachusetts settlers early awoke to the advisability of raising sheep and making woolen cloth. Sheep were permitted to graze on the commons, they were carefully protected from dogs, and it was forbidden to export them. Spinners were drafted, one from each family, into groups of ten persons each, under a separate director, and required to produce a certain weight of thread. In 1642 there were a thousand sheep in Massachusetts, and in a few years the number had tripled.[2] Somewhat later Newport had a wool market to which came buyers from all parts of New England.[3] Before the end of the third quarter of the century New England was exporting wool to France in exchange for linens and to Spain in exchange for wines.[4]

The Puritan spinners were at no loss to secure many and varied dyes for their wool. Indigo from Barbados was used, by the end of the century, for all shades of blue; the bark of the hickory or the red oak provided pretty browns and yellows; madder and logwood gave reds and blues; the goldenrod, mixed with indigo and

[1] Alice M. Earle, *Home Life in Colonial Days* (N. Y., 1898), 166-251.

[2] C. W. Wright, *Wool Growing and the Tariff* (Boston, 1910), 3.

[3] Sylvester Judd, *History of Hadley, Mass.* (Springfield, Mass., 1905), 372.

[4] The growth of the wool manufacture in New England, doubtless much exaggerated by report, soon worried the government in London: "Contrary to the policies and restrictions heretofore observed they have increased a stock of sheep to nearly one hundred thousand, whereby not only the nation and the manufacturers thereof are become less necessary to them, but they may soon supply the Dutch in New Netherland." *Cal. of State Papers, Colon., Am. and W. I., 1661-1668,* 25.

alum, gave a beautiful green; from the juice of the poke-
berry was secured a rich crimson, from the iris a delicate
purple, from sassafras orange, from fustic and copperas
yellow.   The art of wool spinning, an art in which the
women of that day had to be adept, required great dex-
terity and skill.   The spinner stood beside her wheel,
holding in her left hand a long slender roll of carded
wool.   With her right hand she wound the end fibers on
the point of the spindle, started the wheel with a wooden
peg and stepped back quickly three steps, holding high
the long yarn.   At the right moment she came forward
again to let the yarn wind on the spindle.   This operation she repeated over and over again, standing hour
after hour, until all the yarn had been spun.   The wool
industry often kept busy an entire New England family.
On winter evenings one might have seen by the light of
the roaring log fire, the pine torch [1] or the flicker-
ing candle, the grandmother carding the wool, the
mother spinning the rolls of yarn, the older children
mixing the dye in the indigo tub, the sons whittling
hand reels and loom spools, the father busy at the
loom.[2]   By the middle of the century some were "making Cloath and Ruggs of Cotton Wool," from raw cotton brought up from the West Indies.[3]

When at last the work of these patient household
manufacturers was done, the cloth had still to be sub-

[1] Francis Higginson, *New England's Plantation* (London, 1630), reprinted in Alexander Young, *Chronicles of the First Planters of the
Colony of Massachusetts Bay . . .* (Boston, 1846), 254, speaks of
"the wood of the pine tree cloven into little slices something thin, which
are so free of the moisture of turpentine and pitch, that they burn as a
clear torch."
[2] Earle, *Home Life in Colonial Days*, 196-198.
[3] Maverick, *A Briefe Description of New England*, 11; and Winthrop,
History of New England, II, 73.

jected to the process of fulling to remove greasy matter and to secure a more compact texture. For fulling the cloth mills were necessary. In 1643 twenty families from Yorkshire skilled in the making of cloth came to New England bringing with them fulling machinery, and set up a mill at Rowley. So successful were they that various towns followed suit, and soon fulling mills were to be found at Roxbury, Dorchester, Watertown, Andover, Ipswich, Salem, Barnstable, Newbury, Stamford and elsewhere.[1]

Side by side with the fulling mills, at times even under the same roof, were built mills for grinding corn. Tiny, one-story, wooden structures they were, but they performed a service of great value to the colonists. Everywhere the traveler in New England stumbled upon them —beside the picturesque stream, whose waters had been harnessed to the wheel; on some exposed hill, where the winds kept the great vanes in constant motion; beside the ocean inlet, where the tides were forced to do duty as motive power.

In the earliest days, before these mills were constructed, the settlers had ground their corn in primitive mortars, hollowed from a block of wood or the stump of a tree, after the Indian manner. The pestle, which was also of wood, was often fastened to the top of a slender sapling, which aided in lifting it after each blow. These sweep or mortar mills, as they were called, were superseded by hand mills in many localities, which in turn gave way to the more powerful and practical mills run by water, wind or tide. It is said that the Indians at first had a superstitious dread of the windmills, and looked with wonder at "their long arms and great teeth

[1] Weeden, *Economic and Social History*, I, 306, 394.

biting the corn in pieces." The first water mill was erected in 1633 at Dorchester. It was antedated by a windmill, however, for it is stated that in 1632 a mill which had been set up near Boston was taken down and reassembled on a hill in the north part of the town.[1]

Water, tides and wind were also used in running the early sawmills. The first of these establishments, so vital to the shipbuilding and timber-export industries, was constructed by Mason's settlers near Piscataqua, but they soon became general throughout New England. They were usually the crudest of wooden sheds, built on the banks of navigable streams and supplied with slow-moving but noisy vertical saws. At first they were usually placed at the fall line, but as the frontier moved inland, the mills followed up stream. When the neighboring woods became denuded of trees, it was the custom to fell the timber above, and float the logs down with the current.[2]

Although the New England woods failed to supply the mother country with all the naval stores of which Hakluyt and others had dreamed, it did produce one article which the royal navy accepted gratefully—the best masts in the world. The tall straight white pines were eagerly sought out and marked with the king's broad arrow. Since the most desirable were often found miles from navigable water, it was a costly and difficult undertaking to haul them through the woods to the landing place. Judge Sewall, in 1687, noted with wonder thirty-two oxen tugging and straining to drag

[1] The customary charge for milling was one fourteenth part. See D. R. Fox, *Caleb Heathcote* (N. Y., 1926), 56.
[2] R. G. Albion, *Forests and Sea Power* (*Harvard Econ. Studies*, XXIX), 233.

along a huge trunk twenty-eight inches in diameter.[1]
But the reward was proportionate to the task.   In
1644 Sir William Warren offered to sell New England masts, thirty-three to thirty-five inches in diameter,
at from £95 to £115 each.   Some especially large
trunks, which were presented to the king by Massachusetts, cost in all no less than £1,600.   Typical
of the mast trade was the cargo of the *America*, which
sailed from Piscataqua in 1692 with 18 masts, 9
bowsprits, 13 yards, 11,400 feet of oars, 25,000
staves and 46 spars.   Generally speaking, only the
large masts were bought from the colonies; the small
and middle sizes were still imported from the Baltic
countries.[2]

Hardly had the Puritans established their settlements
on the shores of Massachusetts Bay when they set about
the manufacture of salt.   Their important fish industry
made it necessary to have this commodity in large quantities, and the cost of importing it from Europe or the
West Indies was heavy.   John Winthrop, jr., made repeated efforts to produce salt by evaporating sea water,
and others imitated him from time to time.   But the venture apparently met with little success.   The fishermen
of Marblehead and Ipswich throughout the century were
forced to prepare their fish chiefly with salt brought from
other lands.   In 1663, when the staple act was passed
forbidding the direct shipment to the colonies of certain
enumerated foreign goods, salt for the New England
fisheries was omitted from the list, on the ground that to

[1] Samuel Sewall, *Diary* (Mass. Hist. Soc., *Colls.*, ser. 5, V-VII),
I, 189.
[2] Eleanor L. Lord, *Industrial Experiments in the British Colonies of
North America* (Johns Hopkins Univ., *Studies*, extra vol. xvii), 71.

exclude foreign salt would ruin this important industry.[1]

Just as salt was vital to the fishermen, so was iron urgently needed in other industries. The shipbuilder used it for anchors and bolts, the carpenter for hinges and nails, the farmer for plow tips, scythes, pots, andirons and a hundred other articles. Yet Spanish and Swedish bar iron was exceedingly costly, while the English product was hardly to be had at all. Faced with this problem, the settlers made earnest efforts to utilize the bog iron found close at hand in ponds, swamps and meadow lands. Again the enterprising John Winthrop, jr., came to the rescue, journeying all the way to England with specimens of ore from the Saugus ponds, organizing a company to finance the enterprise, and sending back many skilled workmen and much material. To encourage this project the general court gave the company the privilege of working waste places and of constructing dams and watercourses, freed it of all taxes and excused the workmen from muster duty. The furnace was set up at Lynn. By 1648 it was running eight tons a week, and, together with works in other parts of New England, such as Taunton, was providing much of the iron used in the colonies. But so uncertain was the output, so unsatisfactory the quality, that the local manufacturers were forced to continue the importation of the costly foreign iron. There was virtually no technical improvement in the American manufacture of iron until the Revolution.[2]

[1] G. L. Beer, *The Old Colonial System* (N. Y., 1912), I, 78.
[2] V. S. Clark, *History of Manufactures in the United States* (Carnegie Inst., *Contribs. to Am. Econ. Hist.*, Wash., 1916), 170; Maverick, *A Briefe Description of New England*, 22.

The difficulty in securing iron forced the New England to make exceptional use of wood. Plows were fashioned of wood with perhaps a tip of iron, harrows were of wood, cart wheels often were wholly of wood; shovels, flails, rakes, barrel hoops, were of wood; many household utensils—churns, buckets, tubs, piggins, rundlets, firkins, trays, spoons—were of wood. Occasionally these articles were purchased of merchants, but more often they were fashioned laboriously by various members of the family, the "whittling Yankees." [1] The greatest ingenuity was displayed in utilizing natural materials. Gourd shells were converted into dippers, bottles and bowls; clam shells into spoons; crooked saplings into sled runners and goose yokes; sections of birch trees into excellent brooms; oak logs into salt mortars, pig troughs and large bread bowls; smaller pieces of wood into cheese hoops and cheese presses; elm rind into chair seats and baskets. It was such work as this which made the colonists practical, keen-witted, self-reliant and adaptable. Life on the fringe of civilization gave little opportunity for proficiency in the arts and sciences, but it offered ever interesting courses in the great school of nature.

The home life of the average New England rural family was wholesome, practical, arduous. With the first streaks of gray in the east the father was out of bed, to strike a light with flint and steel and kindle a fire in the huge stone fireplace. As the others arose, they took their turns at the wooden basin, perhaps to break the icy surface before washing their faces and hands. The father and older sons then went to the cow yard to milk the cows, while the younger boys fed the hogs. In the mean-

[1] H. E. Nourse, *History of Harvard, Mass.* (Harvard, Mass., 1894), 77.

time, the mother and daughters had been cooking the porridge, and when the reading of the Scriptures and the family prayers had been concluded, breakfast was ready. The family gathered around the long, narrow table-board, perhaps by the light of candles, and reverently gave thanks. After the porridge had been dealt out in small wooden bowls, all sat down to enjoy this early repast.

The father and sons then went forth to the fields for the day's work. If it was spring or early summer, they armed themselves with hoes and brought out the wooden plow, drawn by slow-moving oxen; if late summer or autumn, they carried scythes and two-pronged pitch-forks. While they labored, breaking the soil or mowing wheat or stacking corn stalks, the women of the family were busy at home. One cleared the table and washed the dishes, one labored at the cheese press, one busied herself at the washtub, another at the soap kettle,[1] another prepared the midday meal. The cooking was done over the log fire in the huge fireplace. Here the skillful cook boiled her Indian corn and kidney beans, flavored with a slice of salt venison; here she made her pumpkin pie, slicing the ripe fruit, boiling it in a little water, and adding butter, vinegar and spice.

At noon the table board was set for dinner—the high salt cellar at the center, then clumsy wooden trenchers, round pewter platters heaped with delicious succotash, a great wooden noggin, several wooden tankards, a number of pewter spoons, but no forks, no glassware, no

[1] The colonists used not only butcher's fat in making soft soap, but also oil from the dead whales washed up so frequently on the shores of Long Island and Cape Cod. See Maverick, *A Briefe Description of New England*, 21; Judd, *Hadley, Mass.*, 378; and R. H. Gabriel, *The Evolution of Long Island* (*Yale Hist. Publs., Miscellany*, IX), chap. v.

china, no covered dishes, no saucers. At the summons of the horn the workers hurried in from the fields, and the family seated themselves on long narrow benches on each side of the table to help themselves to the plain but bountiful food.

The midday meal over, the father and the boys returned to the fields for five more hours of labor, while the mother and daughters resumed their separate tasks. As evening approached the hogs and sheep were driven into their enclosures near the barn, where the faithful dog could guard them throughout the night. Supper was simple—for the children milk porridge or hasty pudding, for the father and mother a slice of cold pork, brown bread and a mug of beer. Once more the Scriptures were read, while the family sat with bowed heads. By eight o'clock all were in bed.

The distinctive feature of New England life was the town; for the family whose daily life we have just been following was closely flanked by neighbors. Had Sir William Berkeley visited the colonies east of the Hudson, he would have been deeply interested in this system of community organization, which differed so greatly from that of the South. He would have thought it strange that men who made agriculture their chief pursuit should live in little villages and not in the midst of the fields they cultivated. The villages themselves would have held his attention, with their boarded houses, some having projecting second stories with turned pendants at the corners, some with steep shingled roofs sloping nearly to the ground in the rear, all fronting on the street; the neat back lots, the outbuildings, the fences, the gardens, the orchards. Here he would have seen the meetinghouse, its pointed roof and open belfry standing out above the other houses; here the tavern with its swinging sign; here the dreaded pillories and stocks; here, on the banks of a little stream, the grist mill; here the schoolhouse, with its single chimney in the center and its roof sloping off on all four sides; here, perhaps, the gloomy log blockhouse, to which the people could flee in case of attack by the Indians.

Beyond the village the visitor would have seen the pasture fields where several hundred cattle were grazing under the watchful eyes of two herdsmen; on this side was an expanse of dense woodland where the villagers cut their firewood and at times timber for building; on that, the common meadow; far out to right and left the arable land where workmen were busy amid the patches of golden wheat or Indian corn or waving flax. Here and there, dominating a lovely hillside, was the isolated residence of some farmer who preferred to live apart from the village. A charming, peaceful picture the little community made, a picture which would perhaps have disarmed even the deep-seated prejudice of Sir William for everything that had to do with Puritans.

CHAPTER IV

The Fall of the Wilderness Zion

ALTHOUGH the English government in permitting the settlement of New England was actuated by economic considerations, a large proportion of the settlers themselves journeyed into the wilderness chiefly for religion's sake. Not only did they wish to escape persecution in England, but they were determined to establish in America a retreat for all of like faith with themselves, a bulwark against the forces of Antichrist. "All other churches of Europe have been brought under desolations," they said, "and it may be feared that the like judgements are coming upon us; and who knows but God hath provided this place to be a refuge for many, whom he means to save out of the General Destruction." They hoped to better their condition in a new and fertile country, of course, for the decline of industry and the lack of employment made conditions difficult in England. "The whole earth is the Lord's garden, . . . why then should we stand starving here for places of habitation, and in the mean time suffer whole countries . . . to lye waste without any improvement?"

But their minds were fired chiefly with the hope of establishing a Bible commonwealth, sealed against error from without and protected from schism from within. "What can be a better or nobler work, and more worthy of a Christian," they said, "than to erect and support a

reformed particular Church in its infancy. . . ." [1]   It
is incorrect to infer that most of the colonists were not
deeply religious merely because it is found that church
members were in the minority. Many righteous Puritans
were unable to state an overwhelming religious experience
which would qualify them for membership, yet they
were sympathetic with the church's purpose.

In so large a movement some were unquestionably impelled by one motive, some by another. Of the thousands of men and women who landed on the New England shores in the years from 1629 to 1640, there were
many who felt little sympathy with the erection there of
a powerful theocracy, some who had come on the repre-
sentations of the shipping agents as to the opportunities
to win a competence in America.[2] But they were forced
to conform to the wishes of the leaders, men of the type
of John Winthrop, John Cotton, John Norton and
John Wilson. This latter group enjoyed a prestige
which was born not only of superior education but of
an extraordinary talent for leadership. Schooled in the
bitter controversies of the day, hardened in the fires of
adversity, they were well fitted to play the rôle of Moses
in the removal of this modern host to the promised land.
"Though the reformed church, thus fled into the wilderness, enjoyed not the miraculous pillar," Cotton Mather
tells us, "we enjoyed many a person, in whom the good
spirit of God gave a conduct unto us, and mercifully
dispensed those directing, defending, refreshing influ-

---

[1] Cotton Mather, *Magnalia Christi Americana* [London, 1702]
(Hartford, 1853), I, 65, 70.

[2] A good discussion of the character and motives of the colonists is
found in Carl Becker, *Beginnings of the American People* (W. E. Dodd,
ed., *The Riverside History of the United States*, Boston, 1915, I),
chap. iii.

ences, which were as necessary for us, as any that the celebrated pillar of cloud and fire could have afforded."

These men were intent on establishing a theocracy in which their tenets and their form of worship should be upheld by the hand of the law.   They were not Separatists but Church of England men, and what they designed was an established church in New England.   At the very outset they made it clear that "they did not separate from the Church of England, nor from the ordinances of God there, but only from the corruptions and disorders of that Church: that they came away from the Common-Prayer and Ceremonies." [1]   On another occasion they called the Anglican church "their dear mother, desiring their friends therein to recommend them unto the mercies of God in their constant prayers, as a Church now springing out of their own bowels, nor did they think that it was their mother who turned them out of doors, but some of their angry brethren, abusing the name of their mother." [2]

The migrating preachers had fought in the old country, not only for the right to worship as they chose in their individual churches but also for control of the Anglican establishment.   Had they succeeded, they would have forced the church into complete conformity with their views, driving out those who persisted in opposing them.   Failing in their efforts, they removed to America where there could be no opposition to their plans.   Having set up their reformed church, having transplanted what they believed to be the true Anglican church to their new homes, they intended to protect it from innovation by the authority of the civil law.   "We came hither be-

[1] Cotton Mather, *Magnalia*, 1, 74.
[2] Cotton Mather, *Magnalia*, 1, 76.

cause we would have our posterity settled under the pure and full dispensations of the gospel; defended by rulers that should be of ourselves." [1] These words, delivered at one of the notable election sermons, give the keynote of the movement. Their church they intended to buttress by a state especially designed for its protection.

Obviously toleration had no part in such a plan. It is a singular perversion of history which attributes ideals to the prime movers in this great migration that they themselves would have been the first to repudiate. The fact that the Puritans deserted their homes to settle in the wilderness in order to worship God as they chose led even Charles II to suppose that they had openly espoused the principles of toleration. That the same mistake should be so common today, when religious freedom has been widely accepted as a principle essential to the welfare of mankind, is perhaps natural, if not inevitable. "On no subject dealt with among us," says a son of New England in an address before the Massachusetts Historical Society, "in lectures, orations, sermons, poems, historical addresses, and even in our choice school literature, has there been such an amount of crude, sentimental, and wasteful rhetoric, or so much weak and vain pleading, as on this. . . . The root of the whole error, common alike to those who censure and those who defend those ancient Fathers, is the assumption that they came here mainly to seek, establish, and enjoy liberty of conscience." [2]

The sermons and published writings of the founders of Massachusetts make it clear that they never entertained the thought of opening the doors of their new

[1] Cotton Mather, *Magnalia*, I, 219.
[2] The Reverend George E. Ellis.

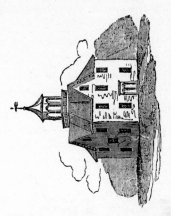

Center: A Sermon in praise of Harvard College, 1655.

Below: The "Old Tunnel" Meetinghouse at Lynn, Massachusetts, 1682-1827.

GODS

MERCY,

SHEWED TO HIS PEOPLE IN GIVING THEM A FAITHFUL MINISTRY AND SCHOOLES OF LEARNING FOR THE CONTINUAL SUPPLYES THEROF.

Delivered in a Sermon preached at Cambridg, the day after the Commencement, by Charles Chauncy, B.D, President of HARVARD Colledg in New-England.

Published with some additions therunto, at the request of diverse Honoured, and much Respected friends, For publick benefit, as they judged.

1 Thes. 5, 12. We beseech you brethren to know them that labour amongst you, & are over you in the Lord, and esteem them very highly in Love for their works sake.

Printed by Samuel Green at CAMBRIDG in New-England 1655.

The Reverend Richard Mather, 1596-1669, the first engraving produced in America, 1670.

Zion to those who differed from them.   So far from being champions of toleration, they opposed it bitterly. " 'T is Satan's policy, to plead for an indefinite and boundless toleration," said Thomas Shepard.[1]   Urian Oakes denounced religious freedom as the "first born of all Abominations," [2] while Increase Mather sternly rebuked the "hideous clamours for liberty of Conscience." John Norton denounced liberty of worship as liberty "to answer the dictates of the errors of Conscience in walking contrary to Rule.   It is a liberty to blaspheme, a liberty to seduce others from the true God.   A liberty to tell lies in the name of the Lord."   The Puritan community thought that heretics should have only the liberty to leave.   As Nathaniel Ward said, "All Familists, Antinomians, Anabaptists, and other Enthusiasts shall have free liberty to keepe away from us." [3]   We gain an insight into the depth of this feeling from the dismay of Edward Johnson when he found Massachusetts rent by the Anne Hutchinson heresy.   He had fled to what he thought would be a safe retreat from heresy, where his soul could rest in peace free from the dread of error.   Now he found controversy raging within the very walls of the new Zion, and he had to choose once more, at the peril of his soul, between truth and falsehood.

We fail to grasp the spirit of these men unless we realize that they considered themselves a chosen people, one to whom God had revealed himself and had led to the promised land far from the sins and corruptions of

[1] Lindsay Swift, "The Massachusetts Election Sermons," Col. Soc. of Mass., *Publs.*, I, 400.
[2] Swift, "The Massachusetts Election Sermons," 401.
[3] Nathaniel Ward, *Simple Cobbler of Aggawamm* (London, 1647), 3-12, *passim*.

the Old World. "The ministers and Christians, by whom New England was first planted, were a chosen company of men," says Cotton Mather, "picked out of, perhaps, all the counties in England, and this by no human contrivance, but by a strange work of God upon the spirits of men that were, no ways, acquainted with one another, inspiring them as one man, to secede into a wilderness, they knew not where." [1]   William Stoughton expressed the same idea in his famous statement that "God hath sifted a nation, that he might send choice grain into this wilderness."   God's concern for the settlement had been lovingly manifested by striking the Indians with a plague a few years before the migration, thus making the waste places safe for his children.[2] Such an attitude does not conduce to toleration.   Convinced that he had been selected by God to receive and expound the truth, the Puritan minister could but look upon those who opposed him as minions of Satan.   The red men, as has just been intimated, were probably of these infernal hosts, and must be ignored or ruthlessly brushed aside; differences in theology as well as in economic circumstances brought about a contrast between the Indian relations of the Puritan and those of the northern Frenchman on the one hand and the southern Spaniard on the other.   John Eliot and the Mayhews, in proportion to their missionary zeal, were exceptions in the priesthood of New England.   But to most of the leaders the Indians seemed far less dangerous than heretics of their own race and neighborhood.

[1] Cotton Mather, *Magnalia*, 1, 240.
[2] Edward Johnson, *Wonder-Working Providence of Sions Saviour in New England* [London, 1654] (J. F. Jameson, ed., *Original Narratives of Early American History*, N. Y., 1906-   ), 41.

The Massachusetts leaders were intent upon establishing, not a government representative of the wishes of the people but an oligarchy in which the clergy would have the deciding voice. The civil authorities of the new state were to serve as handmaidens to the church, and the ministers, although themselves not holding public office, were to be the final depository of power in the colony. This power they exercised chiefly through their control of the franchise. No man was to vote who was not a member of the church, and no man could be a member of the church until he had been admitted by the clergy. The clergy, in turn, took care to admit none who were in opposition to the established order. "In as much as very much of an Athenian democracy was in the mould of the government by the royal charter," says Cotton Mather, "Mr. Cotton effectually recommended it unto them, that none should be electors, nor elected therein, except as were visible subjects of our Lord Jesus Christ, personally confederated in our churches. In these, and many other ways, he propounded unto them an endeavour after a theocracy, as near as might be, to that which was the glory of Israel, the peculiar people." [1]

As for democracy, the New England fathers dreaded it as a form of government inconsistent with the rule of the best and most pious men. "Democracy I do not conceive that God did ever ordain as a fit government for either church or commonwealth," says John Cotton. "If the people be governors, who shall be governed? As for monarchy and aristocracy, they are both clearly approved and directed in the Scriptures. . . . He setteth up theocracy . . . as the best form of government

[1] Cotton Mather, *Magnalia*, I, 266.

in the commonwealth as in the church." [1] Winthrop agreed heartily, averring that democracy had no warrant in Scripture and that "among nations it has always been accounted the meanest and worst of all forms of government."

Thus the earnest men who led the Puritan exodus planned their new Bible commonwealth and thus they built it. Composed in large measure of persons of like faith, protected from invasion by its very isolation, guided by the clergy and by magistrates in close sympathy with them, this wilderness Zion was the culmination of their fondest hopes. Yet from the first the theocracy found itself faced by a multitude of difficulties, which threatened its supremacy and slowly undermined its strength.

The first of these was that love for self-government so universal among Englishmen. All the reverence, all the love, all the admiration which the people had for their leaders, did not reconcile them to the loss of their liberty. In the early days of the colony the outstanding leader was John Cotton. This remarkable man has been spoken of as "the unmitred pope of a pope-hating people." What he advised from the pulpit was usually enacted into law. The chronicler of Christ's wonders in America says that Cotton was the great director, "the father and glory of Boston." [2] Yet even the influence of John Cotton could not prevent a strong faction of the

[1] Thomas Hutchinson, *The History of the Colony of Massachusetts-Bay* (Boston, 1764-1828), I, 437.
[2] Cotton Mather, *Magnalia*, I, 252. The biographical chapter on Cotton (252-286) is very interesting. See also E. D. Mead, "John Cotton's Farewell Sermon," Mass. Hist. Soc., *Proceeds.*, ser. 3, I, 105.

people from demanding that in their new home they should not be deprived of their rights and liberties. According to the charter all important matters of government were left to the discretion of the stockholders, or freemen, in the general court. Only twelve of these freemen had come to Massachusetts in 1630, and all had been made magistrates. Since they were in full sympathy with the leading clergymen, and supported them in all their policies for both church and state, the arrangement constituted the government by the best which Winthrop and Cotton so earnestly advocated. Democratic it was not. When the first general court convened in October, 1630, the magistrates had shrunk in number to eight, and this small group were confronted with a demand from one hundred and nine of their fellow settlers to be admitted as freemen. These men were doubtless all Puritans, but they could see in their demand for citizenship nothing inconsistent with the dictates of their religion.

The magistrates postponed action on this petition until the spring. In the meanwhile they decreed that the assistants and not the freemen should make laws and elect the governor, and that the assistants should hold office during good behavior. This left the freemen only the right to select new assistants when vacancies occurred. The applicants agreed to this arrangement although it left them only the husks of real citizenship, and for some months more the little body of magistrates continued to tax and legislate. In 1632, however, when the assistants voted a levy for fortifications, the town of Watertown entered a vigorous protest. Under the leadership of their minister the people passed a resolution "that it was not safe to pay moneys after that sort, for fear of bringing

themselves and posterity into bondage." [1]   Governor
Winthrop, greatly disturbed at this show of insubordination, summoned the Watertown men before him, and
after they had made their submission, pardoned them.
But the other towns were not less concerned at the limi-
tations set upon their liberty.   When the general court
met in May, the body of the freemen voted that the
governor and his assistants must be elected each year, and
that every town should elect two delegates to act with
them in levying taxes.

Although this was a long step toward representative
government, it still left the deputies without a hand in
making laws.   In 1634 they assumed this right also.
In May two men from each of the eight towns met in
Boston and demanded to view the charter of the colony.
Winthrop dared not refuse, and they at once called his
attention to the fact that the charter gave the making
of laws to the whole body of freemen.   When the general court met a few days later, three deputies appeared
from each town, ready to demand their rightful share in
the government.   Against this action the magistrates and
leading ministers protested.   The very foundations of
the newly established theocracy seemed to be crumbling.
John Cotton threw the full weight of his influence in
favor of upholding the established order, pleading that
the Bible clearly showed that the magistrates ought to
hold office for life.   But the freemen, so far from yield-
ing, refused to reëlect Winthrop governor, and actually
imposed fines upon some of the magistrates for abuse of
power.   They then decreed that henceforth the general

[1] John Winthrop, *History of New England* (J. K. Hosmer, ed.,
in J. F. Jameson, ed., *Original Narratives of Early American History*,
N. Y., 1906-   ), I, 74.

court, consisting of the governor, the assistants and deputies elected by the towns, alone should have the right to tax, make laws and admit freemen.

Thus, four years after the Massachusetts Bay charter was brought to America, the government was changed from a narrow oligarchy to what appeared to be a little republic. Yet, even after the establishment of representative government, very little real liberalism existed, and the theocracy still ruled almost supreme. The freemen were only a small part of the population and the law forbidding the admission of nonchurch-members was rigidly enforced. Moreover, the prestige of the few leading laymen of the colony was such that they were selected as magistrates over and over again. John Cotton insisted "that a magistrate ought not to be turned into the condition of a private man, without just cause, and be publicly convict, no more than the magistrate may not turn a private man out of his freehold, etc., without like public trial." The idea became fixed that every official should be reëlected unless convicted of misconduct. Consequently the governor and his assistants continued to represent only the narrowest aristocratic clique in the colony, and the deputies a comparatively small body of voters, picked by the ministers from church members.

The theocratic form of government not only created internal dissension, but it was a leading cause in weakening Massachusetts by the withdrawal of several congregations to the Connecticut Valley. The liberal views of Thomas Hooker were so greatly at variance with those of Winthrop and Cotton that he could not rest at ease in his Newtown settlement. "There is a great disunion of judgement in matters of religion amongst good minis-

ters and people which caused Mr. Hooker to remove,"
wrote the Reverend R. Stansby to John Wilson, "and
that you are so strict in the admission of members to your
church, that more than halfe are out of your church in
all your congregations, and that Mr. Hooker before he
went away preached against that." [1]   Winthrop ex-
postulated with Hooker about the danger of "referring
matters of counsel or judicature to the body of the people," arguing that "the best part is always the least, and
of that part the wiser part is always the lesser."   Hooker
replied that to leave all power in the hands of rulers who
were not responsible to the people, was to invite tyranny.
I "must plainly profess if it was in my liberty, I should
choose neither to live nor leave my posterity under such
a government. . . . A general councel chosen by all,
I conceive under favour most suitable to rule and most
safe for the relief of the people." [2]

Although those who favored representative government had won a certain measure of success, schismatics
and heretics at first could do nothing.   The magistrates
and ministers were adamant against attempts to break
down the unity of their "City of God on earth."   Yet
both schism and heresy were prompt in showing themselves.   In 1631 the scholarly and liberal Roger Williams arrived, and accepted a pastorate at Salem.   An
avowed Separatist, he at once attacked the established
order for not renouncing fellowship with the Church of
England.   Besides inveighing against legal oaths and
against the validity of titles to land granted by the general
court, he also denounced the union of church and state,
declaring from the pulpit that the magistrates had no

[1] Letter of April 17, 1637, Mass. Hist. Soc., *Colls.*, VII, ser. 4, 10-11.
[2] G. L. Walker, *Thomas Hooker* (N. Y., 1891), 121-122.

right to punish Sabbath breaking or other violations of the first four commandments.

This open attack upon the theocracy could not be passed over. The ministers rendered their judgment "that he who should obstinately maintain such opinions, whereby a church might run into heresy, apostacy, or tyranny, and yet the civil magistrate could not intermeddle," was too dangerous to be tolerated.[1] Williams was cited to appear before the authorities, and after a trial was sentenced to banishment. The decree was suspended until spring, on condition that he refrain from attempting to spread his opinions. This he was unable to do, and when the magistrates decided to keep him on shipboard pending the next sailing for England, he escaped through the frozen forests to the Narragansett Bay region. The theocracy had won an easy victory, but one which was costly because achieved by appealing to the civil authorities. Schism for the moment had been blocked, but physical force cannot prevent the growth of divergent opinions, and before long heresy reappeared in a far more dangerous form.

Anne Hutchinson, who had been a parishioner of John Cotton in England, is described by Winthrop as a woman of "ready wit and bold spirit." Several years after her arrival in Boston she began the dangerous practice of holding meetings in her house to rehearse and discuss the sermon of the previous Sunday. From this she passed to comparing the teachings of the clergymen, and then to the evolution of a doctrine of her own. The ministers were expounding a covenant of works, she maintained, whereas the Bible showed that salvation was based on a covenant of grace. Although Winthrop wrote

[1] Winthrop, *History of New England*, I, 162.

that "no man could tell (except some few who knew the bottom of the matter) where any difference was," [1] he and the other leaders of the theocracy understood clearly enough that her ideas were inconsistent with the established order.   The covenant of grace made religion a matter of direct communication between man and his Maker, while the covenant of works required only obedience to a prescribed code of which the minister was the official interpreter.   Should the former doctrine secure wide acceptance, not only would unity be lost, but a stunning blow would be struck at the theocracy.

For a time Boston supported Mrs. Hutchinson with something like unanimity.   Even the great John Cotton was inclined to embrace her doctrines.   The religion of love which she preached was more in keeping with his naturally kindly nature than the established tenets of law and judgment.   But he drew back in time.   John Wheelwright, Mrs. Hutchinson's brother-in-law, and young Harry Vane bore the brunt of the battle.   The former was summoned before the general court, and although he refused to answer questions because the proceedings were held in secret, was found guilty of sedition and contempt.   To weaken the influence of Boston, a resolution was passed transferring the next court of elections to Newtown.   When the vote was taken, the orthodox party succeeded in restoring Winthrop to the governorship.   Boston, however, sent as its deputies Vane, Coddington and Hoffe, all favorable to Mrs. Hutchinson.   The court at first refused to seat them, but when Boston held a new election and returned them again, "the Court not finding how they might reject them, they were admitted."   In the following summer

[1] Winthrop, *History of New England*, I, 209.

the clergy met in synod and condemned as erroneous and blasphemous the Hutchinson heresies. At the November court Wheelwright was disfranchised and banished, while other members of the dissenting faction were severely punished. Mrs. Hutchinson was "banished from out this jurisdiction as being a woman not fit for our society." [1]

In this way was the church purged of heresy, and the theocracy saved from what to its leaders seemed the most deadly peril. It is folly to condemn these men for bigotry and intolerance. They had given up their homes and had fled into the wilderness for the purpose of establishing a society free from error. How natural, then, that they should have combated what they considered error, when to their horror they found that it had followed them across the Atlantic. "Two so opposite parties could not contain in the same body without hazard of ruin to the whole," said Winthrop. Conformity was gained, but only at the cost of a bitter struggle which left scars that were slow to heal. Theocracy was so weakened that another great heresy might shatter it.

Though for some time no such heresy arose from within, the ministers soon found themselves confronted with a peril from without. In 1656 Quaker missionaries invaded New England with the avowed purpose of making converts. The democratic leanings of the Quakers, their refusal to accord especial respect to magistrates, their denial of the need of an established clergy, combined to make them obnoxious to the Puritan leaders. When Mary Fisher and Ann Austin arrived in Boston,

[1] J. T. Adams, *The Founding of New England* (Boston, 1922), 171.

the colony was stirred to its foundations. "Why was it that the coming of two women so shook ye, as if a formidable army had invaded your borders?" George Bishop inquired of the magistrates.[1] But the magistrates would undoubtedly have been less dismayed at the invasion of an armed host. Powder and shot could only imperil men's lives; the Quakers were assaulting their souls. We gain an insight into the state of mind of these stern Puritans, not so much from their action in arresting these women, denouncing their doctrines and burning their books, as from the care they took to board up the windows of their cell so that the prisoners could not preach to the people. After five weeks of imprisonment they were shipped back to Barbados whence they had come.[2]

A few days later eight more Quakers arrived from London. Governor Endicott immediately put them in prison and at the first opportunity sent them out of the country. In October the general court fixed the fine of any master who should bring in a Quaker at £100, and declared that the Quaker himself should be severely whipped. By a later enactment the offender's tongue was to be bored with a hot iron, his ears cut off, he was to be banished, and if he returned, to be executed. New Haven, Plymouth and Connecticut also passed severe laws against the Quakers, but the death penalty was pre-

[1] George Bishop, *New England Judged by the Spirit of God* (London, 1703), 2.

[2] It must be remembered, however, that the Quakers were rather trying, judged by any standard. One woman, to evidence humility, was wont to exhibit herself in an old sackcloth gown with her face smeared with grease and lamp black; two others, though generally of modest deportment, went naked to church and market place "as a sign." See Bishop, *New England Judged*, 377, 383, and the summary of the *Persecution in New England* in J. G. Palfrey, *History of New England* (Boston, 1892), II, 449, 483; also Charles Deane, "Report on the Belknap Donation," Mass. Hist. Soc., *Proceeds.*, III (1855-1858), 320.

scribed by Massachusetts alone. Rhode Island, under the leadership of Roger Williams, would have none of this persecution. A band of Quakers who landed at Newport were received with kindness. But the other colonies, fearing that the missionaries would use Rhode Island as a base of operations, entered a vigorous protest. Pointing out that the "contagion" could easily spread across the borders, they threatened to take strong action "to prevent the aforesaid mischief." [1]

The reply of Williams might well have given pause to the Massachusetts magistrates and ministers. We "finde that in those places where these people, aforesaid, in this colony, are most of all suffered to declare themselves freely, and are only opposed by arguments in discourse, there they least of all desire to come . . . surely we find that they delight to be persecuted by civil powers, and where they are soe, they are like to gain more adherents by the conseyte of their patient sufferings." [2] The Rhode Island assembly answered in similar vein, reiterating their intention to uphold freedom of conscience which they prized as their greatest happiness.

The Massachusetts magistrates continued their pitiless warfare against the invaders. In September, 1659, Mary Dyer, William Robinson and Marmaduke Stevenson, who had come to Boston courting martyrdom, were all banished. Mrs. Dyer reached Rhode Island, whence she immediately returned, but the two men went only to Salem before facing about. All were sentenced to death. Robinson and Stevenson were hanged, but Mrs. Dyer,

[1] United Colonies of New England, *Acts*, II, 180.
[2] J. R. Bartlett, comp., *Records of the Colony of Rhode Island and Providence Plantations in New England, 1636-1792* (Providence, 1856-1865), I, 376.

after her hands and legs had been bound, her face covered and the rope adjusted about her neck, received word that she had been reprieved. Once more she was sent to Rhode Island, but the efforts of her family to keep her there failed. In the spring she came back to Boston where she too was executed. In November, 1660, another Quaker, William Leddra, suffered the same fate.

Though the theocracy went to these extremes, the battle was going against them. Endicott and Norton had good reason to realize that Roger Williams had been more farseeing than they, for the sufferings of the Quakers won for them the sympathy of thousands who had only contempt for their doctrines. A few days before the execution of Leddra, Wenlock Christison, another Quaker, strode into the court room, and looking into the face of Endicott, said to him, "I came here to warn you that you should shed no more innocent blood, for the blood that you have shed already cries to the Lord for vengeance to come upon you." [1]   He was seized and brought to trial. The magistrates debated long as to what should be done, for public sentiment was turning rapidly against them; but for Endicott there was no hesitancy. Pounding the table he shouted out, "You that will not consent, record it. I thank God I am not afraid to give judgement." Christison was condemned to death, but the sentence was never carried out. Partly from fear of interference from the crown, partly because of the evident opposition of the people, the persecution had to take a milder form. There were no more executions.

It was a severe defeat for the theocracy. The ideal

[1] William Sewel, *The History of the Rise, Increase, and Progress of the Christian People Called Quakers* (N. Y., 1844), I, 338.

of a Puritan commonwealth walled in against heresy had broken down. The suffering Quakers had proved that the New World did not offer so safe a refuge from the "poison of error" as the leaders of the exodus had hoped. Moreover, it had been made apparent that there were limits beyond which the people of Massachusetts would not follow the magistrates and ministers. The sight of a suffering Quaker, stripped to the waist and tied to a cart's tail, his back clotted with blood from frequent whippings, trudging through snow and ice, could but cause revulsion in men's minds against the system which was responsible for it. The Puritan leader in the days of his exile and his sacrifices was an inspiring figure; the Puritan persecutor seemed in contrast unlovely indeed.

In addition, the conflict brought interference from England, and with it the threat of an early termination of the charter upon which the established order was based. Charles II, displeased at the executions, gave orders that the vein of innocent blood opened in his dominions should be closed. The English Quakers actually chartered a ship to carry this message to New England and in six weeks delivered it into Endicott's hands. Accordingly, the laws against heresy were modified, so that many mouths were "opened which were before shutt."

Charles's quarrel with the Massachusetts government was by no means limited to the question of toleration for the Quakers. When this monarch found himself fixed on the throne of his fathers, he turned his attention to colonial matters. Although the policy of his government found its chief expression in the navigation acts, his advisers were also intensely interested in political and social conditions within the individual provinces. When they became aware that Massachusetts had made itself almost independent of the crown, that power there had fallen into the hands of a narrow theological group, that the laws of England were disregarded, the oath of allegiance neglected, the Anglican worship forbidden, they at once took steps to reëstablish the king's authority in the colony. The struggle which ensued lasted for nearly three decades and ended only with the overthrow of the Stuarts. So long as Charles I was uncertain of his ground in England, he refrained from pushing matters to an issue in Massachusetts, contenting himself with warnings, threats against the charter and the sending of agents to represent him in the colony. The magistrates on their part adopted a policy of procrastination. The king's commands were not openly flouted, but there were constant evasions and delay. When the Long Parliament was dissolved, the theocracy was still supreme in political and ecclesiastical affairs in Massachusetts, and paid to the crown but a shadowy homage.

With the advent of the second Stuart despotism the situation suddenly changed. The unprincipled but astute Charles II, having freed himself from the domination of Parliament by accepting a pension from Louis XIV, devoted the last years of his life to the task of ending liberty both in England and America. The liberal charters acquired by Connecticut (1662) and Rhode Island (1663) seemed to have been granted to strengthen settlements lying so near the Dutch frontier, or as an indirect rebuke to Massachusetts, or in a lapse into carelessness; they are marked exceptions to the king's general policy. Supported by the Tories and the Anglicans, he crushed the chief Whig leaders, circumscribed free speech, and set to work to reconstruct the British electorate to suit his own interests. In the colonies he attempted to suppress representative government and to substitute for it the rule of his own appointees. The order forbidding the Virginia assembly to initiate legislation and the withdrawal of the Massachusetts charter were but parts of the king's new policy of aggression, a policy made possible by the political situation in England.

Had Charles confined his attack to the narrow theocratic group in Massachusetts, he would have found powerful support within the colony itself. But he was bent not only upon overthrowing the established order but upon substituting for it the despotic rule of the crown. The people were not to benefit by this transfer of power and even the forms of representative government which had persisted under the old régime were to be swept away in the new. Edmund Andros, who was made governor-general of all New England despite the guarantees of the Connecticut and Rhode Island charters, trampled ruthlessly upon the rights held most sacred by Englishmen. In conjunction with his council he made laws, gave judicial decisions and ordered the collection of taxes. The Massachusetts general court was abolished, and every freeholder was made uneasy by the threat to revoke existing land grants.

Fortunately the tyranny of Charles II and James II in New England proved short-lived. The English nation rose in 1688, drove James into exile and granted the throne to his daughter Mary and her husband, William of Orange. The Glorious Revolution is a landmark in the history of English liberty, a landmark between the period in which the theory of divine right received widespread acceptance, and the period of parliamentary supremacy. In America, especially in New England, the effects were not less far-reaching. The old Massachusetts theocracy which was demolished to make room for royal absolutism was not fully restored when absolutism in its turn was overthrown. Increase Mather went to England to plead for the renewal of the original charter, but fortunately for Massachusetts he was not successful. Mather claimed to be the representative of the whole people; yet we know that public sentiment, while hoping for the restoration of the former status of semi-independence, by no means favored the old narrow administration in local affairs. In other words, the people wanted both autonomy and political liberty, only one of which they had enjoyed prior to the second Stuart despotism, and neither under the rule of Andros. The resolution passed by Watertown in May, 1689, asking that the number of freemen "be inlarged farther than have been the Custom of this Colony formerly," was no doubt representative of opinion throughout Massachusetts.

They had their wish. The new charter, which was issued in 1691, instituted a royal government not unlike that of Virginia. There was to be a representative assembly, while the franchise was based, not on church membership, but on property holdings. The crown appointed the governor, who had the power to veto bills of the assembly, appoint judges and other officials, and put the laws into execution. Members of the council were nominated by the legislature and confirmed by the governor. Religious freedom for Protestants was guaranteed. Thus was established a new order distinctly more liberal than that under which Massachusetts had lived during the past six decades. The power of the clergy was not completely crushed; the social and political structure of the colony was not revolutionized. A full century and more was to pass before Massachusetts became in any real sense democratic. But the old buttressed Bible commonwealth, the Zion which had been the dream of Winthrop and Cotton and for which they had made such sacrifices, was gone forever.[1]

On the other hand, England was never able to establish in practice the close control designed when the new charter was drawn up. The royal governors found themselves weaklings in the hands of the assembly. As the English House of Commons made use of its control of the purse to whittle down the royal prerogative, so the colonial legislatures made use of their taxing power to control the representatives of the crown in America. In Massachusetts they frequently withheld the governor's salary until he had yielded to their wishes. At the end of a half century the colony, in internal affairs, had become practically an autonomous state. For New England, especially for Massachusetts, the victory of liberalism proved the substance of the Glorious Revolution, while the technical tightening of the bonds with England was the shadow.

The decline of the theocracy manifested itself even more clearly in the loss of moral prestige than in the loss of political power. The sermons of the clergy in the last two decades of the seventeenth century are filled with references to the sinfulness of the day and the inattention paid to religion. "I saw a fearful degeneracy, creep-

[1] For a brief general account, see H. L. Osgood, *The American Colonies in the Seventeenth Century* (N. Y., 1904-1907), III, chaps. xiii-xiv.

ing, I cannot say, but rushing in upon these churches, . . ." said Cotton Mather, in his *Magnalia*.[1] "I saw a visible shrink in all orders of men among us, from that greatness, and that goodness, which was the first grain that our God brought from three sifted kingdoms. . . . What should be done for the stop, the turn of this degeneracy?" "Let us, the children of such fathers," wrote John Higginson, "lament our gradual degeneracy from that life and power of Godliness, that was in them, and the many provoking evils that are amongst us." Samuel Torry, so early as 1674, considered the golden age of New England as gone forever. "Truely, so it is, the very heart of New-England is changed and exceedingly corrupted with the sins of the Times," he said, "there is a Spirit of Profaneness, a Spirit of Pride, a Spirit of Worldliness, a Spirit of Sensuality, a Spirit of Gainsaying and Rebellion, a Spirit of Libertinism, a Spirit of Carnality, Formality, Hypocrisie and a Spiritual Idolatry in the Worship of God." [2]

Such was New England as it seemed to the more illiberal preachers of the day. It is easy for the modern mind to translate what they termed rebellion and gainsaying into a spirit of liberalism, the alleged gross licentiousness into merely a natural reaction against the iron bonds of the Puritan moral code. But they were quite right in seeing in the general tendencies of the day a gradual weakening of the influence which formerly had made the people follow their leadership with such unquestioning faith. The Halfway Covenant, introduced

[1] Cotton Mather, *Magnalia*, I, 249.
[2] In his election sermon of that year at Weymouth, Mass. Lindsay Swift, "The Massachusetts Election Sermons," Col. Soc. of Mass., *Publs.*, I, 402.

in 1657, which had allowed baptism to children of pious parents who yet had had no definite religious "experience," seemed to many a terrific inroad upon orthodoxy; and they were not altogether wrong, for it marked a faint beginning of reaction.   The example of Rhode Island and the Providence Plantations, the only community in Christendom where anyone might explain as he would the universe and his relation to it, must have roused some doubts as to the perfection of the surrounding New England system.[1]

It must be remembered that from the first many persons settled in New England from economic rather than religious motives.   Cotton Mather relates that once a Massachusetts minister, who was preaching to a congregation in the northeast region, urged them to continue a "religious people from this consideration that otherwise they would contradict the main end of planting this wilderness; whereupon a well-known person, there in the assembly, cryed out, Sir, you are mistaken, you think you are preaching to the people at the Bay; our main end was to catch fish." [2]

Even at Boston itself there were many who had come to better their fortunes rather than to escape persecution. With the development of trade and industry this group received gradual accessions until a separate merchant class had developed.   Between the merchant and the clergyman there was a distinct and growing divergence of interests.   The former looked out upon the whole world, his vessels wandered from the West Indies to England,

[1] Maryland in its toleration act of 1649 insisted upon professed belief in the Trinity; it was almost inevitable that a Catholic proprietor under an English government should be tolerant, especially when his fellow churchmen were in a minority in the colony.

[2] Cotton Mather, *Magnalia*, I, 66.

and from Chesapeake Bay to the Mediterranean; he learned to know the Catholic Spaniard, the Anglican Virginian, the Quaker of Pennsylvania, and found good in them all. He had no sympathy with the policy which would make of New England a Zion, walled against the contagions of a sinful world. When Boston made it illegal for townsmen to "entertaine any strangers into their houses for above 14 days" without special permission from the authorities, it aroused the merchants to protest.

We find the pious Edward Johnson, so early as 1650, expressing alarm at the growing spirit of commercialism. Merchants and vintners "would willingly have had the Commonwealth tolerate divers kinds of sinful opinions to intice men to come and sit down with us, that their purses might be filled with coyn, the civil Government with contention, and the Church of our Lord Christ with errors." [1] As the century grew older the merchant class increased both in numbers and influence. The prosperity which they brought to New England, the outlet they offered for its products and the employment they gave to thousands of workers, rendered them formidable opponents. The ministers railed at them and warned them that they must not attempt innovations. "New England is originally a plantation of Religion, not a plantation of Trade," thundered Higginson in his election sermon of 1663. "Let Merchants and such as are increasing Cent per Cent remember this." [2] But the merchant class added a leaven to public opinion which the clergy could not ignore and found it difficult to

---

[1] Johnson, *Wonder-Working Providence*, 254.
[2] John Higginson, *The Cause of God and His People in New England* (1663), 11, quoted in Col. Soc. of Mass., *Publs.*, I, 398.

combat.   During the Salem witchcraft delusion it was
Thomas Brattle and Robert Calef, both merchants, who
had the common sense to see the folly of the inquisition
and the bravery to denounce the justices and the ministers for their part in it.

The closing years of the seventeenth century witnessed
in Massachusetts a far-reaching change.   The experiment
of a Bible commonwealth had definitely failed; the influence of the clergy in civil government, although by
no means entirely eliminated, was greatly restricted; their
hold upon the hearts and minds of the people distinctly
weakened.   From the first the theocracy was doomed to
defeat because it set itself against men's natural instincts;
and natural instincts cannot permanently be suppressed.
During the half century of its supremacy the theocratic
establishment had to endure a succession of shocks.   The
struggle for representative government, the Roger Williams and Anne Hutchinson heresies, the Quaker invasion, the annulling of the old charter, the defeat in the
witchcraft prosecutions, each played an important part
in the overthrow.

More powerful than any one incident was the slow,
almost imperceptible change which was coming over
men's minds, the trend toward rationalism, the development of liberalism, the widening of human sympathies.
This movement found no corresponding development
among the old school of churchmen.   So far from attempting to keep in step with the times, to shape their
theology in conformity with new ideals and new points
of view, they remained rigid and unyielding.   Regarding
the leaders of the exodus as saints, they sought to perpetuate their tenets and to pattern their lives after them.   In
this they failed, for the ability of the early fathers to

move the hearts of men lay in their creative force. John Winthrop and John Cotton were living actors in the drama of their times; Cotton Mather was little more than a stereotyped imitator. In the last analysis the New England theocracy fell because it tried to crystallize the Puritan spirit of the early seventeenth century, while the tide of a new civilization swept over and past them.

CHAPTER V

A Transplanted Church

WE have seen how climatic, geographic and economic conditions affected the life of the European settlers in America—how these factors defeated England's chief purpose in founding the colonies, tended to undermine the theocratic structure in Massachusetts, brought the artisan in Virginia and Maryland to drop the saw or the shuttle for the plow or the hoe, changed the New England farmer into a shipbuilder or a merchant, and made fur traders of the French on the St. Lawrence and the Dutch on the Hudson. We may now turn to the profound changes which they wrought in a typical Old World institution, the Anglican church.

During the seventeenth century Virginia was the only English colony on the American continent in which the majority of the people adhered to the established faith of the mother country. In Maryland the church was first set up by law in 1692, and prior to that date there were usually three or four Anglican clergymen in the colony. For a generation after the founding of South Carolina the proprietors opened the doors of their settlements to all kinds of dissenters, so that when at last, in 1704, a conformity bill was passed, the Anglicans are said to have constituted but one third of the population. Elsewhere the Church of England had but few adherents and lived only on sufferance. It is in the Old Dominion, then, that one can study to the best advantage the interesting experiment of transplanting into the New World this religious establishment so vigorous and important in the Old.

It was inevitable that in the American branch there should be many changes. The basic doctrines remained the same, but from the first there was divergence in organization, in government, even in the form of worship. In England the church was controlled by a highly developed hierarchy, while in Virginia it was more democratic. In England the clergy as a body enjoyed a certain degree of independence, and exercised a powerful influence upon civil affairs. In Virginia the church was largely controlled by the people through their vestries, while in state matters it was, at most periods, quite devoid of influence. The ecclesiastical establishment began from the very hour of its foundation a separate and peculiar development: it had to mold itself into something suited to the peculiar requirements of a new country.

The Anglican church, unlike English representative institutions, did not flourish in the soil of Virginia. The democratic tendencies of the colonists and their scattered mode of life proved serious obstacles to the development of a truly religious life. Before the end of the century pious men were noting with misgivings that the character of the clergy was bad, that many parishes were vacant, that the liturgy was neglected and the religious wants of the people imperfectly met. Unless vigorous efforts were made to effect a thorough reform, decay and ruin seemed inevitable.

Thoughtful clergymen in the colony attributed these unfortunate conditions chiefly to the sparseness of the population. The Virginians were a race of plantation dwellers. There were no real towns. Jamestown it-self, for a century the capital and the chief entrepôt of the colony, was no more than a straggling hamlet. Since none but the most fertile lands could be cultivated with profit, extensive untouched tracts lay between the various settlements. Vessels navigating the tributary streams of the James, the York and the Rappahannock frequently had to make their way for miles under the shadows of the virgin forest.

This made it necessary to create parishes of very great size, so great, in fact, that no man could alone minister to any one of them. "The families . . . are dispersedly and scatteringly seated upon the sides of Rivers," wrote a pamphleteer in 1661, "some of which running very far into the Country, bear the English Plantations above a hundred miles, and being very broad, cause the Inhabitants of either side to be listed in several Parishes. Every such Parish is extended many miles in length upon the Rivers side, and usually not above a mile in Breadth backward from the River." [1] As time passed and the population became more dense, the parishes changed in size and shape, but they remained to the end too large to be cared for properly. In 1724 St. Paul's Parish in Hanover County was sixty miles long, Bristol and Hungers were each forty, and Westminster and Westover each thirty.[2] When the parishes were smaller, the difficulty of providing for the support of the pastor often made it

[1] R. G. (pseud.), "Virginia's Cure: or an Advisive Narrative Concerning Virginia [1662]," Peter Force, comp., Tracts and Other Papers (Wash., 1836-1846), III, no. xv, 4.
[2] W. S. Perry, ed., Historical Collections Relating to the American Colonial Church (Hartford, 1870-1878), I, 201, 263-264, 266, 270, 273, 277.

necessary to double his burden by placing two cures under his care.[1]

Neglect of religion was inevitable. Regular attendance at worship was difficult, for few had the constancy to make their way ten or fifteen miles to church through the forests or on the rivers. The roads were execrable. Until late in the seventeenth century the paths which led from plantation to plantation were so unfit for vehicles that the universal mode of traveling overland was on horseback. Upon Sunday mornings when the weather was bad the minister knew that many vacant pews would confront him. The evil was mitigated to some extent by the erection, in remote districts, of chapels of ease. They were very poorly served, however. Usually service was conducted by lay readers, for the pastor could seldom visit them more than once a month. Often even chapels were lacking, and the clergymen found it necessary to ride out to their scattered flocks to preach in private houses. "Sometimes after I have travell'd Fifty Miles to Preach at a Private House," wrote one clergyman, "the Weather happening to prove bad, on the day of our meeting, so that very few or none have met; or else being hindered by Rivers & Swamps rendered impassable with much rain, I have returned with doing of nothing to their benefit or mine own satisfaction."[2]

The great distances made it difficult for ministers to win the friendship and love of their flocks, for they could not be frequent visitors at homes that were perhaps ten or fifteen miles from the rectory. "The inconvenience

[1] In 1702 Stephen Fouace ministered to Martin's Brandon and York Hampton; James Slater to Charles and York; John Frazier to St. Paul and Overworton.

[2] Perry, *Historical Collections*, I, 327-328.

and prejudice of such large bounded parishes are very great," wrote the Reverend Alexander Forbes,[1] ". . . for the Word of God can be preached but seldom among them; the use of the Sabbath day is converted by them into some diversion or worldly business; they cannot be catechized so frequently as their need requires; their sick cannot be visited." Some of the Virginia parsons struggled manfully against these unfortunate conditions. It must have been a familiar sight to see them upon their mud-splashed horses, making their way along the narrow forest paths to bring the comforts of the church to the homes of their scattered parishioners. But the fight was a hard one, and many of the clergy were neither earnest enough nor brave enough to make it.

The clergy themselves were quick to perceive the danger which threatened the church from this source, and their letters to the bishop of London are full of the subject. "In remote and scattered settlements," wrote the Reverend Francis Mackemie, "we can never enjoy . . . privileges and opportunities [of religious worship], for by reason of bad weather, or other accidents ministers are prevented and people are hindered to attend. . . . It is a melancholy consideration how many . . . continue grossly ignorant of many necessary parts of the Christian religion."[2] "Their seating themselves in that Wilderness," declared another writer, "hath caused them hitherto to rob God in a great measure of that publick Worship and Service which . . . he requires to be constantly paid to him. . . . This Sacriledge I judge to be

---

[1] Perry, *Historical Collections,* I, 326.
[2] A Well-Wisher to Both Governments (*pseud.*), "A Plain & Friendly Perswasive to the Inhabitants of Virginia and Maryland for Promoting Towns & Cohabitation [London, 1705]," *Va. Mag. of Hist. and Biog.,* IV, 264-265.

the prime Cause of their long languishing, improsperous condition, for it puts them under the Curse of God." [1]

As the sparseness of the population hindered the clergyman's work, so it made it difficult to provide an adequate salary. No matter how large the parish, it usually embraced but a small congregation. Even at the end of the seventeenth century there were a number of parishes which had less than one hundred families, most of them far from being well-to-do. In Virginia there was nothing comparable to the great endowments in England which did so much to make the church independent and powerful. The colonial clergy were paid almost entirely from funds raised by local taxation, so that relief could be had only by enlarging the size of the parishes. The church was caught in a dilemma. If the parishes were of moderate size, the clergymen could not secure adequate support; if they were enlarged, it became impossible to minister to them properly.

In the first half of the century salaries varied widely. It was the practice to assess each taxable person in the colony an equal amount for church dues, but the money thus raised was not distributed equally among the clergymen. Each minister received only the funds raised in his own parish. His annual stipend might be eighty pounds, it might be less than thirty pounds. For some years the tax was placed at ten pounds of tobacco and a bushel of corn. In 1632, when the clergy petitioned for a better support, the assembly granted them "the 20th calfe, the 20th kidd of goates, and the 20th pigge, throughout all plantations," as an addition to their salaries.[2] The sys-

---

[1] R. G. (*pseud.*), "Virginia's Cure," 4.
[2] This act was soon repealed. W. W. Hening, comp., *Statutes at Large of Virginia* (Phila., 1823), I, 159, 221.

tem worked great hardship upon the clergy in the less populous counties, and in 1662 the practice was changed, an act being passed to make all salaries uniform. The assembly fixed the stipend at eighty pounds, "besides the perquisites and glebes," and ordered each parish to raise this sum.[1] Unfortunately, this caused great inequality in the distribution of church dues, and placed an insupportable burden upon poor or thinly settled parishes.

When the law was first passed it seems to have provided the clergy with a maintenance suited to their calling and their requirements. But when the passage of the navigation acts brought about a radical decline in the price of tobacco, the value of ministers' salaries was cut in half, for the taxpayers had the privilege of making payment in tobacco, at the rate of twelve shillings a hundred pounds. The 13,333 pounds of leaf which the law allotted to each minister, in 1662 brought in the market not much less than the prescribed eighty pounds, but a few years later they were worth only half that sum. The clergy complained bitterly of this unexpected development, and appealed to the assembly to change the valuation of their tobacco so that it would approximate the true market price. After many delays they succeeded in securing a law increasing the amount of tobacco paid each minister to sixteen thousand pounds; but this by no means restored the income to its former value. So late as 1724 we find the clergy complaining that the average stipend was such that any "man of Ingenuity" would prefer a fixed income of forty or fifty pounds a year in England, if such pittance were paid there.[2]

To make a bad matter worse, the tobacco in which the

[1] Hening, *Statutes at Large of Virginia*, II, 45.
[2] "A Proposition," Perry, *Historical Collections*, I, 335.

clergy were paid was by no means uniform in quality. Between the two standard varieties raised in Virginia —Orinoco and Sweetscented—there was a wide divergence in price. The latter, which was much the more valuable, could be grown to perfection only in the Peninsula and the counties north of the Rappahannock. Clergymen holding cures in the Sweetscented counties usually received in actual value stipends double those residing in sections where Orinoco only could be raised.[1]

There was a law enacted in 1661 which required every parish to set aside for its rector a glebe supplied with all necessary buildings and livestock. In most parishes this act was complied with, and the clergy were soon in possession of little plantations which, it was hoped, would add greatly to their incomes. But the results were disappointing. In some places the lands were sterile or inaccessible, in others the buildings were inadequate. In those cases where the glebe was all that could be expected, the clergyman found it difficult to utilize it properly. His tenure was so uncertain that he hesitated to spend time or money upon the upkeep of the property. To repair the buildings or clear tobacco fields might profit only his successor. "Due care is not taken to keep the house in repair," wrote the Reverend John Cargill, "and on the precarious tenure I hold it, without induction, I don't think it my business. Besides the buildings are of wood and require such expenses to keep them tenantable that my poor Salary would be exhausted that way. . . . So I have been obliged to look out for a habitation elsewhere."[2] Nor could the clergy spare the time

[1] Perry, *Historical Collections*, I, 267, 282, 302, 307, 312.
[2] John Cargill, "Southwark Parish in Surry County [June 24, 1724]," Perry, *Historical Collections*, I, 307.

and labor necessary for cultivating a plantation. They could not well desert the prayer book for the plow. It is not surprising that at the end of the seventeenth century many of the glebes were in a sad state of neglect, without orchards or barns, their rectories deserted or decaying. The clergy themselves declared that "one with another" the glebes were "not worth above forty or fifty shillings per annum."

Certain perquisites which were allowed the ministers made a small addition to their incomes. They charged a fee for performing the marriage ceremony amounting often to two hundred pounds of tobacco, and another for preaching funeral sermons of four hundred pounds. One clergyman estimated his annual perquisites at twelve hundred pounds of tobacco, and this seems not to have been far from the average. In 1696 the clergy as a body claimed that their fees were almost negligible. "We have no perquisites except for Marriages & a few funerale Sermons," they complained, "and we find that they do not amount . . . to above five pounds per annum." [1]

All in all the livings of the Virginia clergy were most inadequate. It was a common complaint among them that they could not attend properly to their duties because they were harassed by poverty. They could not supply themselves with books. Many of them were compelled to remain single, for they could not afford to support a family. In 1692 the Reverend James Blair represented to William III, probably with some exaggeration, that the condition of the ministers in Virginia was miserable in the extreme. The salaries had fallen a full half, he said, "and there is no hope that they can

---

[1] P. A. Bruce, *Institutional History of Virginia in the Seventeenth Century* (N. Y., 1910), I, 158-162.

live comfortably upon them, so that many of the better sort who can pay their passage, begin to desert the country." [1] The troubles of the clergy growing out of the fluctuations of the medium in which they received their salaries vividly illustrate the chronic unhealthfulness of an economic system resting on a single crop, and that crop tobacco, so sensitive and unpredictable in itself, and so largely related to distant market conditions which were not well understood.

The scattered mode of living in Virginia injured the church in still another way: it made it impossible for the clergy to conform fully to the liturgy. This was a matter of deep concern to many rectors, but they were powerless to remedy the evil. They discovered that rules and ordinances which were well-suited to the church in the mother country could not be enforced in this remote corner of the world. The common use of lay readers in both churches and chapels was a serious breach of the liturgy; but what could the clergy do? The number of ordained priests was insufficient for the needs of the people, and laymen of "sober life and conversation" had to be employed frequently, or many persons permitted to go for weeks without public worship. The vestries never so far deviated from the church canons as to permit "laicks" to deliver sermons of their own. When they officiated in place of the regular minister they read printed sermons. Dr. Blair wished to restrict them to the homilies, but it was argued that this would make the service so dull that people would not attend.

In plain violation of the liturgy, the Virginians buried their dead in private cemeteries rather than in the con-

[1] "Memorial Concerning Virginia Clergy," C. O. 5: 1306, Doc. 73 (Brit. Pub. Rec. Office).

secrated ground of the parish churchyards. The clergy frowned upon this custom, but they found that it was made necessary by the isolation of the plantations. It was inconvenient and expensive to convey bodies from remote dwellings to the church. Often when the roads were bad it was not to be thought of. Moreover, in colonial Virginia, where people came miles to attend a funeral, the bereaved family had to provide not only food for a large number of guests, but often sleeping accommodations.[1] This would have been impossible had the interment taken place in the far-off churchyard. Some of the old private cemeteries still exist in eastern Virginia, and the traveler comes upon them in unexpected places, perhaps in the corner of a field, or hidden in a little cluster of trees. In 1718 the bishop of London wrote the clergy of Virginia complaining of this matter. Dr. Blair replied that it was beyond their power to effect a change. "It is a common thing all over the country (what thro' want of ministers, what by great distance & the heat of the weather), both to bury at other places than church yards, and to employ laicks to read the funeral service; till our circumstances and laws are altered, we know not how to redress."[2]

Even more serious was the necessity of administering the sacraments without the prescribed vestments and without proper ornaments and vessels. In fact, both clergy and laity became lax in observing many customs considered of importance by the Anglican church. None of the holy days were observed except Christmas and

[1] P. A. Bruce, *Social Life of Virginia in the Seventeenth Century* (Richmond, 1907), 218-222.
[2] "John London to Clergy of Virginia," Perry, *Historical Collections,* I, 201.

Good Friday, the Lord's Supper was often administered to unconfirmed persons, and marriages were solemnized in private residences.[1]

In the matter of government also the Virginia church was different from the parent church in England. In the early years, when the inhabitants were but a few hundred in number, the king had commissioned his governor to look after ecclesiastical matters. This he considered all that was necessary, for the appointing of a bishop or the establishment of a hierarchy was not to be thought of for an infant colony. But the governor proved ill-suited to be head of the church—his other duties required his attention, while his political interests at times conflicted with those of the clergy. Moreover, as a layman he could never become in a real sense the bishop of Virginia. During most of the seventeenth century the governors seem to have neglected their clerical duties and left the church to develop as time and local conditions should determine. This made possible that strange anomaly, a democratic branch of the Anglican church.

In Virginia the church buildings were erected almost invariably by the people, and not, as often was the case in England, by wealthy patrons. Moreover, the clergy were paid, as we have seen, by the people through their vestries. The people, therefore, claimed a major part in the control of the church. They were the true patrons of the parishes, they argued, and as such had the right to select their own ministers. Although the governors, in their commissions, were instructed to induct, or install, ministers upon presentation by the vestries, this power was seldom exercised. Throughout the entire colonial period most of the clergy officiated only as the salaried

[1] Perry, *Historical Collections*, I, 213.

employees of the vestries. In a few cases, where the
ministers showed themselves men of ability and piety,
the vestries presented them to the governor for induction. When this was done, they held their places for life.
But it is probable that not more than one tenth of the
clergy were thus honored.

In the meanwhile circumstances had been making the
bishop of London the diocesan of the colonial church.
At first his duties in this office seem to have been confined to sending ministers to the plantations. Before
the end of the seventeenth century, however, he assumed
a more direct control and appointed in several colonies
commissaries to represent him and uphold his authority.
But neither in Virginia nor later in Maryland, the
Carolinas and Georgia, did this officer exercise great
power, and he by no means superseded the governor
as head of the local church. He was authorized to
hold convocations, make visitations and supervise the
conduct of the clergy. The governor claimed by his
commission the power of giving licenses for marriages,
probates of wills and inductions of ministers. As this
division of authority resulted in frequent clashes between the governor and the commissary, it brought
discredit upon the church, and was a source of great
weakness in its government. Of course neither officer
could ordain or remove a clergyman or confirm a
communicant.

The insufficient salaries and the insecurity of tenure
conspired to bring upon the church still another evil.
It became a matter of the greatest difficulty to secure
able and pious ministers. It is always with reluctance
that men leave their homes to migrate to a distant and
strange land, and great advantages must be shown them

before they will make the venture.[1] Those advantages
the Virginia church could not offer. As a result it was
forced, only too frequently, to content itself with men
of inferior ability and character. There were many
good and earnest ministers in the colony; scores of instances can be cited of men who accepted without complaint the arduous task of upholding religion, and won
the love and respect of their parishioners. Among them
are Robert Hunt who "comforted the wants and extremi-
ties" of the early settlers; Bartholomew Yates, a gradu-
ate of Oxford; Cope Doyley; James Clark; William
Thompson; Charles Anderson of Westover Parish; Andrew Jackson, Christ Church, Lancaster County; Jacob
Ware of Varina Parish; Daniel Taylor of New Kent
County; and Edward Portlock.[2]

But there can be little doubt that the Virginia parson was often ill-suited to his holy calling. Of ministers, as of "all other commodities the worst are sent us,"
wrote Sir William Berkeley with a tinge of bitterness.
Governor Nicholson declared "that the clergy are all a
pack of scandalous fellows." In 1704 the vestry of
Varina Parish complained that often the ministers were
weak men or worse, "being given to many vices not
agreeable to their coats." Their own commissary testified that there were "enormities among them." In 1697,
a certain Nicholas Moreau wrote that the clergy were "of
a very ill example," and that some of them, especially
Scotchmen, had been so scandalous in their conduct that

---

[1] F. L. Hawks, *A Narrative of Events Connected with the Rise ana
Progress of the Protestant Episcopal Church in Virginia* (N. Y., 1836),
87-88, traces the steps in the transit of a typical immigrant clergyman
to his living.

[2] C. O. 5: 1314, Doc. 63, XVII (Brit. Pub. Rec. Office); Bruce,
Institutional History of Virginia, I, 203.

they had created a strong prejudice among the people against the clergy as a whole.[1] Matters became so bad that the bishop of London felt it necessary to warn them that "the faults & miscarriages in the life and conversation of some" must be corrected. This admonition accomplished little, for a few years later it was declared necessary to take severe action against such vices on the part of the clergy as "cursing, swearing, drunkenness or fighting." It was seriously proposed to establish a test to determine how far a minister might proceed in his cups before passing the limits of sobriety. "First let the signs of Drunkenness be proved such as sitting an hour or longer in the Company where they were a drinking strong drink and in the meantime drinking of healths or otherwise taking his cups as they came round . . . ; striking, challenging, threatening to fight, or laying aside any of his Garments for that purpose; staggering, reeling, vomiting, incoherent, impertinent, obscene or rude talking."[2] If the rector were guilty of these things it was felt reasonable to assume that he had exceeded the bounds of propriety.

At first sight it seems strange that the people of Virginia should have submitted to conditions such as these, but they had to accept ministers of poor character or none at all. The vestry of Christ Church Parish, Lancaster County, declared that it was so hard for them to secure pastors that they were glad to take any that offered, "let their lives be never so licentious or their qualifications so unfit."[3] Some parishes were forced for

[1] "Mr. Nicholas Moreau, to the Right Honorable the Lord Bishop of Lichfield and Coventry, His Majesty's High Almoner [Virginia, April 12, 1697]," Perry, *Historical Collections*, I, 30.
[2] "A Proposition," Perry, *Historical Collections*, I, 341-342.
[3] C. O. 5: 1314, Doc. 63, XVII (Brit. Pub. Rec. Office).

years to remain vacant, and throughout the entire colonial period there never was a time when the supply of ministers was equal to the demand. So early as 1611 we find the colonists begging for "godly and earnest" men to fill their pulpits.[1] In 1629 Governor John Harvey tried to impress upon the privy council the crying need for "able and grave" pastors. "Do they not wilfully hide their talents," complained another writer, "or keep themselves at home, for fear of losing a few pleasures? Be not there among them of Moses and his mind, and of the Apostles, who forsook all to follow Christ?"[2]

During the Commonwealth period this want was still so severely felt that special inducements were offered by the assembly to ministers to migrate to the colony. In 1661 the king was implored to ask Oxford and Cambridge universities to furnish the Virginia church with the clergymen they so greatly needed. When Lord Culpeper became governor, thirty-four men were ministering to forty-eight parishes; seventeen years later there were fifty parishes, to serve which there were but twenty-two pastors.[3] "Our condition here in Virginia is very different from that of England," wrote the vestry of Lawn's Creek Parish to Governor Francis Nicholson, in 1704, "for there are always enough in orders there to supply vacancies. Here there has never yet been ministers enough to supply us, neither are there now incumbents in above half our parishes and none unbeneficed to be presented by those that are vacant. Neither can we

[1] Bruce, *Institutional History of Virginia*, I, 118.
[2] William Meade, *Old Churches, Ministers and Families of Virginia* (Phila., 1857), I, 14.
[3] "A List of the Parishes in Virginia [June 30th, 1680]," *Va. Mag. of Hist. and Biog.*, I, 242-244.

get them, tho we have earnestly tried to procure them from England." [1]

Such was the condition of the Virginia church as the seventeenth century drew to a close. To thoughtful men it seemed that things could not be worse. With the clergy poorly paid, too few in numbers and of inferior ability and character, with the liturgy frequently disregarded, with the parishes too large, the church government weak and disorganized, unless radical reforms were instituted, ruin was inevitable.

The great churchmen of England were not ignorant of the danger which threatened. The Virginia clergy, in letters and pamphlets, made frequent complaint of their troubles. Yet no one in England felt a direct responsibility in the matter, and no reforms were made until the accession to the see of London, in 1675, of Henry Compton. This able man took seriously his duties as diocesan of the colonial church. After a careful investigation, he laid before the board of trade a report on ecclesiastical abuses in the colonies. He complained of the laxness of the Virginia governors in not upholding the right of patronage, of the hiring of ministers by the vestries, the payment of salaries in cheap tobacco, the custom of burying in "gardens, orchards and other places," the use of laymen to perform the marriage ceremony.

Neither Compton nor the board of trade realized that these abuses were rooted deep in the economic and social life of the colony. The board had no remedy to suggest, and simply directed the governors to put an end to each abuse, as though those officers by a mere com-

[1] C. O. 5: 1314, Doc. 63, XVII (Brit. Pub. Rec. Office).

mand could revolutionize the colonial church.[1]   Having
directed them to see that adequate salaries be paid the
clergy, that violations of the liturgy be stopped and that
the tenure of the clergy be made secure, they forgot the
whole matter, and turned to their accustomed business
of regulating the trade of the colonies.

In 1681, and again in 1683, they received reports
from Governor Culpeper of Virginia, which must have
opened their eyes to the complexity of the problem.
To put things in "a good method," said Culpeper, would
be very tedious and the labor of years.   The root of the
trouble lay in the smallness of the salaries.   "Which way
to begin," he added, "I know not.   Good ministers
would in time certainly get a better interest in the people, but without encouragement few will go so far, and
the people are not only poor in general, but several parts,
either from barrenness, unhealthfulness or lying too remote are almost totally deserted." [2]

So far from being discouraged by these adverse reports, the bishop of London became all the more determined to effect reform.   Appointing the Reverend
James Blair as his commissary, or representative, he intrusted to his hands the conduct of affairs in Virginia.
He could not have made a better selection.   A man of
energy, ability and perseverance, Blair entered upon the
work with all the zeal of a crusader.   He had the enthusiastic support of the lieutenant-governor, Francis Nicholson.   This strange man, despite his profanity, violent
temper and immoral life, showed himself at all times in
the several colonies where he served the crown, an ardent
friend of the church.

[1] *Cal. of State Papers, Colon., Am. and W. I., 1677-1680*, 117.
[2] C. O. 5: 1356 (Brit. Pub. Rec. Office), 172-174.

1656—James Blair—1743.

✠ Old Trinity, Dorchester County, Maryland. ✠

✠ St. Luke's, Isle of Wight County, Virginia. ✠

This ill-assorted trio—Blair, Compton and Nicholson
—went to work to combat the evil influences which were
undermining the Virginia church. It was Blair who
took the active lead and drew up the scheme of reform.
He counted upon Nicholson's influence to force a bill
through the assembly increasing the ministers' salaries.
Pressure was to be brought upon the parishes to present
their ministers for induction, so as to free them from
their dependence upon the vestries. Ecclesiastical discipline was to be made a reality. A college was to be
founded in which young Virginians could be trained for
divine orders. The clergy were to have a representative
in the council of state to guard their interests in civil
affairs.[1]

Such was the plan for revivifying the Virginia church.
It seemed a practicable scheme, neither violent nor revolutionary, but of far-reaching purport. It had the enthusiastic support, not only of the lieutenant-governor,
but of the powerful prelates in England. The bishop
of London, the archbishop of Canterbury, the bishop of
Worcester and the bishop of Salisbury were deeply interested, and gave their hearty support before the king
and queen, the privy council and the board of trade.
Their influence made it possible for Blair to secure almost any reasonable thing within the power of the royal
government to grant. Yet the efforts for reformation
failed dismally. After years of endeavor, years filled
with bitter contests and heartburnings, no permanent
good had been effected. Nor are the reasons hard to
find. Blair had assailed conditions in the colony which

[1] [Henry Hartwell and others], "An Account of the Present State
and Government of Virginia," sec. xii., Mass. Hist. Soc., *Colls.* (1798),
164 ff.

not even the power of the crown could change. So long as the plantation remained the unit of life in Virginia and the inhabitants retained their scattered mode of habitation, he could do little. Blair finally came to the realization that the Virginia church would never become a counterpart of the church in the mother country.

But at first the commissary met only with success. He secured the hearty coöperation of the Virginia assembly [1] and then sailed for Europe. The bishop of Worcester laid the plan before the queen, while the archbishop of Canterbury explained it to King William.[2] Both monarchs expressed unqualified approval and promised to give financial support. The sum of £1985 14. 10. was set aside from the quitrents for the college, another substantial sum was devoted to increasing the ministers' salaries, Dr. Blair was made a member of the council of state, and a letter was secured from the king requesting the assembly to vote better salaries in money or in tobacco at the current rates.[3]

Despite all this, Blair returned to find that his troubles were just beginning. His old friend Nicholson had been removed in favor of Sir Edmund Andros. The new executive resented Blair's inroads upon the royal funds, and viewed with disapproval the enormous influence which he wielded in England. Before many months had elapsed the commissary was writing to the bishop of London in a tone of bitter complaint. Andros had blocked the bill for increasing the ministers' salaries, he had hindered the building of the college, he had done

[1] House of Burgesses, *Journals*, April, 1691, 25-28.
[2] Perry, *Historical Collections*, I, 6.
[3] C. O. 5: 1358 (Brit. Pub. Rec. Office), 222.

nothing to secure permanent tenure for the clergy, he had opposed ecclesiastical discipline, and he had flouted the king's wishes by expelling the commissary from the council of state. In this crisis the English prelates remained loyal to Dr. Blair and brought such pressure to bear upon Andros that he was compelled to resign.[1] As his successor the king again designated Blair's collaborator, Francis Nicholson. The commissary's triumph was short-lived. Nicholson now took sides against him, and the quarrel between commissary and governor became fiercer than ever. With no little embarrassment Blair once more sought the help of the bishop of London. He had made a terrible mistake in recommending Nicholson as governor, he said, for he had now turned against him and was blocking the scheme of reform. Nothing could be accomplished until he should be removed. And removed he was. Even then Blair was destined to meet only disappointment and defeat in his efforts to reform the church.

The vestries could not be made to present their ministers. In this matter Nicholson had done his best. He had secured an opinion from Attorney-General Edward Northey that if the parishioners did not present, the governor had the right to collate a clergyman to their church by lapse.[2] Against this the vestries protested. One after another they wrote Nicholson, criticizing the opinion, defending their position and refusing to obey.[3] The governor dared not bring matters to an issue. Had he forced his nominees upon the parishes by collation, it

[1] "A True Account of a Conference at Lambeth, Dec. 27, 1697," Perry, *Historical Collections*, I, 36-65.
[2] "Commissary Blair to Bishop of London, July 17, 1724," Perry, *Historical Collections*, I, 320-321.
[3] C. O. 5: 1314, Doc. 43, IIIa (Brit. Pub. Rec. Office).

would have been impossible for them to collect their dues. The governor might arm the minister with all legal papers, but the poor man would starve if he came contrary to the wishes of the vestry. So the tenure of the ministers remained as insecure as ever.

The movement for better salaries was only partially successful. When the assembly met in October, 1693, Andros neglected to recommend a law dealing with this matter. But the burgesses of their own accord passed a clergy bill, reducing the price of tobacco in all payments of parish dues from twelve to ten shillings a hundred pounds. As the equivalent of eighty pounds was allowed by law, this would increase salaries from 13,333 pounds of tobacco to 16,000.[1] Unfortunately this bill, with several others which came before the governor in a general revision of the laws, was vetoed. In 1696 the measure was passed again, but this time the clergy were cumbered with unfavorable conditions of collecting their bulky stipends. Though Andros gave his assent, Blair complained that the measure was far less acceptable than the former bill and left the clergy still too meagerly provided for.[2]

Even the college proved a disappointment. The work of erecting the main building was begun in August, 1695. But the lack of funds and the governor's opposition caused such delays that it was not completed until 1700. Six years later it was destroyed by fire,[3] and it was many years before Blair succeeded in repairing the damage. When the institution first opened its doors,

---

[1] House of Burgesses, *Journals*, Oct., 1693.
[2] Meade, *Old Churches, Ministers and Families of Virginia*, I, art. xii.
[3] Council Minutes (Brit. Pub. Rec. Office), I, 400.

it was no more than a grammar school, with one master and an usher. Advanced courses were begun later, but few young Virginians could be found to take them. With the evidences of the hardship of the ministers' lives before them, it was not to be expected that the sons of the planters would often select that calling. The number of Virginians who were educated at William and Mary in the divinity school and went to England for ordination seems never to have been large.

The attempts to establish ecclesiastical discipline also proved futile. The want of clergymen in the colony made leniency as necessary after Blair's arrival as before. Unless the clergy are "notoriously scandalous," he wrote in 1724, "I have found it necessary to content myself with admonitions, for if I lay them aside by suspension, we have no unprovided clergymen to put in their place." [1] During the thirty-four years that he had been commissary, he said, he had made but two examples of this kind. Yet he himself at times felt that the conduct of some ministers was so flagrant that it would be better to leave the parishes vacant than to fill them with "such as are scandals to the Gospel." The sober part of the clergy are "slothful & negligent," it was testified in 1726, "and the others so debauched that they are the foremost & most bent in all manner of vices. Drunkenness is the common vice and brings with it other indecencies, which among the ignorant creates disrespect to the character and indifferency in matters of religion." [2]

Thus in utter failure ended the movement for the reform of the Virginia colonial church. From the first the undertaking was doomed to disappointment, for

[1] Perry, *Historical Collections*, I, 250.
[2] Perry, *Historical Collections*, I, 347.

Blair and Compton had attempted the impossible. They had tried to make the conditions in the colony conform to the laws and the structure of the Anglican church. Since the ecclesiastical robes did not fit the shoulders of this young wilderness child, they attempted to alter the shoulders. Able men though they were, they could not see that the church would fail of its mission in Virginia unless it shaped itself to conditions in the colony. Commissaries Garden in Carolina and Henderson in Maryland later encountered the same difficulties. The influence of the Anglican church continued to decline until during the American Revolution it reached its lowest ebb. Its history throughout the entire colonial period is one long recital of disappointment, of wasted opportunities, and gradually diminishing strength.

CHAPTER VI

THE INVISIBLE WORLD

THE colonists brought with them from Europe a vivid consciousness of the supernatural. Any variation, great or small, from the known routine of nature was taken as a "sign." Thus, when a calf was born with six eyes, the pious Winthrop shook his head in solemn apprehension: "What these prodigies portend the Lord only knows, which in due time he will manifest." [1] It was an age of magic and witchcraft, an age which believed that thunderstorms were caused by malignant spirits, that persons in league with the devil could sink ships at sea, ruin crops, strangle infants in the crib, cause sickness and death. The powers of the air were everywhere. Like their forefathers, the colonists regarded comets and other such phenomena as supernatural manifestations, set in the sky to mark some event of especial importance, to give warning of God's anger, or to herald the approach of famine or war or pestilence. The wheat blight of 1665 in Massachusetts was preceded by "a great and blazing comet," while the comet of 1680 gave Increase Mather inspiration for a sermon entitled "Heaven's Alarm to the World." When John Cotton died a comet appeared in the heavens as a signal testimony, so it was thought, "that God had removed a

[1] John Winthrop, *History of New England, 1630-1649* (J. K. Hosmer, ed., in J. F. Jameson, ed., *Original Narratives of Early American History*, N. Y., 1906-), 264.

bright star, a burning and a shining light out of the heaven of his church here."

> That comets great men's deaths do oft forego,
> This present comet doth too sadly show.[1]

A spearlike form in the northern lights of 1667 presaged the deaths of three revered clergymen, Samuel Shepherd, Henry Flint and Jonathan Mitchell.[2] The Dutch settlers on the Hudson trembled at the "dreadful comett starr" of 1680 with its "fyery tail or streemer," and, feeling that God had threatened them, petitioned for "a day of fasting and humiliation." In Virginia the people were warned of the approach of Bacon's Rebellion by a comet "streaming like a horse tail westward."

Increase Mather, in his *Remarkable Providences*, tells how certain holy men were preserved at sea, when all others in the ship's company were lost. Lightning he calls "Heaven's arrow," and relates numerous instances in which men were "smitten with the fire of God." The smell of brimstone, which so often accompanies the thunderbolts, he considered proof positive that they were of supernatural origin. He was not a little perplexed that these dreadful visitations should come so often to pious persons, in some cases when they were assembled for prayers and worship. Meteorites he regarded as missiles hurled from heaven. In fact, every manifestation of nature which science had left unexplained he instantly assigned to the sphere of the supernatural. "There is also," he says, "that which is very mysterious

---

[1] Lines from funeral elegy by Reverend John Norton, in Nathaniel Morton, *New-England's Memorial* (Plymouth, 1826), 149.

[2] W. D. Love, *The Fast and Thanksgiving Days of New England* (Boston, 1895), 190.

and beyond human capacity to comprehend, in thunder and lightning." [1]

Cotton Mather, having lost the manuscript of three lectures, satisfied himself that "Spectres, or Agents in the invisible World, were the Robbers." When New England was swept by yellow fever, he ascribed his escape to the intervention of a good angel. In 1696 he set out for Salem, undeterred by a threatening storm, whereupon "the storm strangely held off," until his return more than a week later. He constantly prayed to be protected from magic, and ascribed to the work of a demon the death of his infant.[2] The God of seventeenth-century New England was a God of dramatic revelations. In June, 1647, when no news had come to New Haven of a great ship which six months before had sailed away with some of the finest manhood of that struggling little settlement, a phantom replica appeared in the harbor and rehearsed the tragic wreck before the eyes of the astonished townsmen. The Rev. John Davenport explained "that God had condescended, for the quieting of their afflicted spirits, this extraordinary account of his sovereign disposal of those for whom so many fervent prayers were made continually." [3]

It was a terrible, mysterious world, this world of the imagination which was so real to the colonists, a world in which devils entered men's bodies and expressed

[1] See Increase Mather, *Remarkable Providences* (London, 1852), 2 ff., 51 ff., for discussions of "Sea Deliverances" and "Lightning."

[2] Cotton Mather, *Diary* (Mass. Hist. Soc., *Colls.*, ser. 7, VII), 171, 204.

[3] The Reverend John Pierpont to Cotton Mather, quoted in Cotton Mather, *Magnalia Christi Americana* (Hartford, 1853), I, 84. This experience together with the imperfections of the harbor discouraged New Haven commerce. See Samuel Maverick, *A Briefe Description of New England and the Severall Townes Therein* (Boston, 1885), 23.

things of which they themselves knew nothing, in which goblins stole infants from the cradle substituting for them hideous elves old in sin, in which Satan's agents took strange forms the better to carry out his evil commands, in which the very air was full of unseen spirits, some good, others ever alert to do harm, in which the powers of darkness could destroy crops, bring on pestilence, cause droughts. Human confederates, peradventure might be enlisted in this hideous work.

Witchcraft as a living force in European life is of comparatively recent origin. During the Dark Ages, when faith was universal and doubt almost unknown, men regarded the devil with something akin to contempt. He was usually depicted as an insignificant imp whose malignity was easily rendered harmless by the repetition of a prayer or by making the sign of the cross. With the first traces of skepticism he became more terrible, and the church began to concern itself with his direct relations with human beings. It was in the thirteenth century that theologians worked out their theory of witchcraft, and in the fourteenth that they drew all witchcraft cases into their own jurisdiction. The end of the sixteenth century and the beginning of the seventeenth, a period noted for religious chaos and conflict, marked the height of the witchcraft prosecutions. The Protestant movement had dignified the Bible into a unique authority, and the Bible commanded, "Thou shalt not suffer a witch to live." [1] Many thought that the Roman church had been criminally lenient in this matter.

In an age when Satan had become a vivid reality, when it was believed that he was constantly taxing his

[1] Exodus, xxii, 18.

ingenuity to defeat the divine will and employing his hellish agents to plague and tempt the select of God, the dread of witchcraft was inevitable. The conflagration broke out first in Italy, Spain and France, carrying terror and panic before it, and causing unspeakable suffering to thousands of innocent persons. In the years from 1588 to 1602 the tribunal of St. Claude, under the presidency of Boguet, is said to have burned six hundred victims, most of them for witchcraft. Decrees passed by the parliaments of Rouen, Dijon, Rennes, Paris, Toulouse, Bordeaux and Rheims were followed by a similarly terrible harvest. At Toulouse four hundred persons perished in one execution; in another place a single judge boasted that he had put to death eight hundred witches in sixteen years; the executions at Paris are described as infinite. In Spain the quest for witches was undertaken with such zeal that the countryside was alight with human torches. The craze spread also to Switzerland. In Geneva alone five hundred witches were executed in the space of three months. In Italy a thousand persons were sent to death in a single year in the province of Como, while in other places the epidemic raged with almost equal fierceness. Witchcraft in its most virulent forms was late in appearing in Germany, but made amends for this tardiness by the thoroughness with which it swept over the country. In Osnabrück one hundred and twenty-one witches were burned in 1583 and one hundred and thirteen six years later; at Ellwangen one hundred and sixty-seven perished in 1612, at Würzburg one hundred and fifty-eight between the years 1627 and 1629.

James I of England was so firm a believer in witchcraft that he wrote a dialogue on the subject. Soon after his accession a law was passed making the practice of magic punishable with death irrespective of the injury inflicted. It was during the period of Puritan ascendency that the witch inquest reached its zenith. It is probable that more innocent persons perished in this way in the years from 1642 to 1660 than in all other periods of English history. When the famous witch finder, Matthew Hopkins, declared that Suffolk and the neighboring shires were infected with witches, two distinguished divines were sent by Parliament to ferret them out. As a result no less than sixty victims were hanged in a single year. In many cases the accused were kept awake by the inquisitors until they became half-crazed and confessed.[1]

The English epidemic pales, however, beside the terrible witch inquests of Scotland. In 1603 the Scotch synod enjoined every minister to see to it that "a subtle and privy inquisition" be made in his parish so that not one of the devil's agents should escape. Large numbers of unhappy wretches, often helpless old women, were dragged before the justices, subjected to torture, strangled and burned. In some cases an iron hoop was bound across the face, with four prongs thrust in the mouth, and fastened to the wall by a chain, so that the victim could neither lie down nor sleep. If this proved not sufficient, the thumbscrew was applied, or the legs of the accused were broken, or fire matches were applied to the body. Under such circumstances many a weird story was gasped out to the justices of contracts with Satan, of witch gatherings, of night rides through the air. In 1662 alone there were one hundred and fifty convictions,

---

[1] Wallace Notestein, *A History of Witchcraft in England from 1558 to 1718* (Wash., 1911), 97-101.

and many a traveler was startled to see the highway lit up by groups of burning witches.[1]

Such was the age which saw the establishment of the English colonies in America. The settlers, whether they landed on the banks of the James or in Boston Harbor, shared fully the almost universal belief in the constant presence of the supernatural. In fact, the transition from Europe to America tended to stimulate rather than weaken the dread of the unknown. This vast country with its strange wild coast, its mysterious forests, its savage Indians, seemed a place especially suited to magic and witchcraft, a place for centuries set aside by Satan for his own uses. At the mummery of the Indian medicine men the Europeans looked on, not with incredulity or derision, but with mingled fear and indignation. To them it seemed a direct manifestation of the devil's power. Happily there were no witch panics and probably no executions in America outside the confines of New England,[2] but only the boldest and most skeptical dared question the reality of the crime of witchcraft. Witch trials took place in almost every colony.

Several years before the Massachusetts Bay Company received its charter a grand jury in Virginia was considering charges of witchcraft against a certain Goodwife Wright. To the modern mind the evidence presented was trivial and absurd. She was heard to curse

[1] The reader who desires to compare the seventeenth-century outlook in New England with that in Scotland will find material readily at hand in H. T. Buckle, *History of Civilization in England* (N. Y., 1884), II, chap. v.

[2] W. H. Browne, *Maryland, the History of a Palatinate* (H. E. Scudder, ed., *Am. Commonwealths*, Boston, 1884), 83, citing William Kilty, *English Statutes* (Annapolis, 1811), speaks of an execution in Maryland in 1685; but the records for 1685 are lost.

Sergeant Booth, after which "he having very fair game to shoot at yet he could never kill anything." She was rejected as midwife for Mrs. Giles Allington, who with her husband and infant immediately after fell ill, the infant finally dying. She had come to the home of a Mr. Moore to purchase some little chickens, and when he would sell her none, not only the chicks died but the hen also.[1] Apparently the grand jury did not consider the case against Goody Wright a strong one, as there is no record of a presentation for trial.

Later came the case of Paul Carter and his wife Sarah, who were accused of infanticide and brought before the Accomac court in 1680. Both were compelled to stroke the body of the child, it being the popular belief that the wounds would bleed afresh at the touch of the murderer. This Virginia grand jury reported that when Sarah touched the corpse, they "saw no alteration," but when Paul's turn came, "immediately whilst he was stroaking ye childe the black & sotted places about the body of the childe grew fresh and red so that blud was redy to come through ye skin. . . ."[2] Equally interesting is a case of witchcraft in Northumberland county, Virginia, in which a certain William Harding was accused by the Reverend David Lindsay. The prisoner was found guilty, and although he escaped the death penalty, he was punished with ten stripes on the bare shoulders and banishment. In 1665 Alice Stephens was brought before the general court on a charge of witchcraft. In 1679 Alice Cartwright was accused in the

[1] The Council and General Court, "Minutes for 1622-1629," *Va. Mag. of Hist. and Biog.*, XXVI, 12 ff.
[2] "Ordeal of Touch in Colonial Virginia," *Va. Mag. of Hist. and Biog.*, IV, 187.

court of Lower Norfolk and examined for witch marks by a jury of women.[1]

Of especial interest was the case of Grace Sherwood of Princess Anne County. In 1689 this woman, together with her husband James Sherwood, brought action for slander against John Eisburne for declaring that she had bewitched his hogs and crops, and against Anthony Barnes for declaring that she had ridden his wife and then, in the shape of a black cat, had slipped through the keyhole. In both cases the jury decided against Grace, possibly because they considered the accusations established. Yet she was not brought to trial until 1708, when a formal charge of witchcraft was lodged against her by Luke Hill and his wife. After some delay she was subjected to the trial by water and to examination for witch marks, both tests going against her, "she swimming when therein and bound contrary to Custom and Judgement of all the Spectators, and afterwards being serched by Five Antient weomen who have all declared on Oath that she is not like them." [2] The final records in this famous case are missing, but it seems certain that she escaped severe punishment, for reference to her occurs several times in later records.

On the whole, however, the Virginia justices weighed with a more critical exactness the witchcraft charges than the magistrates in New England. The accused persons were not driven to confession by judicial pressure, there was no disposition to prejudge their cases, the evidence

[1] "Witchcraft in Virginia," *The Lower Norfolk Antiquary*, I (1897), 56.

[2] The records of this case have been carefully printed by E. W. James, ed., "Grace Sherwood, the Virginia Witch," in *William and Mary Col. Quart.*, III, 190-192, 242-245; IV, 18-20, and in *Lower Norfolk County Antiquary*, II, 92-93.

was not twisted to bring about convictions. Above all, when charges of witchcraft were made, either in moments of anger or out of deliberate conviction, so far from bringing the accused to the gallows, they were apt to result in a law suit and a fine for the persons presenting them.[1] This attitude of the courts may have been partly the result of a dawning skepticism among the more enlightened men in this colony, but it is more readily explained by the absence of interference on the part of the clergy. In Scotland, in the Puritan shires of England and in New England, the court which dealt leniently with a suspected witch was certain to incur many a fiery denunciation from the pulpit, but the Anglican ministers who came to Virginia were laggards in this matter. The fear of witchcraft in Virginia seems to have sprung more from folklore than from theology.

Across the Potomac, in Maryland, the strong Puritan element made the charge of witchcraft a more dangerous matter. The justices were instructed "to enquire of all manner of Fellonyes, witchcrafts, inchantments, Sorceries, Magick Arts, etc.," and there is evidence that this order was not neglected.[2] During the reign of Charles II, John Coman, who was accused of "witchcraft, conjuration, sorcery or enchantment upon the body of Elizabeth Goodale," was tried and sentenced to death. In 1675 he petitioned the lower house of the assembly to intercede for him with the governor. The governor, who had a keener appreciation of his own profit than of the perils of witchcraft, commuted the

[1] P. A. Bruce, *Institutional History of Virginia* (N. Y., 1901), I, 278-289.
[2] Browne, *Maryland*, 83.

sentence on condition that Coman work for him in the capacity of a servant. The sheriff of St. Mary's conducted the culprit to the gallows and placed the rope around his neck before informing him that he was not to be put to death.[1]

In William Penn's settlement upon the banks of the Delaware witchcraft attracted little attention. The Quakers believed in the reality of the crime and George Fox himself exclaimed, "Arise, children of God, and suffer not a Witch to live." But the gentle mysticism of the sect was out of harmony with the vivid consciousness of demonology and the spirit of religious militancy essential to every great witch inquest. Having no clergy, inclined to charity, slow to credit evil of their neighbors, the Quaker colonists escaped almost entirely the witchcraft charges and trials so common elsewhere. The most important case was that of Margaret Mattson, who was accused before the governor and council in 1683 of having bewitched her neighbors' cows. Although she was pronounced not guilty "in manner and forme" as indicted, the court declared her convicted "of haveing the Comon fame of a witch." Eight years later Robert Guard and his wife came before the council complaining that John Richards, a butcher, together with his wife Ann, had accused them of witchcraft. "The matter was inquired into, and being found trifling, was dismissed." [2]

In the Dutch colony of New Netherland we hear nothing of witches, because Holland, even in the seven-

[1] Maryland General Assembly, *Proceeds. and Acts for 1666-1676* (W. H. Browne, ed., Balt., 1884), 425-426, 444-446.
[2] G. L. Burr, ed., *Narratives of the Witchcraft Cases, 1648-1706* (J. F. Jameson, ed., *Original Narratives of Early American History*, N. Y., 1906-), 85-88.

teenth century, had largely outgrown the superstition. The country had had its share of witch executions under the Spanish Inquisition, and a wholesome reaction was now in progress. The works of Dutch writers are full of arguments against the reality of demonology and against the use of torture in witch cases. The foes and the victims of the witch prosecutions in other lands were welcomed. So far as is known, there were no trials for witchcraft in Holland after 1610; the Dutch traders who settled on the Hudson were almost entirely free from the current superstition. When the colony came under the rule of England and was expanded to include the Puritan parts of Long Island, one or two witch cases came before the courts.[1] But the authorities not only treated the charges lightly but actually opened their doors to refugees fleeing from the stern witch prosecutors of Hartford and Salem.

In New England witchcraft in America reached its greatest excesses. The Puritan teaching made it appear that supernatural intervention was a commonplace event. The New Englanders sent witches to the gallows in part to champion the cause of God against the devil, in part out of fear of what the witches might do. Back of every witch epidemic was a strong element of terror, and superstition was the soil from which each sprang. Nevertheless, the actual growth required a special preparation, usually the broadcasting of books and pamphlets on the subject. At any time in the seventeenth century the

[1] This is illustrated by a case brought before the court of assizes in 1665, and one before the governor's council in 1670. It is interesting to note that one was from Brookhaven, a New England community, and the other involved a woman from Wethersfield, Connecticut, who lived in Westchester with many other settlers from the east. See N. Y. Executive Council, *Minutes* (V. H. Paltsits, ed., Albany, 1910), I, 52-55.

contortions of sufferers from epilepsy, the vagaries of the insane or the tricks of mischievous children might spread alarm, and place many persons in danger of the gallows. But there would be no frantic searching out of witches, no wholesale trials and executions, without some unusual inciting cause.

In New England there were two well-defined epidemics of witch hunting, one in the years from 1647 to 1663, the other from 1688 to 1693. The first seems to have been inspired by the witchcraft frenzy which swept the Puritan counties of England at the time of the Civil War. Many of the settlers in Massachusetts and Connecticut had left these districts but a few years before Hopkins and Stearne began their notorious proceedings, and the details of trials and hangings must have been almost as well-known in Boston as in London. Bewitched and bewitchers alike were doubtless personally known to many, while no letter from Suffolk or Norfolk could fail to dwell upon the subject which was uppermost in every mind. Moreover, some of that swarm of books and pamphlets generated by the English trials unquestionably found their way across the Atlantic. Matthew Hopkins's *The Lawes Against Witches* appeared in 1645, followed two years later by his *The Discovery of Witches*, while Stearne's *Confirmation and Discovery of Witchcraft*, *The True and Exact Relation*, *Signs and Wonders from Heaven*, and *A True Relation of the Arraignment of Eighteen Witches at St. Edmundsbury*, all were issued in 1645. So profound was the influence of Hopkins and Stearne in Massachusetts that the highest court of the colony in admiration of their achievements was "desireows that the same course which hath been taken in England for the discouery of witches, by watchinge, may also be taken here." [1]

Early in 1647 Governor Winthrop of Massachusetts wrote in his journal, "One of Windsor arraigned and executed for a witch." This short entry long baffled New England historians, for the official records make no mention of the case. The identity of the unhappy victim seems now to be established, however, by the discovery of the following entry in the diary of Matthew Grant of Windsor: "May 26, '47, Achsah Young was hanged." [2] With the details of this, the first execution for witchcraft in any of the colonies, we are still entirely unacquainted.

Massachusetts, as though jealous of Connecticut for having been before her, was quick to follow her example. Margaret Jones of Charlestown was accused because, "after some angry words passing between her and her Neighbours, some mischief befel such Neighbours in their Creatures." Although she was urged on the day of her execution to confess and repent, "she constantly professed herself innocent of that crime." [3]

Trials and executions now followed with monotonous regularity, both in Connecticut and in Massachusetts. In 1648 one Mary Johnson was hanged at Hartford. "Her first familiarity with the Devils came by Discontent, and wishing the Devil to take that and t'other Thing, and, the Devil to do This and That; Whereupon a Devil appeared unto her, tendering her the best service he could do for her." After this he would clear the

---

[1] Governor and Company of the Massachusetts Bay, *Records for 1628-1686* (N. B. Shurtleff, ed., Boston, 1853-1854), III, 126.

[2] H. R. Stiles, *The History and Genealogies of Ancient Windsor* (Hartford, 1891), I, 147.

[3] Burr, *Narratives of the Witchcraft Cases*, 408.

hearth, and when her master would send her to the field "to drive out the hogs that us'd to break into it, a Devil would scowre them out, and make her laugh to see how he feaz'd em about." [1]

In 1651 John and Joanna Carrington of Wethersfield were executed for having "intertained familiarity with Sathan the Great Enemye of God and Mankinde," while a certain Goody Bassit went to her death in the same year for a like crime. The trials continued in Connecticut for another decade, but prior to 1662 there was no panic, and in some cases the juries actually brought in acquittals. The most notable execution of the period occurred in Boston, where Mrs. Ann Hibbins paid the penalty, as has been said, of "having more wit than her neighbors." This lady was the widow of William Hibbins who had served twelve years in the council of assistants and at one time had been the agent of Massachusetts in England. The affair aroused fierce excitement, and doubtless was in part responsible for the long lull which followed in the witchcraft prosecutions in that colony.

In Connecticut there was a recurrence of the craze in 1662 which threatened a panic hardly less terrible than that which occurred at Salem three decades later. Ann Cole, daughter of a Hartford carpenter, "was taken with very strange fits, wherein she (or rather the Devill as t'is judged) made use of her lips and held a discourse." Her ravings were taken down and used as evidence of witchcraft against several neighbors, among them Mr. and Mrs. Greensmith. Both were old and ignorant, the wife probably half-crazy. The poor woman confessed her familiarity with Satan, declaring that he had just

[1] Burr, *Narratives of the Witchcraft Cases*, 135-136.

appeared to her in the image of a deer. The witches had meetings near her house, she testified, in which some assumed one shape, others another. The Greensmiths were both executed, together with Mary Barnes of Farmington, also accused by Ann Cole. Mrs. Elizabeth Seager was tried, but acquitted, while William Ayres and his wife, after submitting to the water ordeal, to see if with Satan's aid they would float, saved themselves by flight.[1]

In all, there were, during this period of sixteen years, eight hangings in Connecticut and six in Massachusetts. This was a terrible toll to take from these infant settlements, a toll which makes it evident that the colonial ministers and magistrates were quite as zealous as those of England in searching out Satan's brood. The executions per capita in New England probably outnumbered five to one those of the mother country during this, the greatest witch-hunting period in English history. To what extent torture to wring confessions was used in the early trials cannot be determined. Since the Massachusetts court advocated the adoption of the methods in vogue in England, it is probable that the "watchings" so vividly described by Hopkins and Stearne were practised in that colony. It was believed that the spirits which attended all witches were accustomed to visit them once in every twenty-four hours, usually in the form of an insect or an animal. If the witch were placed upon a chair in the middle of the room and kept awake, the imps could not approach her. This led to the custom of making the accused person walk in order to prevent sleep, and protracted sleeplessness was productive of

[1] H. C. Lea, *Superstition and Force* (4th edn., Phila., 1892), 325 ff., gives a description and history of the water ordeal.

confessions.[1] Perhaps more frequent in New England was the pressure brought to bear by "Godly Divines," who pleaded with the witches, "laying the hainousness of their sins to them," and depicting the terrible fate which awaited them in the next world should they refuse to confess.

In the quarter of a century from 1663 to 1688 witchcraft obtruded less upon the New England consciousness. In Connecticut there was a trial in 1670, and a few years later the pranks of a mischievous boy caused great apprehension at Newbury. But the impelling forces for a new witch panic seem to have been lacking. The colonists were occupied with other affairs, while in England the restoration of the monarchy had brought about the suppression of the witch hunters and the persecution of the Puritan clergy. Had not the New England synod attempted to arouse anew a vivid consciousness of supernatural occurrences, it is probable that there would have been no further executions. But in the last quarter of the seventeenth century the theocracy was becoming alarmed at the decline of its influence, and was trying to buttress its power. It was Increase Mather who conceived the idea of publishing a record of "illustrious providences" or supernatural happenings, an attempt to prove by a sort of scientific induction that God had special concern for New England.[2] At a synod in 1681 it was resolved that "Divine Judgements, Tempests, Floods, Earth-quakes, Thunders as are unusual, strange Apparitions, or what ever else shall happen that is Prodigious, Witchcrafts, Diabolical Possessions,

---

[1] Notestein, *Witchcraft in England*, 202-203.
[2] See K. B. Murdock, *Increase Mather, The Foremost American Puritan* (Cambridge, 1925), 167-170.

Remarkable Judgements upon noted Sinners, eminent Deliverances, and Answers to Prayer, are to be reckoned among Illustrious Providences." In 1684 this project found expression in Increase Mather's *An Essay for the Recording of Illustrious Providences.* The book met with a ready welcome, went through three impressions before the end of the year, and unquestionably did much to prepare the minds of the public for a new witchcraft epidemic.

When the children of a Boston mason named Goodwin became afflicted with fits, complaining that they had been bewitched, the entire community was alarmed. An old half-crazy Irish Catholic laundress was accused of the crime and brought before the court. The finding of several small rag dolls in her house weighed heavily against her, and she was said to have confessed that by wetting her finger and stroking these images she could torment her victims. Her incoherent and wild answers to questions were accepted as evidence of guilt; she was pronounced sane by a board of physicians, and was led forth to execution. The matter might have ended here had not Cotton Mather, in an effort to confute the Sadduceeism of the skeptical, brought the oldest Goodwin girl into his own home for observation. This was a great event in the life of the child, for Mr. Mather was perhaps the most influential man in the colony. The little child of an obscure workman suddenly found herself the object of the great man's interest. Her every movement was closely watched, her every word weighed and duly recorded in a new work on memorable providences. She knew what was expected of her, and, consciously or unconsciously, played her part.

As she went through her antics the famous minister

looked gravely on, or actually stimulated her imagination by leading questions. She rode imaginary horses, was pulled hither and thither, was strangled by invisible spirits; which so impressed the eminent observer that he seriously set down: "I shall count that man Ignorant who shall suspect, but I shall count him down-right Impudent if he Assert the Non-existence of things which we have had such palpable Convictions of." His witch-craft clinic, to his own mind, had proved a complete success. His account appeared in 1689. "The old Heresy of the sensual Sadduces, denying the Being of Angels either good or evil died not with them," he wrote. "How much this fond opinion has gotten ground in this debauched age is awfully observable; and what a dangerous stroak it gives to settle men in Atheism, is not hard to discern." [1] This heresy the book was intended to combat, a task it accomplished so successfully that within three years New England was beside itself with the witchcraft terror, hundreds of persons had been accused, scores sentenced to death and no less than nineteen executed.

In the household of Samuel Parris, minister of the church at Salem Village, were two West Indian slaves, John Indian and Tituba. This pair, themselves steeped in voodoo lore, gathered around them a group of young girls, who listened with fascination to their stories of fortune telling and witchcraft. The girls, who came to be known as the "afflicted children," began to show all the symptoms of magical possession, falling on the floor, speaking in a meaningless jargon, screaming as though in agony; whereupon they became objects of supreme interest. Ministers and physicians flocked to see them,

[1] "Address to the Reader," *Memorable Providences* (Boston, 1689).

watched their antics with close attention, plied them with questions.

When asked to name their tormentors the girls accused one neighbor after another until it seemed that half the village must have sold themselves to the devil. Terror seized the community. The ministers and the magistrates, triumphant at this manifestation of the supernatural, staunch in their determination to put to rout the forces of evil, proved blind to reason. The accused, some of them persons of blameless life and elevated character, received the mockery of a trial, and were hastened to the gallows. The idle gossip of neighbors counted heavily against them, trivial incidents in their lives received the most sinister interpretations, the obvious meaning of their answers was twisted to their undoing. At the trial of the Reverend George Burroughs the afflicted girls fell into such violent fits that for a long while they were unable to testify. "The chief judge asked the prisoner who he thought hindered these witnesses from giving their testimonies? and he answered, He supposed it was the Devil. That Honourable person then reply'd, How comes the Devil so loathe to have any Testimony born against you?" "Which cast him," Cotton Mather tells us, "into great confusion." [1]

Old Giles Corey pleaded not guilty, but refused to put himself on trial; whereupon he was pressed to death, the old English *peine forte et dure*. "In pressing his Tongue being prest out of his Mouth, the Sheriff with his Cane forced it in again, when he was dying." [2]

[1] Cotton Mather, *Wonders of the Invisible World* (reptd., London, 1862), 122.
[2] See the readable account in W. S. Nevins, *Witchcraft in Salem Village in 1692* (Salem, 1892), chap. vii.

william Stoughton.

A Witchcraft
Judge, 1692.

When Mr. Burroughs was upon the scaffold he made a speech to the assembled crowd, asserting his innocence with such earnestness as to force conviction. As he was concluding with the Lord's Prayer, many eyes were dim, and there was a movement as though some would hinder the execution. But his accusers explained that he was able to simulate innocence through the devil's promptings, and he was quickly dispatched.

Among those accused was the wife of Mr. Nathaniel Cary, a prominent shipmaster of Charlestown and later a member of the general court. "I having heard some days that my Wife was accused of Witchcraft," wrote Mr. Cary, "we went to Salem-Village to see if the afflicted did know her. . . . They all came in, who began to tumble down like Swine, and then three Women were called in to attend them. We in the room were all at a Stand to see who they would cry out of; but in a short time they cried out, Cary; and immediately after a warrant was sent from the Justices to bring my Wife before them. . . . My Wife declared to the Justices that she never had any knowledge of them before that day; she was forced to stand with her arms stretched out. I did request that I might hold one of her hands, but it was denied me; then she desired me to wipe the Tears from her Eyes, and the Sweat from her Face, which I did; then she desired she might lean herself on me, saying she would faint. Justice Hathorn replied, she had strength enough to torment those persons." The poor woman was committed to Boston prison, but Cary succeeded in having her removed to Cambridge, where she was kept in irons. "The Tryals at Salem coming on," he recorded, "I went thither, to see how things were there managed; and finding that the Spectre-Evidence

was there received, together with idle, if not malicious
Stories against peoples Lives, I did easily perceive which
way the rest would go." He then petitioned that his
wife's trial might be held in her own county, but receiving word that it would not be granted, he managed
to deliver her from prison and the two fled to Rhode
Island. Even there she was not safe, and "along with
some others that had escaped their cruel hands," they
made their way to New York where they were courte-
ously received by Governor Benjamin Fletcher.[1]

There were other husbands who lacked either the
foresight, desire or ability to rescue their wives. Some
no doubt believed sincerely that justice would be done
and innocence vindicated, some perhaps were actually
persuaded of their guilt. The trials and executions went
on. The case of Rebecca Nurse furnishes an illustration
of the lack of fairness with which the proceedings were
conducted. This good woman was acquitted by the
jury, but when the afflicted girls heard the verdict, they
"made an hideous out-cry" as if their tortures were at
once resumed. The presiding judge thereupon told the
jury that they must have overlooked one fact—that the
prisoner in an unguarded moment had really confessed
her guilt. It seems that when one of the accused,
Deliverance Hobbs, "who had confessed herself to be
a witch, was brought into Court to witness against her,
she had exclaimed, 'What, do they bring her? she is one
of us.'" An acquittal was out of the question, the
learned judge felt, in the face of such evidence. Unfortunately the old woman, being somewhat deaf, missed
the significance of what was being said, and by her silence

---

[1] Robert Calef, "More Wonders of the Invisible World," Burr, *Narra-tives of the Witchcraft Cases*, 350-352.

seemed to assent to his interpretation of her remark. Thereupon the jury went out again and found her guilty. Later she explained, what to an unprejudiced mind would have been obvious from the first, that she had referred to Goody Hobbs as one of "us prisoners," not as one of "us witches." But this did not save her from the gallows.

The terrible epidemic wore itself out through its own excesses. When a score of persons had been executed, when eight more were under sentence, when fifty others had confessed themselves to be witches, when one hundred and fifty were in prison and two hundred accused, things came to a sudden halt. People began to reflect that it was most improbable that "so many in so small a compass of Land should so abominably leap into the Devil's lap at once." [1] Nor did any man know when his own turn might come. Eastern Massachusetts became a place of terror, where neighbor looked with suspicion upon neighbor. When the afflicted girls began to accuse prominent persons, the magistrates, seeing that things had gone too far, threw out the indictments and opened the jails. The episode proved a boomerang for the clergy. Skeptics appeared on all sides, and it was soon widely recognized that many, if not all, the persons executed had been innocent. Judge Sewall, five years afterwards, got up in the Old South Church and publicly acknowledged his repentance and shame. Ann Putnam, one of the most active of the afflicted children, later admitted that she had been instrumental in the shedding of innocent blood. So far from striking a blow at Sadduceeism, the affair tended to discredit the men, who,

[1] John Hale, *A Modest Inquiry into the Nature of Witchcraft* (Boston, 1702), chap. iv.

by their influence and example, had done so much to stir up the trouble.   The Salem witch executions played an important part in undermining the power of the old theocracy.

The gradual decay of the belief in the supernatural, a decay which was marked in the colonies as well as in Europe, was not, however, the result of one incident, but of a subtle and far-reaching mental change.   The seventeenth century saw the growth of the spirit of rationalism which was destined eventually to sweep the civilized world.   Superstition is the child of ignorance. The ecclesiastical mind, brought into contact with the forces of nature and completely ignorant of the laws which govern them, saw in them the visible manifestation of the spirit world.   The eclipse of the sun was a token of divine anger, the lightning bolt was thought to be the witches' plaything, the hurricane the work of the magician.   The normal person of the fifteenth or sixteenth centuries lived in a realm of the supernatural because he found no ready natural explanation for the phenomena which surrounded him.   Deformed persons, half-wits, the blind, were possessed of devils; disease was produced by magic; drought, hail and tempests were the work of malignant spirits.

When science began to reveal the true causes of these things the world of the supernatural faded away.   The appearance of a comet loses its awful significance when we know just what it is, when we can determine its component elements, estimate its density, measure its velocity, and, if it be periodic in its character, foretell the exact date of its reappearance.   It was Copernicus, Galileo, Kepler, Newton, Halley, Walton, Boyle and hundreds of lesser scientists, working patiently at their separate tasks, who freed the human mind from the chains of the invisible empire. One after another the phenomena of nature were shown to be the result of natural causes, and the conclusion was almost unescapable that all things could be so explained.

The change was not the work of a decade or even of a century; it began in the Middle Ages, and is not yet completed. Before the end of the seventeenth century it had progressed far enough to make many thoughtful men skeptical of the reality of witchcraft. It was the growth of this spirit which the New England ministers noted with apprehension, denounced as Sadduceeism, and combated fiercely in sermon and pamphlet. But they were powerless to sweep back the advancing tide of rationalism. The *Remarkable Providences* and the *Memorable Providences* did indeed for the moment rouse anew the latent fear of the invisible, but they were swept away in the very storm they blew up. There were witchcraft trials in America even in the eighteenth century, the belief in supernatural intervention in human affairs lingered on well into the nineteenth; but the champions of the invisible world had made their last real stand, and had met defeat.[1]

[1] In taking leave of the subject, however, it may be remarked in some astonishment that the latest author to treat of witchcraft states his belief that contracts with Satan must be taken as actualities "then and now"! See Montague Summers, *The History of Witchcraft and Demonology* (C. K. Ogden, ed., *The History of Civilization*, N. Y., 1924-   ), as reviewed by Lynn Thorndike, "A Welter of Witches," *The Nation* (N. Y.), CXXIV (1927), 43.

CHAPTER VII

THE PRACTICE OF PHYSIC

MORE has been done in the past half century to combat disease, allay suffering and prolong life than in all previous history. The dread diseases, which in former times swept over nations, are succumbing one by one. The discovery of the origin of many maladies, the use of effective preventive measures, the production of new specifics, a better understanding of the laws of hygiene, a tremendous advance in surgical knowledge and skill, have made our own age preëminent in the conservation of health. Accustomed to this beneficent progress of science, one turns to the seventeenth century to find a state of mind in sharpest contrast. With the opening of that century, when the English laid the foundations of their empire in America, there was general ignorance of the composition and processes of the human body. This age, the age of Shakespeare and Jonson, of Francis Bacon and Galileo, was also the age of fetish cures and mysterious quack remedies, an age which discouraged anatomical study and looked with contempt upon the surgeon—the barber-surgeon, whose lancet brought him no more prestige than his razor. While all Europe was tingling with the intellectual impulse given by the Renaissance, the Reformation and the opening of the New World, the science of health remained much as it had been in the days of Charlemagne.

The chief cause of error was the belief, widely accepted for many centuries, that disease is caused by diabolic influence. "It is demons which produce famine, unfruitfulness, corruptions of the air, pestilences," said Origen; and Saint Augustine agreed that "all diseases of Christians should be ascribed to these demons." From this conception to a condemnation of the use of medicines was an inevitable step—it was worse than futile to apply natural remedies to supernatural ills. Gregory of Nazianzen declared that pain, being inflicted by devils, should be cured by the laying on of consecrated hands. Saint Ambrose considered it sinful to resort to medicine instead of trusting to the intercession of saints. Martin Luther shared these opinions, declaring that "Pestilence, fever and other severe diseases are naught else than the devil's work." [1]

These views did not prevent a serious attempt by scholars to learn the secrets of the human body. Giles Firmin, indeed, as early as the sixteen forties was "reading" to Massachusetts pupils on the basis of an "anatomy," or skeleton, which he had articulated, probably the beginning of clinical instruction in America.[2] Autopsies were sometimes performed, such as that by Dr. Bryan Rossiter in Hartford in 1662 upon the Kelly child; yet this particular demonstration may have advanced science but little, as it proved to the doctor's satisfaction that the girl had died of witchcraft.[3] In

[1] F. H. Garrison, *An Introduction to the Study of Medicine* (Phila., 1922), 37.

[2] S. A. Green, "Remarks," Mass. Hist. Soc., *Proceeds.*, ser. 2, I, 44-45; and John Eliot, "The Letter . . . to T. S. [Thomas Shepard] Covering the Late Work of God Among the Indians," Mass. Hist. Soc., *Colls.*, ser. 3, IV, 57.

[3] W. S. Steiner, "History of Medicine," N. G. Osborn, *History of Connecticut* (New Haven, 1925), III, 664-666.

southern Europe, where the Saracen influence was strong, medicine was taught in the universities. But it must be said that at the opening of the seventeenth century the science was everywhere still traditional and empirical. There grew up the wildest and most absurd notions concerning remedies. It was reasoned that since the universe was made for man God must have put his sign upon everything designed to serve as specifics for disease—the doctrine of signatures. Eyebright, which is marked with a spot like an eye, was thought to be excellent for diseases of the eye; bugloss, resembling a snake's head, was good for snake bite; celandine, which has a yellow juice, was used in cases of jaundice. "Like by like is to be cured—that is, similar ulcers by similar forms," said Paracelsus.[1]

Amid the general ignorance and superstition, observation and experience had brought to a few men some faint conception of the real causes of disease. It was known that certain maladies were communicated from one person to another and some crude efforts were made to isolate the sufferers. On the vessels which brought immigrants to Virginia in 1610 a number of wretches who developed yellow fever or the plague were promptly thrown overboard. When the *Sarah Constant,* the *Discovery* and the *Goodspeed* set sail for Virginia in 1606, the council in England gave instructions that in selecting a site for their town: "Neither must you plant in a low or moist place because it will prove unhealthfull." [2] *The Laws Divine and Martial,* published at Jamestown some years later, displayed a certain knowl-

[1] Paracelsus, *De Cutis Apertionibus,* folio 62.
[2] "Advice of the Council," Alexander Brown, *The Genesis of the United States* (Boston, 1891), I, 84.

edge of the principles of hygiene. "There shall no man or woman . . . dare to wash any unclean linnen . . . within the Pallizadoes . . . nor rench, and make clean, any kettle, pot or pan . . . within twenty foote of the olde well . . . upon pain of whipping." [1]

These were but faint glimmerings amid general darkness. More typical of the times is a letter of 1643 from Dr. Stafford of London to Governor Winthrop of Connecticut giving detailed information concerning various cures, for example that for smallpox, plague, purples and poison. "In the month of March take toads as many as you will alive," he says; "putt them in an earthen pott, so that it may be half full; cover it with a broad tyle or Iron plate; then overwhelme the pott so that the bottom may be uppermost; put charcoales around about it. . . . Sett it on fire and lett it burn out and extinguish of itself; when it is cold take out the toades, and in an Iron mortar pound them very well. . . . Moderate the dose according to the strength of the partie." [2]

The close affinity in medical ideas between the seven-

[1] William Strachey, "For the Colony in Virginea Britannia. Lavves Diuine, Morall and Martiall, &c. [London, 1612]," Peter Force, ed., *Tracts and Other Papers Relating . . . the Colonies in North America* (Wash., 1836-1846), III, no. ii.

[2] O. W. Holmes, "Receipts to Cure Various Disorders," Mass. Hist. Soc., *Proceeds.*, V (1860-1862), 381. See also his *Medical Essays*, in his *Works* (Boston, 1892, IX), 312-369. In the Redmond Collection of Livingston manuscripts (privately owned, New York City) is a paper marked "Doctor Eales Powder agt ye Stone 1702": "Take anniseeds, Sweet fennel Seeds dell seed . . . tops, ye Root of white Saxifrage, ye husk nib off, of each an ounce, beat them fine, & sift them thro a Tiffany Seive, mix them together, then add crabs Eyes, ye seeds of wild Briar hips & jaw bone of a Pike, of each in fine Powder as much as will lye upon ye point of a knife . . . take ye quantity of a Drahm of this Powder ye day before ye new moon, & ye day after & so at ye full in white wine, or ale." "Crab's eyes" were concretions from the crawfish's stomach.

teenth century and the Middle Ages is clearly indicated by the general belief in the efficacy of the royal touch in curing diseases.[1]   James I and Charles I lent themselves to this practice and supposedly brought relief to many sufferers from epilepsy and scrofula; Charles II touched nearly a hundred thousand during the thirty-five years of his reign.   Richard Wiseman, perhaps the ablest English surgeon of the century, tells us: "I myself have been a frequent eye-witness of many hundreds of cures performed by his Majesty's touch alone, without any assistance of chirurgery, and those, many of them, such as had tried out the endeavors of able chirurgeons before they came thither."   It was in 1687 that a pauper of New Hampshire petitioned the general assembly for permission and assistance to go to England to be healed by the royal touch.   In 1684 several persons, seeking to secure relief from their afflictions, were literally crushed to death in the impetuous rush of the crowd to reach the king.[2]

With such superstitions accepted in England, we are not surprised to find the American colonists profoundly ignorant of medicine.   The most enlightened men often sought to cure disease by a hodgepodge of quackery and magic.   "Lett me tell you an easy medicine of mine owne," wrote Governor Winthrop in 1656, "that I have seene do miraculous cures in all sortes of Ulcers, and in knitting soddainly broken bones. . . . Beate to subtile powder one ounce of crabbes eyes, then putt upon it in a high glasse four ounces of strong wine-vinegar. It will instantly boyle up extremely; lett it stand till all

[1] A. D. White, *A History of the Warfare of Science with Theology in Christendom* (N. Y., 1896), II, 47.
[2] Edward Eggleston, *The Transit of Civilization* (N. Y., 1901), 91.

be quiett; then strain it through a fine linen; and of this liquor (which will then taste like dead beere, without sharpnesse) give two spoonefuls att a time to drinke, three times a day; and you shall see a strange effect in a weeke or two." "For all sortes of agewes," says the same authority, "I have of late tryed the following magneticall experiment with infallible success. Pare the patients nayles when the fever is coming on; and put the paringes into a little bagge of fine linen or sarenet; and tye that about a live eeles necke, in a tubbe of water. The eele will dye and the patient will recover." [1] Equally efficacious must have been "pricking the gums with the bill of an osprey" to cure toothache, or the use of bear's grease "for aches and cold swellings." Things bad for the heart, we are told, are "beans, pease, sadness, onions, anger, evil tidings and the loss of friends." To cure insomnia "bruise a handful of anise-seeds, and steep them in Red Rose Water and make it up in little bags, and binde one of them to each Nostril." For fevers one should take "two salt white herrings and slit them down the back and bind them to the soles of each of the patient's feet." [2]

Frequently today, in metaphorical phrase, we say that a disease has taken hold of a patient; once it was no mere figure of speech. This may be gleaned, for example, from a letter written by George Alsop of Maryland. "A throng of unruly distempers have crowded into the Main-guard of my body," he says, "when the drowsie Sentinels of my brain were a sleep. Where they got in, I know not, but to my grief and terror I find them pre-

---

[1] Winthrop had learned this from Sir Kenelm Digby; see *Conn. Mag.*, II, 37.
[2] Danvers Historical Society, *Colls.*, IV, 73-88.

dominant." He received from his cousin, Mrs. Elinor Gories, "an antimonial cup" [1] which effected a perfect cure. "As soon as I received it, I went to work with the Infirmities and Diseases of my Body," he tells us. "At the first draught, it made such havock among the several humors that had stolen into my body, that like a Conjurer in a room among a company of little Devils, they no sooner heard him begin to speak high words, but away they pack, and happy is he that can get out first." [2]

The colonists, themselves filled with superstition, valued highly the hocus-pocus of the Indians, and their medical men were pronounced "as able physicians as any in Europe." The savages used herbs for cathartics and emetics and as remedies for various diseases. These medicines were soon borrowed by the white men, some actually being sent to Europe where they came into wide repute. Tobacco, which was supposed by the Indians to possess extraordinary medicinal powers, was used by the English as a specific for a number of maladies. It was thought to be a sure antidote for all poisons and to have the power of "expelling rheums and sour humours." As for healing wounds, it was better than St. John's wort, hitherto accounted the sovereign remedy. Some persons used it in cases of gout or ague, others to relieve hunger and weariness or to neutralize the effects of drunkenness. [3]

[1] ". . . A drinking vessel made of that metal, which like our quassia-wood cups might be filled and emptied *in sæcula sæculorum* without exhausting its virtues." O. W. Holmes, *Medical Essays*, 341.

[2] George Alsop, *A Character of the Province of Maryland* [1666] (N. D. Mereness, ed., Cleveland, 1902), 100, 105.

[3] Anon., "Tobacco in England in the Reign of James I," *Va. Mag. of Hist. and Biog.*, XXIX, 108.

The doctors were not only relatively inefficient and ignorant, but there were never enough of them for the needs of the people. In New England conditions were more favorable than elsewhere because of the character of the settlements, for the physicians found it easier to earn a living in the shipping towns and in village communities than among the scattered plantations of the South. Frequently the healing office was practised by the clergymen—an "angelical conjunction," as Cotton Mather called it—and such men as Giles Firmin of Massachusetts and Gershom Bulkley of Connecticut were prized as much for their physic as for their divinity.[1] Among the first New England practitioners was Lambert Wilson, who was engaged by the Massachusetts Company to settle in the colony. Winthrop spoke of him as "our chief surgeon." He agreed to educate several youths in medicine so that they could assist him in his work and succeed him when he retired. In 1690 Boston had four doctors, while every town of any size had at least one. During the last decades of the century Dr. William Avery was the most noted physician of New England. He is said to have been notably skillful in physic and to have invented some useful instruments for surgery. He was also an investigator, making many experiments in chemical physics.[2]

A writer states in 1686 that Dr. Thomas Oakes had acquired great skill in his profession, and was notably successful in rescuing patients from the jaws of death.

[1] J. W. Dean, *Memoir of Giles Firmin* (Boston, 1866), 8; H. R. Stiles, *Ancient Wethersfield* (N. Y., 1904), I, 215.
[2] G. L. Kittredge, ed., "Letters of Samuel Lee and Samuel Sewall Relating to New England and the Indians," Col. Soc. of Mass., *Publs.*, XIV, 142-166.

Of Dr. Benjamin Bullivant it was said that "he was intimate with Gallen and Hypocrates," and

> so conversant with the great variety of nature, that not a Drug or Simple can escape him; whose Powers and Virtues are known so well to him, he needs not practice new Experiments upon his Patients, except it be in desperate cases, when death must be expelled by Death. This also is Praise-worthy in him, That to the Poor he always prescribes cheap, but wholesome medicines, not curing them of a consumption in their Bodies, and sending it into their Purses; nor yet directing them to the East-Indies to look for Drugs, when they may have far better out of their Gardens.[1]

In Virginia the most noted physician was Dr. John Pott. This man acted as physician-general for the colony and was active during the terrible epidemics which swept over the infant settlement during the early years of the century. He is described as "a Master of Arts . . . well practiced in chirurgery and physic, and expert also in distilling of waters, [and possessing] many other ingenious devices." [2] On one occasion he made use of his accomplishments to poison a number of hostile Indians, a feat which drew down upon him the displeasure of the Earl of Warwick. A letter from Charles Gordon to his brother Dr. John Gordon gives an interesting picture of conditions prevailing in the medical profession in New Jersey in the ninth decade of the century. "If you design to come hither yourself," he says,

> you may come as a planter, or a merchant, or as a doctor of medicine. I cannot advise you, as I can hear

[1] John Dunton, *Letters Written from New England, A. D. 1686* (Prince Soc. *Publ.*, IV, Boston, 1867), 92.
[2] E. D. Neill, *Virginia Company of London* (Wash., 1868), 221.

of no diseases here to cure, but some agues and some cutted fingers and legs, but there are no want of empiricks for these already. I confess that you could do more than any yet in America, being versed in Chirugery and Pharmacie, for here are abundance of herbs, shrubs and trees, and no doubt medicinal ones for making drugs, but there is little or no Imployment this way.[1]

In New York it was said that "Quacks abound like the locust in Egypt, and too many have recommended themselves to a full practice and profitable subsistence." [2]

In the colonies medical practice was not regulated as in England, where every accredited doctor belonged to the College of Physicians. The governments seldom concerned themselves with the training of the practitioner; no licenses were required; and anyone who had a superficial knowledge of medicine was at liberty to put up his sign. The extent of his practice would be determined by his success with his patients. If his treatments were ineffectual, he was deserted, but a tolerable degree of skill would insure him a fair living in the more thickly settled communities.[3]

Drugs were secured in various ways. There were local apothecaries who sold their wares either to the physician or directly to the patients, but it was usual for the doctor to make his own physic and add the cost to his bill.[4] The manufacture of powders and pellets, hard

---

[1] Stephen Wickes, *History of Medicine in New Jersey and of its Medical men . . . to 1800* (Newark, 1879), 15.

[2] Wickes, *History of Medicine in New Jersey*, 17.

[3] Kittredge, "Letters of Samuel Lee and Samuel Sewall," Col. Soc. of Mass., *Publs.*, XIV, 142-166.

[4] Kittredge, "Letters of Lee," etc., 142.

work with mortar and pestle by the master and his apprentices, made his residence appropriately known in some places as the "doctor's shop." In Virginia there were many complaints of overcharging for medicines. In 1658 a law was passed by the assembly giving the patient the privilege of appealing to the courts in case he considered "the account of his phisitian or chirurgeon to be unreasonable either for his pains, druggs or medicines." [1] Some drugs, which were beyond the opportunities or the skill of the American pharmacists, were purchased from the London dispensary. The most important of these was mithridate, which was considered indispensable in cases of poison, plague, madness, leprosy, cancer, gout or dysentery.

According to the standards even of the seventeenth century the colonial doctors were usually sadly deficient in skill. There were no facilities for medical training in America, while inducements for able English practitioners to migrate were lacking. Dr. Samuel Fuller, who came over in the *Mayflower*, was typically ignorant of his profession, if we may believe Thomas Morton. "Dr. Noddy did a great cure for Captain Littleworth," he says, "he cured him of a disease called a wife." [2] Dr. John Clark, who died at Boston in 1661 and whose interesting portrait has come down to us, according to tradition was the first regularly educated physician in New England.[3] Quacks appeared on every hand. It was complained that "Shoemakers,

[1] W. W. Hening, comp., *Statutes at Large of Virginia* (Phila., 1823), I, 450.
[2] Alexander Young, *Chronicles of the First Planters of the Colony of Massachusetts Bay* (Boston, 1846), 131.
[3] James Thacher, *American Medical Biography* (Boston, 1828), I, 222.

A Seventeenth Century Physician—Dr. John Clark,
of Newbury and Boston.

Weavers and Almanack makers . . . have laid aside
the proper business of their lives to turn Quacks."
In 1649 a law was passed in Massachusetts to regu-
late the practice of medicine by "chirurgeons, Midwives, Physicians and others," but it seems to have
accomplished little.   In many communities, as we have
seen, the minister acted as a doctor, and mingled with
his prayers for the sick of his parish applications of
plasters and doses of "physick."   Bleeding was almost
universal.   It was supposed to free the patient of hostile
humors.   The infant in the cradle and the tottering
octogenarian alike were subjected to this treatment,
which often weakened them at the very time when their
strength was most needed.   The pernicious practice continued even into the nineteenth century.   It was the
bleedings of a country doctor, seconded by a bad case
of laryngitis, which cost George Washington his life.

The medical profession should have been foremost in
pointing out the folly of the belief in witchcraft, but
unfortunately it often lent its support to the delusion.
Many a physician, when his concoctions failed to bring
relief, excused himself by complaining that the patient
had been bewitched.   Few seem to have had any conception of the real nature of insanity or of epilepsy, and the
ancient theory of demoniacal possession was generally
accepted.   Dr. John Swinerton, of Massachusetts, was
a notable exception to the rule, and throughout the
Salem witchcraft craze used his influence on behalf of
the victims.   Other doctors fully concurred with the
ministers and the judges in diagnosing the troubles of
the Goodman children and the "afflicted" girls of Salem
as magic.   When on rare occasions physicians ascribed
mental disturbances to natural causes, their judgment was

still ridiculously at sea. In Massachusetts a case is recorded of a man who sent for a doctor to treat him for hallucinations. The physician was unable to come in person, but "sent word that the vapours ascending from his sore legg had caused a water in his eyes, and disturbance in his braines, by means whereof he was troubled with such Visions; and sending an eye water to wash his eyes with, and a cordial to take inwardly, upon the use of these, this disturbance vanished in half a quarter of an hour." [1]

In the Southern colonies, where the settlements were scattered and the means of communication very poor, it was difficult even for the best of doctors to make a living. Consequently there were few practitioners, and among them many quacks. Alsop, upon his arrival in Maryland, complains that he fell into the hands of "a Galenist with his bag-pipes of physical operations," who could not put him to rights. The London Company, solicitous for the health of the first settlers in Virginia, took pains to send over several able physicians. Among the settlers of 1607 were William Wilkinson and Thomas Wotton, both skilled in medical science. The First Supply, or relief expedition, which arrived in January, 1608, brought "Walter Russell, a Doctor of Physic and Post Guinnot, a chirurgeon." Lord Delaware brought with him in June, 1610, Dr. Lawrence Bohun, who had been educated "among the most learned surgeons and physicians in the Netherlands." But Russell died, Bohun was killed in the West Indies, and some years later Governor Harvey wrote that Dr. John Pott was the only physician in Virginia. The records contain many references to practitioners in the colony

[1] Danvers Hist. Soc., *Colls.*, IV, 85.

during the period from 1635 to 1690, but it is certain that skilled physicians were at all times rare.[1]

It was customary for the planter and his wife to make a superficial study of medicine, so that when a physician could not be had, they themselves could care for the sick of the family. We find in almost every colonial library treatises on the practice of medicine. Among Madam Wormeley's books were "A Chirurgicall old Book," *The Chyrurgan's Mate, Treatis of the Gout,* Galen's *Art of Physick, Universall Body of Physick, The English Physitian* and Dr. Willis's *Practice of Physick.* In the library of Matthew Hubbard we find Riverius's *Book of Physic, Physician's Library* in folio, Culpeper's *Dispensatory,* Culpeper's *Anatomy* in folio, and the *Institution of Physick.* Unfortunately, what was learned from these books could have done little good, unless to help the patient along to a speedy conclusion of his earthly sufferings.

In the South the care of the sick was intrusted especially to the planter's wife, who was always armed with an assortment of remedies and upon the larger estates made periodic rounds in the slave or servant quarters. Obstetrics everywhere in the colonies was very largely in the hands of women. In 1690 the Reverend Samuel Lee, writing to Dr. Nehemiah Grew from New England, stated that "of midwifes everyone takes whom they please."[2] For this service the compensation varied with the skill and success of the practitioner. In

---

[1] A. Brown, *Genesis of the United States,* II, 601, 830, 907, 988; John Smith, *Works* (E. Arber, ed., Birmingham, 1884), 94, 390; E. Eggleston, *Transit of Civilization,* 74.

[2] Samuel Lee to Nehemiah Grew, June 25, 1690, in Colon. Soc. of Mass., *Publs.,* XIV, 147.

1634 Agnes Williams, who lived in Virginia, paid the Widow Hollens a dozen hens for attending her in confinement. In the eastern Long Island communities midwives were elected in town meeting.

All the colonies were subject to epidemics which took a terrible toll in human life. In tidewater Virginia the mosquitoes and the unwholesome drinking water made malaria and dysentery almost universal. Three months after Captain Newport's first landing, sickness and death appeared at Jamestown. "If there were any conscience in men," said Captain George Percy, "it would make their harts to bleed to heare the pitifull murmurings and outcries of our sick men without relief, every night and day for the space of sixe weeks; in the morning their bodies being trailed out of their cabines like Dogges, to be buried." [1]   The settlers who came in succeeding years had a like experience. The Spaniard Molina, writing in 1613, declared that fully fifty per cent of the newcomers died before they had been in the colony twelve months. "June, July, and half of August," writes De Vries, "are very unhealthy there for those who have not lived there a year. The English die there at this season very fast." [2]   The Company took no adequate precautions to exclude infected persons from the immigrant vessels, with the result that epidemics frequently occurred at sea. One ship is said to have lost one hundred and thirty persons out of one hundred and eighty-five. On the fleet which left for Virginia in 1609, both yellow fever and bubonic plague appeared. In this way these diseases were brought to the colony, where they spread rapidly.

[1] John Smith, Works, lxxii.
[2] D. P. De Vries, Voyages from Holland to America, A. D. 1632-1644 (N. Y., 1853), 109.

The Virginia physicians were incapable of coping with the situation. They knew little of the principles of quarantine or of sanitation; their remedies were inadequate. The epidemics, running their course unchecked, threatened to depopulate the country. It is true that Governor Harvey wrote that Dr. John Pott was "skilled in the Epidemicall diseases of the planters," but it is probable that his treatments did little real good to his patients.

The London Company, which saw all of its efforts jeopardized by these epidemics, urged a more careful observance of religious matters, so that God might be induced to withhold his chastening hand. They also sent directions for the erection of four guest houses or hospitals. But all this was to little purpose. In the year ending March, 1621, over a thousand persons died on the way to Virginia or after landing. During the next twelve months twelve hundred perished, and George Sandys wrote that the worst fever ever known in Virginia was raging. The epidemic, he thought, had been introduced by the *Abigall,* many of whose passengers had died on the way over. Immigrants who escaped death from the diseases indigenous to Virginia were said to be "seasoned" or immune, and could feel reasonably safe from their recurrence. But they were still susceptible to epidemics of the London plague and yellow fever.

The introduction of cinchona bark proved a great boon to the planters. It is related that the wife of Count Cinchona, Viceroy of Peru, was cured of an intermittent fever by the native physicians through the use of this remedy. In the year 1640, the count's own physician brought the Peruvian bark to Spain, and fourteen years later it found its way to England. Although the price was £8 a pound, it was introduced into the tobacco colonies, and greatly reduced the mortality from malaria. Formerly not one servant in five survived the first year, wrote Berkeley in 1671, but now most of them escape.

The Chesapeake Bay colonies were not the only ones to suffer from epidemics. In New England smallpox appeared early in the century, and throughout the colonial period continued to exact a heavy toll.[1] In the winter of 1633-1634 a smallpox epidemic raged among the Indians, but the white men seem to have escaped. In 1636, however, the general court sat at Roxbury in order to avoid the smallpox at Cambridge. In 1677 the Reverend Thomas Thacher issued a *Brief Rule to Guide the Common People of New England; How to Order Themselves and Theirs in the Small Pocks, or Measels.* This work proved timely, because in 1678 occurred the worst smallpox epidemic of the century. Cotton Mather, then but fifteen years old, wrote to John Cotton, describing the ravages of the disease. "Never was it such a time in Boston," he said. "Boston burying-places never filled so fast. It is easy to tell the time when we did not use to have the bells tolling for burials on a Sabbath day morning by sunrise; to have 7 buried on a Sabbath day night, after Meeting. To have coffins crossing each other as they have been carried in the street;—To have, I know not how many corpses following each other close at their heels,—to have 38 dye in one week,—6, 7, 8 or 9 in a day. Yet thus hath it lately been; and thus it is at this day. Above 340 have died of the Small Pox in Boston since it first assaulted this place. To attempt a Bill of Mortality, and number

[1] Cf. J. T. Adams, *Provincial Society* (*A History of American Life,* III), 270.

the very spires of grass in a Burying Place seems to have a parity of difficulty and accomplishment." [1]

Despite all, despite the prevalence of epidemics, the ignorance of hygiene and the crudeness of medical practice, it was not uncommon for the men and women of the time to attain a ripe old age. Of this fact the genealogical history of the town of Hingham, Massachusetts, supplies interesting evidence. The records of this place, which have been carefully preserved from its first settlement in 1635, give the ages of hundreds of the inhabitants. The family histories have been carefully worked out and published under the direction of the town. Of the eight hundred and twenty-seven persons mentioned as belonging to this period and whose length of life is recorded, one hundred and five reached the age of eighty or over, nineteen lived to be ninety or over, and three— Daniel Stodder, John Beal and Sarah Gardner—attained the century mark. This is a truly notable record; it would be difficult to find a community in the twentieth century which can match it.

The explanation lies partly in the sturdiness of the stock, partly in the simplicity of the people's lives. Their food was plain and wholesome, their work hard but not enervating; their houses were not over-heated; they were free from the nervous strain attendant upon life today. They were prepared to offer a sturdy resistance to organic diseases, and if they escaped epidemics or accidents, were apt to live to a ripe old age. Notwithstanding the fact that a number of Hingham men lost their lives in the unfortunate expedition of Sir William Phips against Quebec in 1690, the expecta-

[1] Letter of Cotton Mather to John Cotton, Nov., 1678. Mass. Hist. Soc., *Colls.*, ser. 4, VIII, 383-384.

tion of life for persons attaining the age of twenty-one was excellent. For males it seems to have been 41.3 years, for females 39.7 years, as compared with a general average of about 43 in the registration area of the United States in 1920.

This record, especially that of the women, is all the more remarkable because of the large families which were so common during the seventeenth century. For the one hundred and fifty-three married graduates of Harvard in the years from 1658 to 1690, the recorded number of children is eight hundred and eight, giving an average family of 5.21. This compares with an average of 3.09 for graduates in the years from 1872 to 1879. Of these men one had twenty children; one had fifteen; three, fourteen; three, thirteen; two, twelve; seven, eleven; four, ten; and fourteen, nine.

Cotton Mather gives some interesting testimony concerning the size of New England families. Mr. Sherman, he tells us, was twice married, having six children by his first wife and twenty by the second. "Another woman had no less than twenty-three children by one husband, whereof nineteen lived unto men's and women's estate. A third was mother to seven-and-twenty children, and she that was mother to Sir William Phips, the late Governor of New England, had no less than twenty-five children besides him; she had one and twenty sons and five daughters." [1] The Reverend Samuel Willard, the first minister of Groton, had twenty children, and was himself one of seventeen children. The Reverend Abijah Weld of Attleboro had fifteen children, the Reverend Moses Fiske had sixteen, Samuel

---

[1] Cotton Mather, *Magnalia Christi Americana* (Hartford, 1853), I, 517.

Green, the Boston printer, was the father of thirty. William Rowson had twenty children by one wife. Of the Hingham matrons Hannah Beal had twelve children, Sarah Cushing twelve, Christian Dunbar thirteen, Rebecca Hersey, twelve, Hannah Jacob twelve, Mary Joy fifteen, Elizabeth Stodder twelve, and Remember Ward twelve.

It might be imagined that such large families would result in a heavy mortality among the mothers. Indeed, many cases may be cited in which they succumbed to the cares and dangers of incessant child bearing. The following inscription is one of many to be found upon the seventeenth-century tombstones: "Here lyeth the body of Elizabeth Haynie, daughter of Richard and Jane Bridger. Was born July 16th, 1665, married Richard Haynie Oct 10th 1681, by whom she had 8 children & died his wife 2. . . . 1697." Cotton Mather's first wife was married at the age of sixteen, bore him ten children, and died at the age of thirty-two. "The Women, like Early Fruits, are soon Ripe and soon Rotten," says an unfriendly English critic of the New Englanders. "A Girl there at thirteen," he adds with obvious exaggeration, "thinks herself as well Quallified for a husband, as a forward Miss at a Boarding School does here at Fifteen for a Gallant." Many cases of early death may be found among the Hingham matrons, some of them easily traceable to excessive childbearing. Thus, Elizabeth Lincoln died at forty, having had seven children; Sarah Cushing had twelve children and died at thirty-eight; and Jail Cushing had ten, dying at forty-six.[1]

[1] Some other examples are equally striking. Thus, Sarah Hawke had seven children, dying at 36; Rebecca Hersey had twelve, dying at

On the other hand, the cases of those who had very large families and yet lived to old age are even more numerous. Ruth Andrews, who had ten children, lived to be ninety-seven; Hannah Beal, with twelve children, died at ninety-three; Sarah Gardner lived to be one hundred and one despite her nine children; Mary Joy had fifteen children, yet lived to be seventy-seven; Triphary Lane, with nine children, died at ninety-five; Elizabeth Stodder, with ten children, died at eighty-eight. The average life of the married women of Hingham during the seventeenth century seems to have been 61.4 years. There were one hundred and five women, concerning whom we have data, who had five or more children. The combined number of their offspring was eight hundred and eighteen, giving an average of 7.8 for each family. The average age at death was 65.5 years. These figures apply to one little town only, and cannot be accepted as conclusive for conditions throughout the colonies, yet they permit of the strong presumption that much which has been written concerning the short expectation of life for women of large families is based upon insufficient evidence.

The dangers which surrounded childhood during the seventeenth century were numerous. Ignorant of hygiene, without competent medical assistance, possessing but a hazy conception of infant dietetics, mothers frequently lost their children in rapid succession. The

45; Joanna Hobart had seven, dying at 41; Mary Russell had eleven, dying at 50; Sarah Lane had five, dying at 34; Sarah Lewis had seven, dying at 37; Sarah Lincoln had seven, dying at 41; Deborah Hersey Lincoln had nine, dying at 40; Deborah Hobart Lincoln had ten, dying at 37; Mary Loring had eleven, dying at 40; Sarah Pratt had eleven, dying at 42; Elizabeth Stodder had twelve, dying at 46; Abigail Thaxter had seven, dying at 30. See George Lincoln and others, *History of the Town of Hingham* (Hingham, 1893), passim.

case of Cotton Mather's family as set forth in his *Diary* is typical. This noted clergyman had sixteen children and survived them all except his son Samuel. Abigail I, William, Mary, Joseph, Mehitabel, Samuel I, Nathaniel, Eleazer and Martha all died in infancy. Jerusha succumbed to measles at the age of two years and seven months. Katherine and Abigail II both lived to be twenty-seven, Hannah twenty-four, Increase twenty-five, Elizabeth twenty-two and Samuel II seventy-nine. Four of the children contracted smallpox, several had scarlet fever, while most of them had measles and three died of it. The *Diary* contains many references to these misfortunes and to Mather's agonized prayers for the recovery of his children.

Joseph Joy of Hingham had fifteen children and lost eight of them before they were two years old. A Plymouth gravestone tells a significant story: "Here lyeth ——— with twenty small children." Cotton Mather himself tells us of the case of a woman who had twenty-two children, "whereof she buried fourteen sons and six daughters." [1]   The old family Bibles have preserved many of these stories of blighted hopes. In one case a matron, the mother of many children, lost her first child four days after the birth of the second. Five times she suffered the death of a child with an infant in her arms, and after being married nine years, had but one living child. Of Judge Sewall's fourteen children, three only outlived their father.

Of the eight hundred and eight children of Harvard graduates for the years from 1658 to 1690, one hundred and sixty-two died before maturity. This gives a recorded child mortality among this selected group of

[1] Cotton Mather, *Magnalia Christi Americana*, I, 517.

twenty per cent. As it is fairly certain that there were cases of deaths especially of infants, for which no records have been left, it may be taken for granted that the actual percentage was higher. These were the homes of ministers and magistrates, where fortune and intelligence provided exceptional care, and if their family histories can show so many gloomy pages, it is a safe inference that death was an even more frequent visitor in the households of their humbler neighbors. The child mortality for Hingham was 33.3 per cent, two hundred and seventy-six of the eight hundred and twenty-seven persons whose ages are known, dying before reaching twenty-one. The mortality among infants accounts for the greater part of these deaths, the percentage of males dying under two being 22.2 and of females 17.8.[1]

Perhaps fewer children would have succumbed, had the diseases from which they suffered been left to run their courses. But the suffering child had to encounter the additional peril of the doctor with his bleeding and his physic. It is not hard to imagine the effect upon cases of measles or smallpox of such concoctions as mithridate or Venice treacle. The latter was a compound of vipers, white wine, opium, spices, licorice, red roses, St. John's wort and some twenty other ingredients. We are left much in the dark concerning the feeding of the colonial baby, but there is reason to believe that its food was not only often unwholesome, but administered without regard to regular intervals or stated amount. Several of Mather's children had convulsions, among

[1] In J. A. Doyle, *The English in America* (London, 1887), II, app. C, may be found some interesting records of early marriages and infant mortality. As Doyle remarks (II, 8), the land was "abundantly replenished and ruthlessly weeded."

them Samuel I, who died in this way. Children suffered often from rickets, and went through life hopeless cripples. The remedies applied were typical of the age, for example:

> Dip the child in the morning, head foremost in Cold Water, don't dress it Immediately, but let it be made warm in the Cradle & sweat at least half an Hour moderately. Do this 3 mornings going & if one or both feet are Cold while other Parts sweat Let a little blood be taken out of the feet the 2d Morning. . . . Before the dips of the child give it some Snakeroot and Saffern Steep'd in Rum & Water, give this Immediately before Diping and after you have dipt the Child 3 Mornings. Give it several times a Day the following Syrup made of Comfry, Hartshorn, Red Roses, Hog-brake roots, knot-grass, petty-moral [penny-royal?] roots; sweeten the Syrup with Melosses.

In Europe the seventeenth century, despite all its backwardness, was marked by certain great figures who were pointing the way to better things in medical science. In 1628 William Harvey published his treatise on the circulation of the blood which revolutionized modern medicine and gave a death blow to the slavelike adherence to Galen. In 1661 Malpighi, by the use of the compound microscope, was able to exhibit the corpuscles of the blood, while Robert Boyle, in the latter half of the century, was laying the foundations of the science of analytical chemistry. But these things found no reflection in America. Colonial medicine was less efficient in 1690 than in 1640, for the physicians of the second generation had a more imperfect training than those who migrated from England. An apprenticeship with an older doctor and a short course of reading in medical books were probably the extent of the equipment of the native practitioner.   If he had ever heard of Harvey, he probably distrusted his conclusions and had no conception of the significance of his discovery.   To the end he remained engulfed in the clouds of ignorance and superstition.

CHAPTER VIII

THE RULE OF CONDUCT

To the Puritan this world, as we have seen, seemed a place of temptation and danger. On trial before an exacting God, he was constantly subjected to the wiles of Satan and his minions. In what form the spirits of evil would assail him he knew not, so that safety lay only in unceasing vigilance. "Was ever man more tempted . . . ," wrote Cotton Mather in his *Diary*. "Should I tell, in how many Forms the Divel has assaulted me, and with what Subtilty and Energy, his Assaults have been carried on, it would strike my Friends with Horrour." Again and again this eminent divine implored "the Help of Heaven" against "the Buffetings of Satan." [1] With eternal happiness or eternal punishment hanging in the balance, the Puritan had for earthly pleasures a mingled feeling of contempt and fear. They were but baubles placed before him in seductive forms by the Evil One to divert him from the great goal of salvation.

This state of mind brought about constant self-searchings and a rigid code of personal conduct. The Puritan had few diversions, and these few he took with some qualms of conscience. To go out into the country in quest of chestnuts, to smoke a pipe, to read a beautiful poem, to play shuffleboard, amusements innocent in themselves, might afford some opening to Satan to lure

[1] Cotton Mather, *Diary* (Mass. Hist. Soc., *Colls.*, ser. 7, VII), 51, 75, 475.

the godly man from the path of duty. Safety could be assured only by constant meditation on religious matters, regular attendance at divine service, copious reading of the Bible, much prayer, and sobriety in the tasks of everyday life.

Nor was the Puritan content with maintaining this rigid standard for himself—he insisted that his neighbor should conform to it also. Sin and worldliness, dread diseases of the soul, are no less contagious than diseases of the body, and like them must be stamped out in order to insure the safety of the community, save the elect from annoyance, and protect God from mockery. The New England leaders set up for their Zion the most severe moral code; that their system interfered seriously with individual liberty did not in the least give them pause.

Laws for the observance of the Sabbath were everywhere rigidly enforced. In Massachusetts a law was passed in 1653 which made it a misdemeanor to waste time by taking walks on the streets or by visiting ships in the port on Sunday. It was forbidden to travel, cook, sweep or make up beds on that day. In New London, John Lewis and Sarah Chapman were brought before the court in 1670, "for sitting together on the Lord's Day, under an apple tree, in Goodman Chapman's Orchard." James Rogers, jr., for sailing in a vessel on Sunday was fined twenty shillings, while Steven Chalker was punished for driving cattle on the day of rest.[1] Long hair for men was considered a dangerous vanity, and the Massachusetts court inveighed against it so late as 1675. When John Gatchell was fined ten shillings for build-

[1] Alice M. Earle, *The Sabbath in Puritan New England* (N. Y., 1891), 246 ff.

ing on the town land at Marblehead, he was advised that
if he would "cut of the long hair off his head into a sivil
frame," half the sum would be remitted and permission
granted to proceed with the building. The art of smoking, early learned from the neighboring Indians, was
popular with men and women alike,[1] though in time
it came to be condemned and was constantly subjected to
regulation. The Connecticut court forbade its use "Pub-
liquely in the street, highways, or any barnyards, or
uppon traineing days in any open places." Massachusetts prohibited shuffleboard and bowling, and imposed
fines on innkeepers who permitted their guests to indulge
in these games. From time to time laws were passed in
various New England colonies against observing Christmas, indulging in mixed dances, playing cards, or performing on certain musical instruments. God's time
must not be frittered away, as anyone who read the book
of Proverbs well understood.

This asceticism entailed no great hardship upon the
moving spirits of the theocracy themselves. For them
there were many compensations—the interest that comes
from creative leadership, the inspiration derived from
reading and study, the anticipated joy of a heaven easily
within the grasp of their imaginations. Beyond doubt the
virile, rosy-cheeked John Cotton delighted in his religion
quite as today the great surgeon and the captain of industry feel the thrill of accomplishment. But for those
in the humbler walks of life—the farmer, the fisherman, the ship carpenter or the blacksmith—the system

[1] Edward Ward, "A Trip to New-England [London, 1699]," G.
P. Winship, ed., *Boston in 1682 and 1699* (Providence, R. I., 1905),
51. Mary Rowlandson, *The Sovereignty and Goodness of God* (Boston, 1682), 24, 56, tells how a pastor's wife finally broke the habit.

of repression must have been irksome. The reverence which they entertained for their leaders, their fear of damnation, their respect for the law might keep them within the narrow limits of Puritan life, but the effort was hard. Even in the days of the exodus, when men's minds were fired with zeal for the new state which they were building in the forests of America, there must have been in many a humble breast the fierce beating of suppressed desire.

We know that not every soul who followed the Puritan leaders out of England was possessed of their religious spirit. Among the immigrants was a sprinkling of servants and laborers, some of them, it was said, remarkable for profligacy. It is this fact which accounts in large measure for the most serious offenses against the moral code in the first few decades of the settlement. Governor Bradford was grieved that "so many wicked persons and profane people should so quickly come over" to join what had been a religious foundation made for "religions sake." He explains that the need for labor in "building & planting" made it necessary to import workers, and where men of good character could not be had, the settlers "were glad to take such as they could." And he adds:

> many untoward servants, sundry of them proved, that were thus brought over, both men & woman kind; who, when their times were expired, became families of them selves . . . so allso ther were sente by their friends some under hope y^t they would be made better; others that they might be eased of such burthens, and they kept from shame at home y^t would necessarily follow their dissolute courses. And thus, by one means

or other, in 20 years time, it is question whether ye
greater part be not growne ye worser.[1]

The Puritan leaders found it a difficult matter to force
such persons to conform to their moral code.   The records show many cases of gross impurity.   In a single
day, in 1633, at Plymouth, we find three instances of
this kind: a certain John Holmes being fined and placed
in the stocks for drunkenness; "John Hows & Jone, his
wife" condemned "to sitt in the stocke because the said
Jone conceived with childe by him before they were pub-
lickely married;" "John Thorp & Alice his wife" accorded similar treatment for the same offense.   On September 3, 1639, Mary Mendame of Duxburrow, for
"uncleannesse" with an Indian, was sentenced "to be
whipt at a carte tayle through the townes streete, and to
weare a badge upon her left sleeve."   The Plymouth
records show many whippings for sodomy, and one execution for "bestiality." [2]   It was the latter case which
so discouraged Governor Bradford, a case which he felt
constrained to mention only because "the truth of ye historie requires it."   Similar conditions existed in other
parts of New England.   "Violations of modesty and
purity before marriage were but too frequent," says one
writer, "and this in the face of a stern magistracy and
strict Puritan usage." [3]   At New Haven, Medford, Bos-

---

[1] William Bradford, "History of Plymouth Plantation," Charles
Deane, ed., Mass. Hist. Soc., Colls., ser. 4, III, 398-399.

[2] Bradford, "Plymouth Plantation," 397-398.

[3] Frances M. Caulkins, History of New London, Connecticut (New
London, 1852), 247.   The Reverend William DeLoss Love declares
that offenses against social morality at Hartford were matters of frequent
record, but he considers this an indication rather of the close Puritan surveillance than of an especially low moral standard.

ton and elsewhere there are many instances of gross misconduct.

The testimony shows, however, that in the early years offenses of this kind were generally confined to servants and freedmen. The mass of the Puritan settlers lived pure and godly lives, in strict conformity with the ideals which led them to the New World. "These English live soberly," said a Dutch visitor to Hartford in 1639, "drinking but three times at a meal, and when a man drinks to drunkenness, they tie him to a post and whip him as they do thieves in Holland." The innate soundness of early New England society needs no further proof than the picture which the records afford us of the sober, industrious, clean life of the average man and woman, the goodman and his wife. The harsh Puritan theology did not rob them of their human charity; the contemplation of the future world could not deny them a few simple pleasures in this one. The ministers might thunder that "no carrion in a ditch smells more loathsomely in the nostrils of man, than a natural man's works do in the nostrils of the Almighty," [1] but on all sides they saw living testimony that there is nothing nobler than a gentle, pure heart.

The rigid standards set by the ministers eventually proved harmful to morality itself. In all ages waves of asceticism have been followed by periods of moral relaxation, and New England proved no exception to the rule. The laxness which marked British society under Charles II and James II had a faint counterpart in Boston, Providence and Hartford. As the licentiousness of the Restoration period was a reaction against the rigid

[1] J. T. Adams, *The Founding of New England* (Boston, 1921), 372.

code of Cromwell's time, so the stern censorship of Endicott and Norton was, in part at least, responsible for the general loosening of moral standards in New England during the last three decades of the seventeenth century. A régime which will not compromise with human nature must sooner or later succumb. "An examination of the court records," says a New England historian, "fixes upon the mind an impression that this second state of the settlement was one marked with more coarseness, ignorance and vice, than the one before or after it." [1]

This development was accelerated by the large influx of new settlers which accompanied the extension of commercial enterprise. The sailing masters, some of whom had found their way to the ports of Europe and the West Indies, brought back thousands who were strangers to the Puritan habits of the people. The movement which Bradford bewailed in the earlier days received a new impetus from the hangers-on of a constantly increasing commercial class. Boston, which for two generations had been given over in large measure to its God-fearing, church-going families, gradually assumed the character of a thriving port, where holdups occurred on the Common and sailors were kidnapped at the wharf ends. In New London, "Men who had long been rovers and unaccustomed to restraint gathered," and flouted the Puritan magistrates and their laws. Yet the loosening of moral standards was by no means confined to the seaports, for many an inland town which had not felt the touch of a defiling commercialism yielded to the general tendency.

[1] Caulkins, *History of New London*, 246. *Cf.* the strictures of Mather and Torry; above, 110.

The sermons of the clergy ring with admonitions against the degeneracy of the day. In 1673 Increase Mather, in his *Two Sermons against the Sin of Drunkenness,* bewailed the multiplication of unlicensed taverns and ale houses.

> I know that in such a town as this, there is need of such houses [he says] and no sober Minister will speak against the Licencing of them; . . . but see that you keep a vigilant eye over these private, dark Houses, where wicked Persons sell Drink and Destroy Souls to get a little Money; and which do more mischief, than all the publick Houses do good, as being the very Sinks of Sin, whereby Youth is wofully corrupted amongst us.

"Sin and daring Prophaneness gets head, and is becoming exceeding bold amongst us," he declared nine years later. "Time was when in New-England they durst not continue whole nights in Taverns, in drinking and gaming, and mispending their precious Time." [1] Again, in 1712, he asks: "Is not that worse than brutish Sin of Drunkenness become a prevailing Iniquity all over the Countrey? How has Wine and Cyder, but most of all Rum, Debauched Multitudes of People, Young and Old?"

In 1702 Mather declared that "the Apostocy and Iniquity of the People" were causing the glory of the Lord to depart from New England. "How many are there amongst us whose Fathers in coming into the Wil-

---

[1] Instances of punishment for "mispending time" are frequently found. For example, see *Records and Files of the Quarterly Courts of Essex County, Mass.* (Salem, 1911), I, 58, and W. B. Weeden, *Economic and Social History of New England* (Boston, 1890), I, 407. E. W. Capen, *The Historical Development of the Poor Law of Connecticut* (Columbia Univ., *Studies,* XXII), 35, states the severe regulation of 1650 in that colony as to idleness.

derness, designed nothing but Religion. But *they* are for
another Interest. Their Hearts are not but for the
World. . . . That there is a general defection in New
England from Primitive Purity and Piety in many re-
spects is so plain that it cannot be denied." A few
years later we hear him denouncing "stage-players and
mixed dancings, and those diversions in which Cruelty
is exercised on Dumb Creatures." "Those infamous
games of cards and dice," he felt were corrupting the
young generation, while many persons frequented public houses and tarried long at their wine. "It may make
a man's heart tremble to think what account some
Church-members will give to Christ at the Day of Judgement, for the time they have spent at the Tavern and at
the Coffee House." In 1692, Cotton Mather declared
that "some of our Rising Generation have been given up
to the most abominable Impieties of Uncleanness,
Drunkenness, and a Lewd, Rude, Extravagant sort of
Behaviour. There are the Children of Belial among
them, and Prodigies of Wickedness."

One must be wary in accepting at their face value the
words of these eminent ministers. Not only would comparatively innocent amusements assume monstrous proportions in their eyes, but in sermons of admonition it
is almost impossible to escape exaggeration. Nor can
we trust such obviously prejudiced and hostile descrip-
tions of New England life as those left by Edward Ward
or Edward Randolph. "Rum, alias Kill Devil, is as
much ador'd by the American English, as a dram of
Brandy is by an old Billingsgate," says Ward. " . . .
Notwithstanding their Sanctity, they are very Prophane
in their common Dialect. They can neither drive a
Bargain, nor make a Jest, without a Text of Scripture

at the end on 't." [1]   "There is a penalty for cursing
and swearing, such as they please to impose," says Jasper Danckaerts in 1680. "Nevertheless you discover little difference between this and other places. Drinking
and fighting occur there not less than elsewhere; and as
to truth and true godliness, you must not expect more of
them than others." [2]

"The first English that came over hither . . . forced
thereto by the severe Treatment they met with from
the Bishops in England," says John Dunton in 1686,

> were certainly the most Pious and Religious Men in the
> World, . . . and were the lively Patterns of Primi-
> tive Zeal and Integrity; and would have converted all
> the World, if they cou'd; especially their own Pos-
> terity: but alas, this blessed Wind of the Spirit blows
> where it listeth; Many of them were converted . . .
> and these walk to this Day in the steps of their Pious
> Fore-fathers: But there are others of them, who never
> knew the Power of Converting Grace, who yet retain
> a form of Godliness, and make a strict Profession of
> the out-side of Religion . . . ; and these are the most
> Profligate and Debauched Wretches in the World; their
> Profession of Religion teaching them only how to sin
> (as they think) more refinedly.[3]

Not the least of the causes for this moral lapse was
the failure of the Puritan leaders to discriminate properly between serious and trivial offences. In a community where cooking breakfast on Sunday might bring
a heavy penalty, transgression was inevitable, and from

[1] Ward, *A Trip to New-England*, 52.
[2] Jasper Dankers [or Danckaerts] and Peter Sluyter, *Journal of a
Voyage to New York, and a Tour in Several of the American Colonies,
1679-1680* (H. C. Murphy, ed., L. I. Hist. Soc., *Memoirs*, I), 394.
[3] John Dunton, *Letters from New-England* (Prince Soc., *Publs.*, IV),
66.

one transgression to another was an easy step. When one is faced on all sides by prohibitions, it becomes difficult, especially for young minds, to differentiate between great matters and small. Certain it is that cases of sex immorality increased rapidly in the closing decades of the seventeenth century. A writer declared in 1682 that "there hardly passes a Court Day but four or five are convened" in Boston for offenses of this character. "Now most certainly if Justice finds out so many Transgressors of this kind, how many must the private ones amount to? I may without being uncharitable think, they include a great part of the Town." [1]

In many New England churches parents who had a child within less than seven months after marriage were required to make a public acknowledgment before the congregation on pain of having baptism refused their children. The number of confessions brought forth by parental fear of infant damnation is surprisingly large, especially in some of the more isolated communities. It must be remembered, however, that the New England betrothal was a solemnity of moment, regarded by many as a halfway marriage. However severe the church may have been in punishing intimacy prior to the wedding ceremony, public sentiment seems to have minimized the offense. Obviously the evidence of a general decline of moral standards in New England in the last three decades of the seventeenth century is ample. Hundreds of families continued to adhere to the earlier rigid morality, and hundreds of others, while participating in innocent

[1] J. W. (pseud.), "A Letter from New-England," G. P. Winship, ed., Boston in 1682 and 1699, 4. Neither J. W.'s account nor that of Edward Ward, which Winship also reprints, is flattering, but one hesitates to give them full value as fair pictures.

amusements, maintained a code which today would be considered extremely high. But many, in defiance alike of law and tradition, went to excesses.

Although the New England of the early years was notably sober, in Maryland and Virginia from the very first there seems to have been much drinking and no little drunkenness. So early as 1624 the Virginia assembly took action to stop "swearing and drunkenness," and ordered all church wardens to present offenders to the commanders of the plantations. Eight years later a law was passed making all who lingered too long at their cups liable to a fine of five shillings. In 1658 the assembly urged that "all good meanes be used in the severall countie courts and parishes" for "the suppression of the odious sin of drunkenness," declaring "that all such persons & persons of what degree or qualitie soever be severely punished and generally to be held incapable of being a witness betwen partie and partie, and of bearing any publique office in the government."

In addition to these measures, at least two attempts were made to limit the available supply of intoxicating liquor. In 1662 a duty of sixpence a gallon was placed on imported rum, because it "hath by experience bin found to bring diseases and death to diver ople, and the purchasing thereof made by the exp   nd unfurnishing the country of its owne   nad le commodities." In June, 1676, when   drink, qua dominated by the strong hand of N   used the jus- was passed suppressing all "or   rely dealt wi other tipling houses," with the   that unl Jamestown and the two main ferr   nent.[1] hese licensed inns were permitted to sell   er, "but no other strong drink," and whoe   d "to sell any sorte of drinke or liquor whatsoever by retail, under any colour, pretence, delusion or subtile evasion whatsoever to be drunke or spent in his or their house or houses, upon his or their plantation," was to be fined a thousand pounds of tobacco.[1] After the suppression of Bacon's Rebellion this measure was repealed and a substitute passed permitting two inns in each county.

In Maryland drunkenness was at first punishable with a fine of thirty pounds of tobacco or five shillings, but in 1642 the sum was increased to one hundred pounds of tobacco. If the offender were a servant, he was to be imprisoned or set in the stocks for twenty-four hours. Even severer laws were enacted during the Commonwealth period, when in certain cases drunkards were to be whipped. Inns soon sprang up near courthouses and ferries, where many varieties of liquors were sold. The list included French brandy and wine, Canary, Madeira, cider, claret, strong ale, rum, perry, quince, Rhenish wines, sherry and mum. The legislature, disgusted at the debauchery in unregulated tippling houses, passed a bill in 1662 to license taverns, a business up to that time untouched by law in that colony; but these ordinaries became centers of dissipation in which the idle and the i   erate could assemble for drinking and playin   evil became so pronounced that in 16   ry to limit the number of licensed

          he half-jesting account in the *Sot-*
          s of the county courts in Mary-
          heavy drinking. The author

[1] W. .   atutes at Large of Virginia (Phila., 1823), II, 361.
[2] J. A. Kro   of Prohibition (N. Y., 1925), 6-7.

says that upon arriving at Battletown he found many
"roaring Planters" sitting in a circle on the ground.
Others were stretched out dead drunk, while still others
were contending and fighting.   At the inn he found that
"all the bedding was possest by one or other drunken
Guest," while even the justices on the bench had taken
more strong liquor than was good for them.   This picture is perhaps not greatly exaggerated.   The Virginia
and Maryland planters looked forward to the meeting
of the court as a time of relaxation and amusement.
The round of life upon the isolated plantations, while
by no means monotonous, afforded little opportunity for
conviviality.   None save the most hopeless tippler can
get enjoyment from a solitary spree; and it is probable
that many a planter, who in the merry company at the
courthouse took his turn with the best of them, in his
own home seldom drank anything stronger than cider,
ale or quince.

Court day was so universally regarded as a day of
revelry that servants and slaves often selected it as the
best time for running away from their masters.   About
1680 a servant testified before the Northampton justices
that he had planned to steal a bridle and saddle to aid
him in getting away, but had been waiting for a court
day, when he knew everyone would be too intoxicated
to observe him.   In 1678 several persons who had made
a practice of gathering at the courthouse to quarrel and fight entered the court room and a[ffronted jus]-
tices to their faces.   These men were seve[rely dealt wi]th,
and the near-by innkeeper was warned [that unl]ess better order was preserved in his establish[ment, h]is license
would be withdrawn.   In 1682 George Mayplis petitioned the court of Lancaster in Virginia "to have ye

privilege of selling of cider at ye courthouse in court time," and received his permit, "provided it be in no ways injurious or prejudicial in ye disturbing of ye court in their time of sitting." [1]

House parties, marriages and funerals all furnished opportunities for indulgence in strong drink of which convivial spirits among the planters were quick to take advantage. The guests at weddings, in order to reach the home of the bride where the ceremony took place, often had to travel many miles, and entertainment was always provided for them. That various kinds of intoxicating liquors were served and the bounds of sobriety often passed may be taken for granted. It might be supposed that reverence for the dead would have prevented similar indulgence at funerals, but such was not the case. "Having observed in the daies of my pilgrimage the debauches used at burialls tending much to the dishonour of God and his true Religion," declared a testator in York County, "my will is that noe strong drinks bee provided or spirits at my buriall." [2]

The presence of many servants and slaves in the Southern colonies almost of necessity led to a certain amount of sex immorality. Instances of improper relations between masters and the women in their service, however, seem to have been of infrequent occurrence. Persons guilty of this crime not only incurred the contempt of their neighbors, but were apt to feel the heavy hand of the law. In 1639 Robert Sweet, who ranked as a gentleman, was ordered to appear in the parish church in a white sheet, while the guilty woman received a sound whipping. In Lower Norfolk County a case

[1] Hening, *Statutes at Large of Virginia*, II, 384.
[2] York County Records for 1671-1694 (Va. State Library), 115.

is recorded in which both the white man and the Negro woman, who was party to his guilt, were forced to stand in church dressed in white sheets and holding white rods in their hands. In addition to this humiliation, masters guilty of criminal intimacy with slave women were subjected to a heavy fine.

We gain an insight into the general disapprobation of misconduct of this kind from a suit brought in the Maryland court. "The Complayn^t prosecuting against the Def^t upon an action of Defamacōn," reads the indictment in the quaint spelling of the original, "for that the Defd reported here that he had heard one Thomas Gutridge in Virginia Say, that the p^{lt} had got one of his Negroes wth Child and that he had a black bastard in Virginia, wch Report the Complayn^t Saith tends much to his disgrace an defamacōn wch he values at twenty thousand pounds Sterling. . . ." [1] The accusation against Richard Lawrence, a man whom we know to have possessed many admirable characteristics, of intimacy with a female slave—which was probably false— brought heavy reproaches upon this champion of freedom in Virginia. In September, 1630, the governor and council of Virginia sentenced a certain "Hugh Davis to be soundly whipped, before an assembly of Negroes and others for abusing himself to the dishonor of God and shame of Christians, by defiling his body in lying with a Negro; which fault he is to acknowledge next Sabbath day." [2]

It must be remembered that it was only late in the

---

[1] Maryland Provincial Court, *Judicial and Testamentary Business, 1649-1657* (W. H. Browne, ed., *Archives of Maryland*, Balt., 1883-   , X), 114.

[2] Hening, *Statutes at Large of Virginia*, I, 146.

seventeenth century that there were many native-born
Negroes in the colonies, among them not more than a
handful of mulatto women. To the well-to-do planters,
who at this time were almost the only class to own
slaves, the pure-blooded African could not have seemed
very attractive. It is not reasonable to suppose, and
there is no evidence to show, that they proved false to
their marriage vows because of the half-savage black
women of their plantations. Substantiation of this conclusion is suggested by the infrequency of applications
for divorce upon the grounds of inconstancy, though, of
course, few divorces occurred on any score. In 1655
Alice Clowson of Northampton secured a separation
from her husband because he refused to give up his Indian concubine, but in 1681 William Fitzhugh declared
that he knew of only one case of divorce in all Virginia.

On the other hand, the presence of Negro women on
the plantations offered a serious temptation to the lower
class of indentured servants. These men were seldom
married, and in some cases had led dissolute lives before
coming to America. Working side by side with Ne-
gresses in the tobacco fields and deprived of the association of white women of their own class, it was inevitable
that some should yield to temptation. Although such
intercourse was strictly forbidden by law, it is unlikely
that the offenders were often punished. Masters were
seriously concerned when a female indentured servant
was found with child, for it lessened her value as a
worker, while the infant was born free. But the child
of a slave remained a slave irrespective of the race or
status of the father. "Whereas some doubts have arisen
whether children got by an Englishman upon a negro
woman should be slave or free," reads an act of the Vir-

ginia assembly in 1662, it is enacted "that all children born in this country shall be held bond or free only according to the condition of the mother."

There was no legal provision in Virginia in the seventeenth century for the union of slaves. Custom demanded, however, that marriages should be conducted, with religious services by ministers of the Gospel. Such unions received a certain legal status from the fact that when children were born out of wedlock the mothers were handed over to the sheriff to be punished. But it is extremely probable that the masters, in most cases, felt no great interest in the matter even when the father was white. The large proportion of mulattoes among the Virginia and Maryland Negroes, even in the eighteenth and nineteenth centuries, were chiefly the result of the association on the larger plantations of white servants and slaves.

The importation of female servants necessarily led to immorality. Some of these women, of course, were of good character, and after their term of service, married well. "The Women that go over into this Province as Servants, have the best luck here as in any place in the World besides," says George Alsop, "for they are no sooner on shoar than they are courted into . . . Matrimony." [1] On the other hand, there were among them some whose antecedents made marriage unlikely. The lower class of female servants usually worked, not only at menial household tasks, but in the tobacco fields side by side with the men. The *Sot-weed Factor* gives an interesting picture of a slovenly servant in the house of

[1] George Alsop, *A Character of the Province of Maryland* [1666] (N. D. Mereness, ed., Cleveland, 1902), 59; and William Gowans, *Bibliotheca Americana* (N. Y., 1845, 1869).

his host, who acted as a kind of chambermaid in addition to hoeing corn and feeding the swine. The frequency with which such women gave birth to illegitimate children caused the enactment of special legislation. Virginia required that the servant "in regard to the losse and trouble her master doth sustaine by her having a bastard shall serve two years after her time by indenture is expired or pay two thousand pounds of tobacco to her master besides the ffine or punishment for committing the offence." [1] This fine was fixed at five hundred pounds of tobacco, and if she could not pay it or her master refused to pay it for her, she was to be whipped on the bare back until the blood came.

A few cases are on record of women servants being guilty of intimacy with Negro slaves. Having just arrived from England, they had not yet acquired the feeling of racial antipathy for the African. But public sentiment, even in the seventeenth century, regarded this crime with abhorrence, and the law spoke of all mulattoes as an "abominable mixture." The maid servant guilty of intercourse with a Negro man was punished by public whipping, and at the expiration of her indenture was sold again by the church wardens for another full term. In the case of Ann Wall, an English woman who had two children by a Negro, the Elizabeth City court sold her as a servant for five years. If she returned at the end of this time, she was to be banished to Barbados.

It will be seen that there existed in the colonies a considerable amount of dissipation, misconduct and even vice of the lowest order. But the life of the colonists as a whole was cleaner than that of the people of the

[1] Hening, *Statutes at Large of Virginia*, II, 115.

mother country or of other European lands.   Nowhere in America was there to be found those sinks of corruption which rendered the slums of London so loathsome, no Lewknor's Lane.   The lack of large towns, the ease with which employment was to be had, the wholesome life upon the farm or in the artisan's shop, all tended to elevate the standard of personal conduct.   The youth, taken from the cellars of London and placed at work in a New England shipyard or on a Maryland plantation, not only found his material position bettered, but also had a better chance of escaping moral ruin.   The native influences of early colonial life—the great forests, the open spaces, the hard work, the higher standard of living and the ease with which material well-being was attained—all acted as purifying forces upon the immigrant stream which poured upon these shores. Despite the natural reaction in New England against the prying Puritan censorship of personal conduct, and despite the evils which came from servitude and slavery in all the colonies, but especially in the South, the morals of these first Americans were, for the age, distinctly high.

CHAPTER IX

Man's Treatment of Man

THE people of the seventeenth century had very crude ideas concerning crime and its prevention. Since it was necessary to protect society by inflicting punishments, they believed that the severer the penalty, the greater would be the measure of protection. At the same time the horizon of their sympathies was too restricted to include the criminal himself. They had no conception of the possibilities of reforming offenders, or of preventing crime by alleviating poverty, drunkenness and bad social environment. A terrible fate was meted out to them, inflicted usually in public that others might beware.

In England, even so late as the reign of Elizabeth, persons sentenced to death were hanged, drawn and quartered. This meant that, after being strung up, the doomed man was cut down while yet alive, dragged at the tail of a horse, and then hacked to pieces. When the Jesuit, Edmund Campion, was executed at Tyburn in 1581, as the attendants were about to cut him down, a voice from someone in authority cried out, "Hold, till the man is dead." This foreshadowed a change in the law, requiring that the culprit be hanged by the neck until dead.

Late in the seventeenth century, when Thomas Ellwood was sent to Newgate, he saw lying in a little closet the "Quartered bodies of three men who had been recently executed." In time these bodies were turned over

to the relatives, "but not the Heads, which were ordered
to be set up in some parts of the city. . . . The Hangman fetch'd them in a dirty Dust Blanket, . . . and
setting them down among the Felons, he and they . . .
took them by the Hair, Flouting, Jeering, and Laughing
at them; and then giving them some ill names, box'd
them on the Ears and Cheeks." [1] Such was the terrible
penalty inflicted upon offenders in England, and such
the indignities to which the human body was subjected.
Such a scene, one is happy to observe, has no parallel
in the history of the American colonies.

It has been estimated that at the beginning of the
seventeenth century the annual executions in England
were not less than eight hundred. The number of crimes
for which the death penalty could be exacted, long
enough in the days of James I and Charles I, continued
to grow until well into the nineteenth century. [2] In the
years from 1660 to 1820 no less than one hundred and
eighty-seven capital offences were added to the code,
and one could be led to the gallows for picking a pocket
or stealing a pewter pot.

In such an age severity would be expected in the colonies; but, with the exception of the drastic administra-
tions of Dale, Gates and Argall in Virginia, and perhaps
the persecution of the Quakers in New England, punishments were far milder than in the mother country. In
1610, the London Company, upon receiving information that insubordination was causing trouble at Jamestown, sent Sir Thomas Gates to restore order. Gates

---

[1] Thomas Ellwood, *The History of the Life and Times of Thomas
Ellwood* (London, 1714).
[2] H. E. Barnes, *The Repression of Crime* (N. Y., 1926), 43, 90-97,
157.

brought the "Divine, Moral and Martial Laws," which later, upon the arrival of Dale, were carried out with savage harshness. "The Colony . . . remayned in great want and misery under most severe and Crewell lawes sent over in printe," said the Virginia assembly of 1624,

> and contrary to the expresse Letter of the Kinge in his most gracious Charter, and as mercylessly executed, often times without tryall or Judgment. [Many of the people fled] for reliefe to the Savage Enemy, who being taken againe were putt to sundry deaths as by hanginge, shooting and breakinge uppon the wheele and others were forced by famine to filch for their bellies, of whom one for steelinge of 2 or 3 pints of oatmeale had a bodkinge thrust through his tounge and was tyed with a chaine to a tree untill he starved, if a man through his sicknes had not been able to worke, he had noe allowance at all, and soe consequently perished.[1]

When several men stole a barge and a shallop in an attempt to get back to England, they "were shot to death, hanged and broken upon the wheel." But with the ascendancy of Sir Edwin Sandys in the company, and the establishing of the first representative assembly in America, this cruel régime came to an end.

From this date a noteworthy feature of the administration of law in Virginia and Maryland was the relative leniency of the courts. For crimes, which in England would have brought death, the colonial judges would often impose fines, imprisonment or at most whippings. This wide difference is explained by the fact that crime was more common in the mother country and

---

[1] L. G. Tyler, ed., *Narratives of Early Virginia* (J. F. Jameson, ed., *Original Narratives of Early American History*, N. Y., 1906-), 422-423.

human life cheaper. The decay of commerce and industry in the first years of the seventeenth century in England, which produced so much poverty, left many the alternative of starvation or a life of crime. The jails were always filled and the hangman always busy. No wonder it was said, "The land grows weary of her inhabitants, insomuch that man, which is the most precious of all creatures, is here more vile and base than the earth he treads upon." [1] The gallows constituted a poor remedy for unemployment and its results, but the English courts were bent on suppressing crime rather than altering the conditions out of which crime grew.

In the colonies, on the other hand, where natural resources were abundant and labor scarce, human life was held in high esteem. Charles II took the normal view of this matter when he called Sir William Berkeley an "old fool" for hanging so many men "in that naked country." [2] Often servants and slaves received only light punishment for crimes which even today might be thought to merit the death penalty. In 1679 Thomas Jones, a servant who had made a felonious assult upon his mistress, instead of being sent to the gallows, received thirty-nine stripes of the whip and was made to wear an iron collar. In Westmoreland, when a Negro attempted to incite his fellow slaves to insurrection—one of the worst crimes in the eyes of the planters—his punishment consisted only of several severe floggings and the wearing of an iron collar for life.

[1] Cotton Mather, *Magnalia Christi Americana* (N. Y., 1853), I, 70.
[2] T. M. (*pseud.*), "The Beginning, Progress, and Conclusion of Bacon's Rebellion in Virginia, in the Years 1675 and 1676," Peter Force, ed., *Tracts and Other Papers* (Wash., 1836-1846), I, no. viii, 24.

In America, of course, there was less incentive to crime than in England. Unemployment was unknown, land cheap, food abundant, wages high. No one had the excuse of desperate poverty for adopting a life of crime. The situation is the more interesting in the light of the attempts of the English authorities to export criminals to the colonies. The belief that America was settled by jailbirds—a belief voiced by Dr. Samuel Johnson when he spoke of the colonists as "a race of convicts"—has no foundation in fact. All save a very small percentage, even of the indentured servants, consisted of honest men who made the trip on their own initiative. On the other hand, we know that from time to time the authorities in England did lighten the expenses of maintaining their prisons by emptying them upon the shores of America.[1] Among these persons, most of whom had been guilty only of petty offenses, were a few hardened criminals. Under such circumstances it might be expected that robbery and murder would be frequent in the colonies. That such was not the case gives interesting confirmation to the contention that usually it is not heredity or naturally depraved instincts which produce the cutthroat, but the environment of poverty and misery.

To what extent the transported jailbirds acquired their freedom and entered into the social fabric of the colonies it is impossible to say. In *Moll Flanders* we find the following: "Hence, child, says she, many a

[1] The vast bulk of the newcomers to Virginia during the seventeenth century were English. An examination of the lists in the Land Office at Richmond shows here and there an Irish or a Scotch name, but in normal periods fully 95 per cent were unmistakably Anglo-Saxon. Even in the years 1655 and 1656, after the Drogheda tragedy, when one sees such names as O'Lanny, O'Leaby, O'Mally and Machoone, the list is predominantly English. See T. J. Wertenbaker, *Planters of Colonial Virginia* (Princeton, 1922), 36.

Newgate-bird becomes a great man, and we have . . .
several justices of the peace, officers of the trained band,
and magistrates of the towns they live in, that have been
burnt in the hand." This obviously is an absurdity,
for notorious criminals as a rule served their masters for
life, and, even when they escaped from bondage, were
forced to flee to the remote frontiers for safety. Yet
many a man, whom poverty had driven to petty crimes
in England, became in the New World a substantial, law-
abiding citizen. "All villanous Outrages that are committed in other States are not as much as known here,"
says George Alsop in his *Maryland*. "A man may walk
in the open Woods as secure from being externally dis-
sected, as in his own house or dwelling. So hateful is a
Robber, that if but once imagin'd to be so, he's kept at a
distance and shun'd as the Pestilential noysomness."
He adds: "Those whose lives and conversations have had
no other gloss nor glory stampt on them in their own
Country, but the stigmatization of baseness, were here
by the common civilities and deportments of the Inhabitants of this Province, brought to detest and loath their
former actions." [1]

In the Southern colonies the life penalty was seldom
exacted save in cases of murder, treason and insurrection. When a conspiracy was discovered among the
slaves of Surry and James City counties in 1710, two
or three only were executed. "I hope," wrote Colonel
Jennings, "their fate will strike such terror in the other
Negroes as will keep them from forming such designs
for the future." [2] Of the rioters who went from plan-

---

[1] George Alsop, *A Character of the Province of Maryland* [1666]
(N. D. Mereness, ed., Cleveland, 1908), 48.
[2] C. O. 5: 1365 and 1406 (Brit. Pub. Rec. Office), 189-191.

tation to plantation in Virginia in 1682, cutting down the tobacco plants, only two were hanged. A notorious exception to the mild treatment of rebels was the savagery of Sir William Berkeley toward the followers of the ill-starred Nathaniel Bacon. Despite King Charles's letter of amnesty, the vengeful old governor strung up the offenders as fast as he could secure convictions, and some of the executions were accompanied by unnecessary cruelty. Anthony Arnold, who had declared that "if the King should deny to doe him right he would make noe more to sheathe his sword in his heart or Bowels then of his own mortall Enemyes," was hanged in chains.[1] When William Drummond was executed, his clothes were stripped from his back and his ring torn from his finger. But Berkeley's vindictive acts were inconsistent with the general practice of the colonies, and it is significant that his hand was finally stayed by his own henchmen in the assembly.

In Maryland a severe law was passed in 1638 which fixed the penalty for treason. If the culprit happened to be a woman, she was to be burned at the stake; if a man of ordinary rank, he was to be hanged, drawn and quartered; if a lord of a manor, he was to be beheaded. Apparently, however, none of these stringent provisions were ever carried out.[2]

In Massachusetts the list of crimes for which the death penalty was inflicted was much larger than in the South. Under the stern Puritan rule persons were hanged for heresy, murder, treason and unnatural vices as well as for witchcraft. As we have seen, several Quakers paid with their lives for their attempt to gain converts, while

[1] C. O. 5: 1371 (Brit. Pub. Rec. Office), 152.
[2] J. T. Scharf, *History of Maryland* (Balt., 1879), II, 40.

many innocent persons were hanged for their supposed contracts with Satan. But when the offense was against the civil code rather than against religion, the New England courts were not overharsh.[1] In 1654 Edward Sanders, convicted of rape in Massachusetts, was sentenced, not to the gallows, but to be whipped and to carry a rope around his neck hanging down two feet. A Negro woman who murdered her bastard child in 1674 was placed on the gallows with a rope around her neck and then whipped "at the Carts Tayle." On the other hand, James Brittaine and Mary Lothain were both condemned to death for adultery, while there were several executions for "beastiality." Most unusual was the case of Marja and Cheffaleer Jack, Negroes who pleaded guilty to arson, the first being burned at the stake, the other first hanged and then burned. In New England, as in other colonies, there were also executions for piracy.

Mutilation was not uncommon in New England in the early years of the century. In 1631 Phillip Ratcliffe, "for uttering mallitious & scandalous speeches against the government & the Church of Salem," was sentenced to "be whipped, have his eares cut of, fyned 40 shillings and banished." Nine years later it was ordered that James Luxford "be bound to the whiping poast," and "have his eares cut of . . . for his forgery, lying & other foule offences." For contempt of court Maurice Brett was to stand in the pillory, to which his ears were to be nailed, "& after an hours standing there to be cut of." In 1684 Joseph Gatchell, convicted of blasphemy, was to stand in the pillory, "have his toung

---

[1] John Noble, "Notes on the Trial and Punishment of Crimes," Colon. Soc. of Mass., *Publs.*, III, 51-66; esp. 59-60, for the examples in the text.

drawne forth out of his mouth, & peirct throyh with a hott iron." During the Quaker persecution, three of the invading missionaries had their ears cut off.

In Virginia and Maryland mutilation was of less frequent occurrence. In 1624 a certain Edward Sharpless, for betraying the secret correspondence of the Virginia government, was sentenced to "stand in the Pillory and there to have his Ears nailed to it, and cut off." His punishment was modified, however, so that he "lost but a part of one of his eares." [1] In 1630 a man found guilty of perjury was sentenced in Virginia to stand in the pillory and lose his ears. On the whole, however, this punishment for free white men was extremely rare; even Berkeley seems to have refrained from mutilation in taking his revenge on Bacon's followers. But for slaves who had run away, it was not uncommon that the ears should be nailed to the pillory and later cut off. This served the double purpose of warning other Negroes not to imitate the offense and of identifying the offender forevermore. Mutilation, though rarely practised by the Dutch settlers of New Amsterdam, was not infrequent after the English conquest of 1664. The hangman at Fort Albany, himself found guilty of "Divers Thefts and Robbings . . . escaped his neck through want of another Hangman to truss him up, soe that all the punishment he received . . . was only 39 stripes at the Whipping Post, loss of an Ear and banishment."

In Maryland there were very severe laws against "wittingly, maliciously and advisedly, by writing or speech, blaspheming or cursing God, or denying the Saviour's divinity, the Trinity or the God head." Any person convicted of these offenses was to have his tongue

[1] C. O. 1: 3 (Brit. Pub. Rec. Office).

bored through and then be fined; for the second offense, to be branded on the forehead with the letter B and fined forty pounds; and for the third offense, to be executed without benefit of clergy.[1] An act of 1647 prescribed for various offenses the boring of the tongue, slitting of the nose, cutting off one or both ears, and branding with a hot iron. It is probable, however, that these harsh penalties were seldom, if ever, enforced.[2] When Captain Josias Fendall was found guilty of speaking seditious words against the government, thus rendering him liable under the law to mutilation, the court contented itself with a fine and banishment.

Branding was a form of punishment not infrequently employed in the colonies, especially in New England. In 1632 Richard Hopkins, for selling "peeces & powder & shott to the Indenes," was sentenced by the court in Massachusetts to be severely "whipt, & branded with a hott iron on one of his cheekes." Nicholas Frost, found guilty of theft, fornication and drunkenness, in addition to other punishments, was to be branded in the hand. A few years later Robert Scarlett, who is described as a known thief, was branded with the letter T. William Brumfield, "for his stealeing, ploting to run from his m^r, lying, drunkenness & idlenes," was branded and whipped. Uriah Clements, for burglary was to be "branded with the letter B. on ye forehead & have his Right eare cutt of." [3]

[1] That is, escape death at the mercy of the court through showing his ability to write his name. In the Middle Ages this was accepted as a sign of the clerical character, and therefore not a fit subject for the civil court. The criminal code of Maryland is summarized by N. D. Mereness, *Maryland as a Proprietary Province* (N. Y., 1901), 277-278.

[2] Scarf, *History of Maryland*, II, 40n.

[3] Noble, "Notes on the Trial and Punishment of Crimes," Colon. Soc. of Mass., *Publs.*, III, 56-57.

All through the seventeenth century whipping, branding, cutting the ear, and other corporal punishments were commonly practised in all the colonies.[1] Today the lash is considered unnecessarily cruel and, save in a few states, is no longer in use in this country. Three centuries ago it was a humane substitute for the gallows. In Virginia the whipping post was resorted to on innumerable occasions, for offenses ranging from petty larceny to attempted murder or rape. In 1640 Thomas Bates, who had wronged his master by seducing his wife, was sentenced to nothing worse than thirty lashes to be laid on at the fort in Jamestown.[2] In contrast to this was the case of Christopher Bryant who was whipped for milking Goodwife Powell's cow by stealth. About 1666 a woman was condemned to twenty lashes in Lower Norfolk County for stealing two smocks; in Accomac another was whipped for making off with a handkerchief, a pillowbere, a hood and a towel. In 1627 the Virginia general court condemned Margaret Partein to "forty stripes" for "concealing the offence of Thomas Hayle lately executed." [3]. In the same year Alice Thornburg was given forty lashes "for her offence in fighting with Anne Snoode and beating her, whereby just suspicion may be had that she" caused abortion. A whipping post was erected near every prison and courthouse in the colony.[4] In Maryland thieves were usually whipped. Forgeries were punished with

[1] Barnes, *The Repression of Crime*, 27.
[2] Conway Robinson, ed., "Virginia Council and General Court Records, 1640-1641," *Va. Mag. of Hist. and Biog.*, XI, 277.
[3] Robinson, "Virginia Council and General Court Records, 1626-1628," *Va. Mag. of Hist. and Biog.*, IV, 246.
[4] W. W. Hening, comp., *Statutes at Large of Virginia* (Phila., 1823), I, 75.

thirty-nine lashes, while to counterfeit the great seal of the province might entail whipping, the pillory and banishment.

In New England whipping was in common use for many offenses and was administered usually in conjunction with fines, imprisonment and branding, but it seems not to have been applied with excessive harshness save in the case of heretics. Of the many whippings during the Quaker persecution, that administered to William Brend was perhaps the most brutal. After being subjected to a severe lashing he was put into "Irons, Neck and Heels, lockt so close together as there was no more room between each, than for the Horse-Lock that fastened them on," in which condition he was left without food for sixteen hours. The next day he was whipped again with a tarred rope until "his Flesh was beaten Black, and as into a Gelly; and under his arms the bruised Flesh and Blood hung down, clotted as it were with Bagges." [1] On another occasion three women were stripped to the waist, tied to the cart's tail and forced to trudge through the December's snow to the frontier. At eleven intervals they were given ten lashes each on the bare back.

The first codes of New Jersey, passed in 1668 and 1675, show the stern influence of Connecticut, whence many of the settlers came. Twelve offenses were punishable by death, and there was frequent resort to the branding iron, the mutilating knife, the stocks and the whipping post. But there was one feature of seventeenth-century criminal law here and elsewhere which modern legislators might study with profit: the offender was compelled to rectify, so far as possible, the wrong

[1] George Bishop, *New England Judged* (London, 1661), 67.

he had done. One guilty of arson had to make good the losses of his victim, just as the burglar and the robber had to restore stolen goods. Fornication brought compulsory marriage unless the parents of the girl preferred the payment of damages. All this savored of the Levitical code or that of the northern European tribes rather than of Roman law, under which the offense was considered to be against the state rather than against the individual.[1]

Imprisonment was far less common in the colonies than in England. In a thinly settled country, especially where there was practically no criminal class, the people were reluctant to vote funds for erecting and maintaining prisons. To give a culprit a sound lashing was quite as effective as keeping him in jail and far less expensive. The Virginia assembly early empowered each county to erect prisons and passed a law making the sheriffs responsible for the escape of prisoners. That this provision was neglected, however, its repeated re-enactment makes obvious. In 1658 and again in 1662 the assembly directed the local authorities to construct jails of ample size and strength.[2] In 1684 the law was passed once more, with the added provision that a certain amount of land was to be laid off adjoining the prison to serve as "a place of liberty and privilege" for prisoners held for minor offenses.

The prisons in most cases were merely places of temporary confinement. Often they seem to have been no more than dwellings or rooms leased by the authorities,

[1] H. E. Barnes, *A History of the Penal, Reformatory and Correctional Institutions of the State of New Jersey* (Trenton, 1918), 27-35. See also Philip Klein, *Prison Methods in New York State* (Columbia Univ., Studies, XC, no. 1), 26-27.

[2] Hening, *Statutes at Large of Virginia*, II, 76-77.

and were so insecure that it was easy for the inmates to escape unless securely manacled and guarded. Governor Culpeper writes that he could hardly sleep for fear the men under sentence for participation in the plant-cutting riots of 1682 would get away.[1] In fact, one of the prisoners, although loaded down with chains, did break through the walls and could not be recaptured. After Bacon's Rebellion John West and John Turner, both condemned to death for their part in the uprising, "made their escapes by breaking prison." [2] In Massachusetts, as we have seen, Nathaniel Cary saved his wife from almost certain death as a witch by delivering her from prison and fleeing the colony. In Hartford an Indian girl charged with murder broke out of the town jail.

When in 1664 John Scott took sudden leave of the Hartford jail, leaving a bill for twelve weeks' "diet," it was thought especially dishonorable. To charge a prisoner for his board was then a general and accepted practice; there were also other means of mulcting a culprit of whatever he had saved. It was recognized as a victory for philanthropy when the Quaker proprietors of West Jersey put into their liberal "Concessions and Agreements" the promise that "no Person nor Persons imprisoned upon any account whatsoever within this Province, shall be obliged to pay any Fees to the Officer or Officers of the said Prison either when committed or discharged." [3]

The American jails of the day could not duplicate

[1] Thomas Culpeper, "Report on Virginia in 1683," *Va. Mag. of Hist. and Biog.*, III, 231.

[2] C. O. 2; 39 (Brit. Pub. Rec. Office), 31.

[3] W. A. Whitehead and others, eds., *N. J. Archives* (Newark, 1880-1906, ser. 1), I, 257.

the ghastly conditions existing in many English prisons. "Here's no Newgates for pilfering Felons," says George Alsop, "nor Ludgates for Debtors, nor any Bridewels to lash the soul of Concupiscence into a chast Repentence." [1] The crowding together of prisoners, the immorality, the foul air, and spread of contagion, must have been unknown in a tumble-down country jail. When the prisoners were laden with chains and put in damp cellars, suffering and sickness often followed; but such cases were rare.   James Barrow, one of Bacon's followers who was locked up at Governor Berkeley's home, complained "of the extremity of Cold, hunger, lothsomnesse of Vermin, and other sad occasions." But Barrow would have felt his Virginia prison quite comfortable had he ever seen the inside of Newgate.[2]

Solicitude for the creditor demanded the imprisonment of the man who did not pay his debts; yet the laws of the seventeenth century dealing with this subject were milder than those of the eighteenth.   Some, indeed, actually protected the debtor.   In the Duke's Laws, proclaimed in New York in 1664, it was provided that "no man shall be longer in prison for debt or fine than he can find sureties."   Twenty years later

[1] Alsop, *Maryland*, 49.
[2] Thomas Ellwood (1639-1714) in his autobiography gives us a vivid picture of this famous place in the seventeenth century. "In the night we were all lodged in one room, which was large and round, having in the middle of it a great pillar of oaken timber, which bore up the chapel that is over it.   To this pillar we fastened our hammocks . . . three stories high, one over the other. . . . The breath and steam that came from so many bodies . . . was enough to cause sickness amongst us. . . ."   The foreman of a jury, which held an inquest over the body of a prisoner who died during the night, lifted up his hands, exclaiming, "I did not think there had been so much cruelty in the hearts of Englishmen, to use Englishmen in this manner."   *The History of Thomas Ellwood, Written by Himself* [1714] (London, 1885), 160, 163.

a law was passed which forbade the imprisoning of
minors for debt except in cases of indebtedness for food
or apparel.[1]

A favorite mode of punishment in the colonies was
to fasten the hands and feet of the offender in a wooden
frame and put him on public display. As we have
already seen, the Quaker, William Brend, suffered in
this manner for defying the laws against heretics in
Massachusetts. In 1638 several men in Virginia were,
for various offenses, "set up by the heels in the stock."
In 1630 three men were laid neck and heels during
divine service for "nicknaming houses abusing men &
their wives & night walking. . . ." [2] During one
of the early wars in Virginia a certain Richard Bickley
was sentenced to lie neck and heels for twelve hours for
refusing to take arms in the defense of the country.[3]
Similar treatment was meted out to a man named
Crooks for calling his neighbor a liar, and declaring that
his house was unfit for any man's entertainment.[4] In
1634 John Holloway of Accomac was sentenced for
contempt of court to lie neck and heels at the door of
the parish church when the worshipers should assemble.
For intimating that Charles I was a papist Stephen
Reikes was, in 1642, condemned to "stand in the pillory
with a paper on his head expressing his offense." [5]
During the seventeenth century the pillory and the

---

[1] *New York Colonial Laws* (Albany, 1894-1896), I, 14, 160.

[2] Conway Robinson, "Notes from the Council and General Court Records," *Va. Mag. of Hist. and Biog.*, XIII, 389.

[3] "Decisions of Virginia General Court, 1626-1628," *Va. Mag. of Hist. and Biog.*, IV, 159-160.

[4] B. H. Wise, comp., "Northampton County Records in 17th Century," *Va. Mag. of Hist. and Biog.*, IV, 402-403.

[5] F. L. Hawks, *Contributions to the Ecclesiastical History of the United States of America* (N. Y., 1836), I, 50-51.

stocks came into almost universal use in the colonies. Thus, the Virginia assembly passed an act in 1662 requiring the erection in every county of stocks, pillory and whipping post. The use of the pillory was often accompanied by other and harsher punishments, as we have seen, when the ears were nailed to the post or cut off, or when the tongue was bored.

Ducking was reserved especially for women whose tongues outran their prudence. In Northampton County, Virginia, Joan Butler was convicted of slander and given the option of doing penance before the congregation or of being dragged at the stern of a canoe over King's Creek.[1] In 1626 the general court ordered that Margaret Jones, for adultery, should be fastened to the stern of a boat in the James River. The next year Amy Hall was condemned to be "toughed aboard the Margaret & John & ducked three times." [2] The use of torture to extract confessions from the accused, while by no means unknown in the English colonies, was infrequent. In New England some of the persons accused of witchcraft seem to have been subjected to the watching method of Matthew Hopkins—a kind of torture which often brought confessions. The pressing to death of old Giles Corey is the only recorded case in the history of the colonies in which a man was legally tortured to death. Running the gauntlet was a form of punishment which seems to have been especially reserved for soldiers. Thus, in 1624, a man in Virginia was forced to pass forty soldiers, every one of whom

[1] Wise, "Northampton County Records in 17th Century," *Va. Mag. of Hist. and Biog.*, IV, 406.

[2] "Decisions of Virginia General Court, 1626-1628," *Va. Mag. of Hist. and Biog.*, IV, 250.

butted him, after which he was "kicked downe & forced out of the fort." [1]

The colonists often made the punishment of offenders symbolic of the offense. When Richard Buckland, in 1646, defamed Ann Smyth in a libelous poem, the Virginia court ordered him to stand in the church door with a paper on his hat bearing the inscription *Inimrius Libellos*.[2] Two years later Robert Warder had to stand at the church door with a great pot tied about his neck, "thereby signifying the merit of being drunk." Another culprit was sentenced to ride the wooden horse with an empty pitcher in one hand, to indicate his propensity to strong drink. Sometimes, too, the community made the culprit do some useful public work, as when in Virginia a man convicted of fornication had to build a ferry boat.[3]

The system of indentured labor involved a very special relation of man to his fellow man. Obviously the community had to confide to the master certain rights of correction and discipline; but it was equally obvious that the servant needed certain legal safeguards against harsh and abusive treatment. Since the servant was bound for a limited number of years, beyond a certain point the master was not impelled by self-interest to conserve his health and strength. Indeed, masters were known to treat servants with intentional cruelty shortly before their period of indenture expired, so that they would be glad to relinquish, in return for

[1] "Minutes of the Council and General Court, 1622-1624," *Va. Mag. of Hist. and Biog.*, XIX, 230.
[2] "Northampton County Records in 17th Century," *Va. Mag. of Hist. and Biog.*, IV, 407.
[3] O. P. Chitwood, *Justice in Colonial Virginia* (Johns Hopkins Univ., Studies, XXIII, nos. 7-8), 90.

immediate freedom, the clothing, food or land to which they were entitled. The Virginia assembly itself testified to the fact that servants were not always well treated. "The barbarous usage of some servants by cruell masters bring soe much scandell and infamy to the country in generall," reads an act of March, 1662, "that people who would willingly adventure themselves hither, are through feare thereof diverted, and by that means the supplies of particular men and the well seating his majesties country very much obstructed." [1]

The most notorious case of brutality to servants in Virginia occurred in 1624 when a certain Mr. Proctor was brought before the general court accused of causing the deaths of Elizabeth Abbott and Elyas Hintone. The woman had been subjected to repeated whippings until "her flesh in some places was raw and very black and blew." [2] At length she ran away to the woods and fourteen days later was found dead. As for Hintone, he was at work in the fields when Proctor struck him a number of blows with a hoe. Complaining to his fellow servants that his master had done him mortal hurt, he too ran away and died.

The assembly and the courts, appreciating the possibilities of cruelty under the indenture system, made every effort to protect the servants. A statute of 1643 provided that, if any servant had just cause for complaint against his master or mistress by "harsh or unchristianlike usage or otherways for want of diet," he could enter complaint with the nearest justice, and the

[1] Hening, *Statutes at Large of Virginia*, II, 117.
[2] "Minutes of the Council of General Court 1622-1624," *Va. Mag. of Hist. and Biog.*, XIX, 388-389.

county court was to give him redress and protection.[1] This law was reënacted in 1658, while in 1662 it was required that "every master shall provide for his servants competent dyett, clothing and lodging, and that he shall not exceed the bounds of moderation in correcting them beyond the meritt of their offences." [2]   Nor were these laws lightly disregarded.   In Lower Norfolk County, when Mrs. Deborah Farneshaugh was accused of failing to provide adequate food and clothing for a young servant, the court ordered her to give the boy better treatment, and finally withdrew her right to hold him when she persisted in her cruelty.   In 1680 the general court issued an order forbidding a certain woman who had been guilty of brutality, to keep servants.

In Maryland it was provided by law that servants refusing to carry out their masters' orders were to be whipped by direction of a magistrate.   On the other hand, if the master failed to provide the servant with proper food and care, he was to be imprisoned by the magistrate until surety was furnished for the performance of his duty.   By a later law a master who failed to provide adequate meat, drink, lodging and clothing, or who overworked the servant or refused to permit him to take proper rest and sleep, was to be fined for the first and second offenses, and for the third to lose all claim to the servant.[3]   Masters were forbidden to administer more than ten lashes unless so directed by a magistrate. The records show a number of cases in which masters were summoned before the courts upon accusations of cruelty to their servants.   In 1652 an inquest was held

[1] Hening, *Statutes at Large of Virginia*, I, 255.
[2] Hening, *Statutes at Large of Virginia*, II, 118.
[3] Scharf, *History of Maryland*, II, 15.

by the court over a Scotch servant whose death followed
a whipping. The jury gave it as their opinion that the
man had died of a fever and not as a result of the lashes.
A few years later a woman was acquitted by the provincial court of causing the death of her servant.

Several contemporaneous writers, who describe conditions in Virginia and Maryland, have testified to the
good treatment generally accorded indentured servants.
"The Servants of this Province," says George Alsop,
"which are stigmatiz'd for slaves by the clappermouth
jaws of the vulgar in England, live more like Freemen
than the most Mechanick Apprentices of London, want-
ing for nothing that is convenient and necessary, and
according to their several capacities, are extraordinary
well used and respected." He was at a loss to understand why the poor of England should hesitate to come
to Maryland because of "the debarment of a foure years
sordid liberty." The servants worked five and a half
days weekly in summer, with a long intermission at
midday. In the winter there was little work save cutting
wood for fires or hunting game.[1]

Hammond, in his *Leah and Rachel*, says that "those
servants that will be industrious, may in their time of
service gain a competent estate before their freedoms,
which is usually done by many. . . ." And he adds:
"There is no master but will allow his servant a parcel
of clear ground to plant some tobacco in for himself,
which he may husband at those many idle times he hath
allowed him, and not prejudice but rejoice his master to
see it."[2] The labor required of the servant, he asserts,

[1] Alsop, *Maryland*, 55, 94.
[2] John Hammond, "Leah and Rachel, or, the Two Fruitfull Sisters
Virginia, and Mary-land [1656]," Peter Force, comp., *Tracts and Other
Papers*, III, no. xviv, 14.

was much lighter than that of the husbandman or the handicraftsman of England.

Although these accounts give only the bright side of the picture, there is no reason to think that they are greatly exaggerated. Not only was it to the interest of the planter to keep the worker strong and healthy, but with food so abundant, the expense of his keep was insignificant. It required a heavier outlay to clothe a servant, and during the period of distress following the passage of the navigation acts, when thousands even of the freemen were in rags, it is quite probable that the servants were ill-supplied. This was not a matter of great moment, however, because of the mild climate of tidewater Virginia and Maryland, and the servant was not often required to work out of doors in winter. But that the system was open to grave abuses is obvious.

An indication of the bad conditions that existed on some plantations is seen in the frequency with which servants ran away. This evil became so pronounced that both Virginia and Maryland were forced to take the most vigorous measures to stop it. In the former colony the absconding servant, when brought back, was required to serve at the end of his indenture double the time lost by his absence; and if the offense were committed a second time, he was branded on the cheek and shoulder.[1] In 1640, when Hugh Gwyn recovered two white servants and a Negro who had fled to Maryland, the court ordered that the runaways each receive thirty lashes on the bare back. Of those who ran off from their masters, it is probable that the larger part were either kidnaped persons brought to the colonies against their will or prisoners under life sentence. In most

[1] Hening, *Statutes at Large of Virginia*, I, 254-255.

cases the man who signed his indenture voluntarily lived peacefully and in comparative comfort.

The problem of social control was further complicated in the colonies by the introduction and spread of slavery. The appearance of this institution excited little moral disapprobation in the seventeenth century. It was generally held that any hardships suffered by the African—in the stifling hold of the slaver or later in the service of his master—was more than offset by his fortunate delivery from a life of idolatry and savagery. To be sure, here and there a voice was raised in protest. After the Pequot War Roger Williams pleaded with the Massachusetts authorities that the remnants of the tribe should not be sold into slavery, while John Eliot many years later declared that "to sell soules for mony seemeth to me a dangerous merchandize." [1]   In 1688 some of the Pennsylvania Quakers addressed a memorial to the Philadelphia yearly meeting, protesting against the perpetual bondage of men and women. Twelve years later Judge Sewall atoned for his mistakes in the witchcraft trials by denouncing the slave trade.

These lone voices found little response. Even in New England it was thought that to enslave an African and bring him under Christian influences was an act in every way commendable. The doctrine of election accepted by the Puritans did not incline them to gentleness in their dealings with inferior races. The savage Negroes and the savage Indians were accursed peoples whom it was quite proper to destroy or to enslave. "We know not when or how these Indians first became inhabitants of this mighty continent," says Cotton Mather, "yet we may guess that probably the Devil decoyed these miser-

[1] J. T. Adams, *Founding of New England* (Boston, 1921), 362.

able savages hither, in hope that the gospel of the Lord
Jesus Christ would never come to destroy or disturb his
absolute empire over them." Efforts were made to con-
vert the Indians, but with very little success; and in the
end they were swept out of the way of the Puritan state
by force of arms. After the Pequot War some of the
prisoners were turned over to the Narragansetts for in-
corporation into that tribe, some were kept by the
English, and others were sent to be sold as slaves in the
West Indies. Of the captives taken in King Philip's
War many were distributed among the whites as servants
for a limited period.[1]

The clergy not only sanctioned these acts but took
their share of the Indian slaves. "Mr. Endecot and
my selfe salute you in the Lord Jesus," wrote a minister
to Governor Winthrop after the Pequot War. "Wee
haue heard of a diuidence of women and children in the
bay and would bee glad of a share viz: a young woman
or girle and a boy if you thinke good." [2] When some
gentlemen of Cotton Mather's church purchased for him
a valuable Negro slave, it seemed to that noted clergyman "a mighty Smile of Heaven" upon his family.
More interesting still as an illustration of the fact that
there was no necessary connection between Puritanism
and opposition to slavery is the will of John Bacon of
Barnstable, which provided that, if his slave Dinah
should survive his wife, she should be sold and the money
laid out in buying Bibles for his heirs.[3] During the

[1] A. W. Lauber, *Indian Slavery in Colonial Times within the Present Limits of the United States* (Columbia Univ., *Studies*, LIV), 124.
[2] William Appleton, ed., *The Winthrop Papers* (Mass. Hist. Soc.,
Colls., ser. 4, VI), 91.
[3] Frederick Freeman, *The History of Cape Cod* (Boston, 1869), II,
293.

Quaker persecution Daniel Southick and Provided Southick, children of one of the missionaries, were sold into bondage in Virginia and the West Indies to pay the fines levied on their parent.[1] Slavery never became general in New England because the industries of that region required intelligent, skillful labor, not because public sentiment condemned the institution as a moral evil.

In the tobacco colonies the demand for slaves was urgent throughout the seventeenth century; but it was only in the last two decades that they could be secured in quantity, and not until after the Treaty of Utrecht in 1713 that they became cheap. By that time the British had established themselves so firmly in the slave trade that they could supply the needs not only of the sugar colonies but of the Chesapeake Bay region as well. Prior to 1690, however, the number of slaves in Maryland and Virginia together probably did not exceed five thousand. On the whole, their treatment on the tobacco plantations seems to have been better than that of the indentured servants. Docile by nature, feeling themselves utterly helpless in a strange land, easily acclimated, the Africans proved easier to handle than the white men. Moreover, since they served for life, there was every incentive for their masters to keep them in good condition. To break the health of a Negro by brutality or overwork was a costly bit of folly.

It is true, however, that slaves often fled from their masters. Perhaps this was to be expected of savages fresh from Africa, unaccustomed to a life of toil and restraint, and uncertain as to their eventual fate. The poor wretches while in transit often fancied that they were to be eaten, and so, when once on shore, took the

[1] Bishop, *New England Judged*, 108-112.

first opportunity to escape.   If the new slave happened
to find himself upon a plantation with native-born
Negroes, their influence and assurances tended to allay
his fears and reconcile him to his new life.   But if he
were placed in the company of unruly white servants,
their example was apt to increase his natural desire to
escape.

The laws concerning runaway slaves were harsh.   In
case they fled to the wilderness, there to maintain themselves by raiding the nearest plantations, they might be
outlawed.   In 1672 an act of the Virginia assembly declared that, since "many negroes have lately beene, and
now are out in rebellion in sundry parts of this country,
and that noe meanes have yet beene found for the apprehension and suppression of them," it should be lawful
for any person to arrest, or in case of resistance, to kill
them.[1]   In 1627 Captain Sampson brought to Virginia
a number of native West Indians and delivered them into
the custody of the council.   They made their escape,
however, in an attempt to reach the Virginia Indians,
and, hiding in the woods, lived by pillaging the planters.
The council considered them so great a menace to the
colony that they issued an order that they should be
taken and hanged.   The Negro was always reckoned a
potential adversary, and there were laws forbidding him
to carry arms.   On June 8, 1692, the court of sessions
in Westchester County, New York, ordered that "noe
Negro [or] Malatto bond slave be Permitted to have
with them Any gunn Doge or Staffe when out of their
Masters plantations." [2]

[1] Hening, *Statutes at Large of Virginia*, II, 299.
[2] D. R. Fox, ed., *Minutes of the Court of Sessions, Westchester
County* (White Plains, 1924), 66-67.

The Virginia laws of the seventeenth century gave the master full power to correct his slave. "If any slave resist his master, or other by his master's order correcting him," reads the act of 1669, "and by the extremity of the correction should chance to die . . . his death shall not be accompted a ffelony . . . since it cannot be presumed that prepensed malice, which alone makes murder ffelony, should induce any man to destroy his owne estate." [1]   In some instances the records show that the masters took advantage of this provision to treat their slaves with excessive cruelty. The Reverend Samuel Gray, when his runaway boy returned, bound him to a tree and compelled another slave to beat him until he died. [2]   In 1662 a woman was tried in the Maryland provincial court for causing the death of a slave. This Negro, often having been put in chains for misdemeanors, refused to work and pretended to be in a fit. For this new offense hot lard was poured on his back, he was tied to a ladder and left in a cold wind. As a result he soon died. In extenuation of this barbarous treatment the overseer testified that the slave had been "an ugly, yelling, beast-like brute," who ran away and lived by stealing. [3]

Measured by the standards of the twentieth century it cannot be said that in their treatment of their fellow man the colonists were always inspired by enlightened and humane instincts. Toward those who transgressed there was harshness and even some terrible cruelty. But

[1] Hening, *Statutes at Large of Virginia*, II, 270.
[2] *Middlesex County Records for 1694-1705*, 238, cited in P. A. Bruce, *Economic History of Virginia in the Seventeenth Century* (N. Y.), 1895), II, 108.
[3] J. R. Brackett, *The Negro in Maryland* (Johns Hopkins Univ., Studies, extra vol. vi), 142 n.

measured by the contemporaneous European standards, the settlers were notably humane.   The translation to the New World, however detrimental in narrowing the intellectual interests of the immigrants, gave them a more advanced conception of the value of human life and the dignity of man.[1]   The wretch who in the slums of London inspired only scorn and contempt assumed in the forests of Virginia or the New England hills his rightful place as a man among men.

[1] The care of the poor naturally engaged less attention in America than in England.   In the South it was the concern of the parish vestry, a self-perpetuating body.   In New England it fell under the jurisdiction of the town, whose officials exercised a close surveillance over strangers, bachelors and others.   See E. W. Capen, *The Historical Development of the Poor Law of Connecticut* (Columbia Univ., *Studies*, XXII), chap. i.

CHAPTER X

THE BEGINNINGS OF AN INTELLECTUAL LIFE

IT was not to be expected that the colonists should display any marked degree of literary or scientific activity. The settlers had to devote their energies to the enormous task of conquering the American wilderness and developing its resources. These first Americans were pioneers in opening to civilization a vast continent, not pioneers in chemistry, anatomy, zoology, engineering or literature. From Maine to the Carolinas we look in vain for a single figure of note in such matters, one standing out above the level of mediocrity. This does not mean that the New England trader or the Virginia planter was inferior in natural capacity to the men they left behind in England; it means rather that their energies turned to the practical problems of clearing the forests, building homes, planting crops, constructing ships, trading and fishing; to the subtleties of Indian warfare; to the unceasing political struggle with the crown.

In New England, where the inclination to investigation and study was greatest, the intellectual streams were in large measure dried up in the arid wastes of theological disputation. Of the one hundred and fifty-seven books put out by the press at Cambridge from its establishment through the year 1670, sixty-three were upon religious subjects.[1] The really vigorous minds of the

[1] Sermons and religious proceedings were often taken down in shorthand. See H. R. Stiles, *The History and Genealogies of Ancient Wind-*

period were interested in discussions of the covenant of grace and the covenant of works, or were writing treatises on religious melancholy or the maxims of piety. John Norton devoted himself with burning zeal to writing *The Orthodox Evangelist,* "wherein he handles the abstruse points of the existence and subsistence and the efficience of God;" John Cotton produced his *Ecclesiastes and Canticles*—John Cotton, who, after his daily study of twelve hours, loved "to sweeten his mouth with a piece of Calvin." [1]   If there appeared among the laity some person of more than ordinary mental activity, he too was almost inevitably drawn into the field of theological discussion.

Nor were the clergy content with guiding the course of intellectual activity through example and leadership, for they exercised a strict censorship over the ideas and reading of the people.   The man who showed a "novile disposition" was asked to leave the colony; the church member found with a heretical book in his possession was frowned upon or even severely disciplined. The spirit of the early magistrates is illustrated by the reception accorded a work by the lawyer Thomas Lechford, entitled *Of Prophesie.*   He intrusted the manuscript to Thomas Dudley, with the request that he

sor (Hartford, 1891), I, 11; S. E. Baldwin, "Rev. John Higginson, of Salem," Mass. Hist. Soc., *Proceeds.*, ser. 2, XVI, 487-489; W. P. Upham, "Remarks [on shorthand]," same vol., 475-476.   All we know of Thomas Hooker's famous sermons of 1638 and 1639 comes to us through Henry Wolcott's notes, taken according to his modification of the Willis system.   See J. H. T. (*pseud.*), "Abstracts of Two Sermons by Rev. Thomas Hooker.   From the Short-hand Notes of Mr. Henry Wolcott," Conn. Hist. Soc., *Colls.*, I, 19-21.   See also John Hull, "Diary," Am. Antiq. Soc., *Trans.*, III, 151-154; and MSS. by C. C. Beale and J. E. Rockwell in N. Y. Public Library.

[1] Cotton Mather, *Magnalia Christi Americana* (Hartford, 1820), I, 250.

advise him as a "private friend" whether it ought to be published. Dudley was so aroused by what he read that he wrote Winthrop, "I find the scope thereof to be erroneous and dangerous, if not hereticall. I have sent you the book herewith that instead of puttinge it to the presse as he desireth it may rather be putt into the fire as I desire." [1]

The first printing press in Massachusetts—and for a generation the only one in English America [2]—was set up in 1639, and for some years thereafter no legal restrictions were put upon its output. This is explained by the fact that it was so under the influence of the theocracy that there was no fear of its turning out anything of which they did not approve. That little actual freedom of the press existed, however, is shown by the reception in 1650 of a pamphlet entitled *The Meritorious Price of Our Redemption*, written by William Pynchon of Springfield. The general court, finding the work "erronyous and hereticale," ordered it to be burned by the common executioner in the market place at Boston. [3] Four years later, when certain books appeared in Massachusetts teaching the tenets of the Quakers, the general court required every inhabitant having copies in

[1] Charles Deane, "Report on the Belknap Donation," *Mass. Hist. Soc., Proceeds.*, III, 311-312. Lechford's own account is found in his "Note-Book" printed in Am. Antiq. Soc., *Trans.*, VII, 48-49.

[2] For example, the Duke's Laws for New York in 1663 had to be printed in Boston. Isaiah Thomas, *History of Printing in America* (Am. Antiq. Soc., *Trans.*, V-VI), I, 38-75, 290. William Bradford, the first Pennsylvania printer, came in the *Welcome* with Penn himself in 1682, his earliest imprint bearing the date of 1685; in 1693 he established the first press in New York. See G. H. Payne, *History of Journalism in the United States* (N. Y., 1920), 37, 46. No press was set up in Connecticut till 1709. See J. A. Doyle, *The English in America, The Puritan Colonies* (London, 1887), II, 195.

[3] C. A. Duniway, *Development of Freedom of the Press in Massachusetts* (*Harvard Hist. Studies*, XII), 32.

his possession to bring them at once to the nearest magistrate upon pain of a fine of ten pounds; "And as many of the said books as can or may be found to be burned by the executioner at Boston." Later it was decreed that any person who "shall knowingly import into any harbor of this jurisdiction any Quaker books or writings concerning their divilish opinions, shall pay for every such booke or writing, being legally prooved against him or them, the some of five pounds." In 1669 the general court, learning that a reprint of *The Imitation of Christ* by Thomas à Kempis was in press, ordered it to be revised before being issued to the public.[1] The loss of the right of censorship, which came with the Andros régime, was bitterly resented by the clergy.

Suppression of opinions and of free discussion [2] was by no means confined to New England. In 1671 Sir William Berkeley boasted that there was no printing press in Virginia; and the Quaker or Puritan who came to that colony with the purpose of making converts found himself outside the pale of the law. But in none of the Middle or Southern provinces was there anything comparable to the rigid control over men's thoughts and opinions exercised by the New England theocracy.[3] Thus circumscribed, the mental activities of the people of this section were marked by neither progressiveness nor breadth of interest. Increase Mather, whose reading may easily be traced through his habit of citing or quoting the writers with whom he was acquainted, seems to have read something of Sir Thomas Browne, Thomas

[1] T. G. Wright, *Literary Culture in Early New England* (New Haven, 1920), 37.

[2] Duniway, *Freedom of the Press*, 32-33, 35-37, 54.

[3] L. C. Wroth, *A History of Printing in Colonial Maryland* (Balt., 1922), chap. i.

Fuller and Robert Boyle, but to have known nothing
of Shakespeare, Ben Jonson or Bunyan. Apparently
though Cotton Mather read Milton and quoted from
him in his *Magnalia*, and shows a wide acquaintance
with ancient and medieval writers, he too failed to keep
abreast the most progressive thought of his own day.

Some idea of the subjects which held the New England mind at the end of the seventeenth century may be
gained from the inventories of books sent to the Boston
booksellers. The volumes delivered by Chiswell of
London to John Usher in May, 1684, were two Bibles,
thirty Greek grammars, three copies of *Bythner on the
Psalms*, six copies of *Sincere Converts*, ten copies of
Flavel on the Sacrament, ten copies of *Cattechise*, two
copies of the *Cambridge Concordance*, two of Sellers'
Practice of Navigation, two of Wilson's *Christian Dic-
tionary*, five of Clark's *Tutor*, four of Burroughs' *Gospel
Remission*, and four of the *State of England* in two
volumes.[1]

Though the Puritan was not up to date in English
literature, in amount his reading was nevertheless considerable. The libraries of the leading men, even in the
early years of the settlement, not infrequently contained
several hundred volumes.[2] William Brewster left at his
death in 1643 nearly four hundred books, Miles Standish
about fifty; John Winthrop, jr., possessed in 1640 over
one thousand; the volumes left to Harvard College by
John Harvard numbered three hundred and twenty. In
many cases these private libraries were brought over by
the settlers when they migrated from England, but from

[1] W. C. Ford, *The Boston Book Market, 1679-1710* (Boston,
1917).

[2] J. H. Tuttle, "The Libraries of the Mathers," Am. Antiq. Soc.,
Proceeds., XX, 269 ff.

the first numerous additions were made by shipment across the Atlantic. In 1632 Edward Howes wrote to John Winthrop, jr., "For new bookes I writt to you of Dr. Fludds works and sent you a cattalogue of them by Mr. Hetherley; there is a booke lately come out of mathematicall conclusion and recreations, which I bought purposely for you. . . . I have sent you two other books vizt. *Malthus Fireworks,* and the *Horizontall Quadrant."* The same year F. Kirby wrote Winthrop that he had secured a catalogue of books from Frankfort for the "Autumnall mart 1631," and would send other lists by the next ship. In 1657 John Eliot wrote of "a smal packet of books from Mr. Jessy," while two years later John Davenport was delighted with a consignment of "letters & bookes, & written papers . . ." containing "sundry rarities of inventions." [1]

From the first the New Englanders were prolific writers. The leading ministers were quick to expound their doctrines or to answer their opponents in books, pamphlets and published sermons. In the years from 1682 to 1689 inclusive, of the one hundred and thirty-three works published in Boston, fifty-six were sermons, thirty-nine others were religious in character, while of the remaining thirty-eight, twelve were almanacs and seventeen proclamations or public pamphlets. In the earlier days a considerable number of books were printed in England describing conditions in New England, such as Johnson's *Wonder-Working Providence* and Winslow's *Good News from New England.* Bradford's *History of Plymouth Plantation* and Winthrop's *History of New England* were published only after the

[1] Wright, *Literary Culture in Early New England,* 25, 28, 30, 33, 46, 73.

lapse of centuries. Although probably neither writer was a conscious artist, both works, for style as well as content, immediately took their place in the body of American literature.

The most interesting figure in early New England literature is Anne Bradstreet. Although the mother of eight children this good woman found time to write more than seven thousand lines of verse. Very poor poetry most of it is, but that she should have written at all amid the hardships of colonial life is remarkable. Her purely didactic poems are typically dreary, but one finds passages in her *Contemplations* which suggest that she was not incapable of finer things:

> When I behold the heavens as in their prime,
> And then the earth (though old) still clad in green,
> The stones and trees, insensible to time,
> Nor age nor wrinkle on their front are seen;
> If winter come, and greeness then do fade,
> A Spring returns, and they are youthfull made;
> But Man grows old, lies down, remains where once
>   he's laid.

The most widely read and perhaps the most representative poet of early New England was Michael Wigglesworth. His *Day of Doom,* first published in 1662, a poem of two hundred eight-line stanzas, tells the story of the last judgment. The passage which gives God's explanation to the reprobate infants will serve to illustrate the whole:

A Crime it is, therefore in bliss you may not hope to dwell;
But unto you I shall allow the easiest room in Hell.

The glorious King thus answering, they cease and plead no
    longer:
Their consciences must needs confess his reasons are the
    stronger.

At times the colonial muse found expression in elaborate, if not very beautiful, epitaphs.   The following
lines are typical:

> The knight starre of ovr cavallrie lyes here
> And to ye state a covnsellour fvll deare
> And to ye truth a friend of sweet content
> To Hartford towne a silver ornament
> Who can deny to poore he was reliefe
> To Marchantes as a patterne he might stand
> Adventring dangers new by sea and land.[1]

Under the most favorable circumstances it was not
to be expected that a new settlement would produce
poetry of a high order.   It was natural for the New
Englanders to avoid seventeenth-century court poets like
Lovelace, Suckling, Carew and Herrick, and Catholic
poets such as Crashaw.   But, on the other hand, it is surprising that they read so little from the Puritan group
represented by Milton and Marvell.   George Herbert,
with his introspection, abstract thought and intense consciousness of sin, seems to have been their favorite.
Milton had shown that Puritanism was not incapable
of lofty flights of imagination and beauty, but the spirit
of *Paradise Lost* found little reflection among the founders of New England.

But it was in New England that the colonial common
school found its highest development.   Though pioneer
conditions obviously are not conducive to an efficient

---

[1] Epitaph of Captain Richard Lord, d. 1662, in Hartford.

educational system, in New England the compactness of the settlements—which were usually grouped around the church, the meetinghouse and the village school—made it possible to gather in one schoolhouse enough pupils to provide at least a fair living for a capable teacher. Important also was the insistence of the clergy upon education. The need of schools, especially elementary schools, was constantly urged in the sermons of the day. The leaders of the theocracy saw that unless the people were educated it would be impossible to maintain an adequate ministry. The Anglican church in Virginia secured its clergymen from England, but no such course was possible for the New Englanders. Whatever their theory, they had in fact broken with the old establishment, had formed a reformed church of their own, and, before many years, were out of touch and sympathy even with the Puritan group of which they had formerly been a part. Moreover, it was necessary that all serious people should read the Bible in order to learn the tests by which each might be certain of his own election and that of his neighbor.

While the clergy encouraged education, they took pains to control and direct it. The textbooks were carefully selected with a view to inculcating the precepts of the established church, while no appointments of teachers were made without the full approbation of the ministers. The schools in one sense were church schools, supported out of church funds.[1] In Massachusetts a law of 1642 made it compulsory that all children be taught—either by their parents or otherwise—

[1] Harlan Updegraff, *The Origin of the Moving School in Massachusetts* (Teachers Col., Columbia Univ., *Contribs. to Educ.*, no. 17), chap. i.

to "read and understand the principles of religion & the capitall lawes of the country." This act did not establish schools nor did it direct the employment of schoolmasters. The results proving unsuccessful in thwarting "the ould deluder Satan," the famous statute of 1647 was passed for expressly establishing a school system and thus preventing knowledge from "being buried in the graves of our fathers in church and commonwealth."

The primary teaching was done partly at home and partly in dame schools, kept perhaps by a busy housewife or a schoolmaster's daughter. Here were taught the alphabet, spelling, primary reading and the catechism. First came the old hornbook,[1] then the so-called a-b-c's, and finally the primer, containing prayers and religious meditations. Later the primer was made to include the hornbook and the a-b-c's. Reading was taught also from books of verse "full of precepts of civilitie." The pupil was now ready to enter the grammar school, where he was supposed to make a beginning in Latin, which was still the sacred language of religion and learning. The Massachusetts law of 1647 required that every town of fifty householders or more should establish an elementary school, and those of one hundred householders a grammar school as well. This provision, although by no means fully enforced, was of far-reaching importance in setting a standard toward which the community must strive. Many of these grammar schools in reality taught but little Latin, and confined their attention largely to the English primer. Some idea of the books used in the schools may be gained from the lists of the Boston book-

[1] The hornbook was a leaf of paper, usually containing the alphabet, the nine digits and the Lord's Prayer, fixed to a wooden frame with a handle, and covered over with transparent horn to protect it from destructive fumbling by the child.

A
Hornbook
for little children,
about 1675
(left).

A
popular
catechism
by a leading
minister
(right).

Seventeenth Century Schoolbooks.

seller, John Usher.   Among his purchases for 1684 we
find a hundred copies of *Sententiae Pueriles*, forty of
Strong's *Spelling Booke*, fifty of Cato, ten of Dugard's
Rhetorick, ten of Smith's *Rhetorick*, eighteen Greek
grammars, thirty copies of *Token for Children*, fifty
Latin grammars and fifty "Construeing books." [1]

To New England belongs the distinction of establishing the first college in British America.   The failure
of the London Company to complete its design for an
Indian school at Henrico in Virginia left the field vacant
until 1636 when the Massachusetts general court voted
four hundred pounds for the erecting of "a schoole or
colledge."   Two years later, when the project still hung
fire for lack of adequate funds, John Harvard, a minister
of Charlestown, bequeathed to the institution his entire
library and half his estate; and the same year the institution was opened as Harvard College at Cambridge.
Other gifts came from time to time, and before the end
of the century £6134 had been received, together with
large bequests of land and books.   The first teacher, a
certain Nathaniel Eaton, had been educated in Holland,
and Cotton Mather says that he "marvellously deceived
the expectations of good men concerning him, for he
was fitter to be master of a Bridewel than a Colledge."
He was soon succeeded by Henry Dunster, under whose
direction a class of nine graduated in 1642. [2]

From the first the requirements seem to have been
rigid.   "When any schollar is able to understand Tully,
or such like classicall Latine author extempore, and make
and speake true Latine in verse and prose . . . and

[1] Ford, *The Boston Book Market*.
[2] Eaton went to Virginia and thence to England.   J. H. Littlefield,
Early Massachusetts Press, 1638-1711 (Boston, 1907), 70.

decline . . . the paradigms of noune and verbes in the Greek tongue: Let him then . . . be capable of admission." The course of study included logic, physics, ethics, geometry, astronomy, Greek, Hebrew, rhetoric and Latin. "The President inspected the manners of the students," wrote Cotton Mather "and unto his morning and evening prayers in the hall joined an exposition upon the chapters; which they read out of Hebrew into Greek, from the Old Testament in the morning, and out of English into Greek, from the New Testament in the evening; besides what Sermons he saw. cause to preach in publick assemblies on the Lord's day at Cambridge where the students have a particular gallery allotted unto them." [1] It is improbable that these high standards were rigidly adhered to, and we know that the attempt to compel conversation in Latin among the students failed. About 1670 Copernican astronomy, it appears, was getting a little foothold in Harvard, a century after its promulgation in Europe, but it was not formally taught until much later.[2]

Like the schools of Massachusetts, Harvard was founded primarily to train ministers for the New England churches; and in this it seems to have succeeded admirably. In 1696, of the eighty-seven Massachusetts clergymen seventy-six, and of the thirty-five Connecticut clergymen thirty-one, were graduates of Harvard. The fame of the institution spread across the Atlantic, for as Edward Johnson writes in his *Wonder-Working Providence,* "Some gentlemen have sent their sons hither

---

[1] Cotton Mather, *Magnalia,* II, 12.
[2] Edward Eggleston, *Transit of Civilization* (N. Y., 1901), 35-36; see also T. F. Waters, *A Sketch of the Life of John Winthrop, the Younger* (n. p., 1899), 57.

from England, who are to be commended for their care of them, as the judicious and godly Doctor Ames, and divers others." [1] At the same time certain New England graduates went to England where they attained distinction in the ministry and other callings. "Europe, as well as America, has from this learned seminary, been enriched with some worthy men," says Cotton Mather. From the hour of its foundation "Old England has had more ministers from New than our New England has since then from Old." "In the perusal of this catalogue," he tells us with pride, "it will be found that, besides a supply of ministers for our churches . . . we have hence had a supply of magistrates, as well as physicians." [2]

During the last quarter of the century Harvard became the battle ground of the conservative and liberal groups in Massachusetts, and suffered much in consequence. For several years it was without a president, its attendance fell away, and it became little more than a divinity school. The Dutch scholar, Jaspar Danckaerts, who visited the institution in 1680, gives a most unfavorable account of it.

> We found there eight or ten young fellows, sitting around, smoking tobacco. . . . We inquired how many professors there were, and they replied not one, that there was not enough money to support one. We asked how many students there were. They said at first, thirty, and then came down to twenty; I afterwards understood there are probably not ten. They knew hardly a word of Latin, not one of them, so

[1] Edward Johnson, *Wonder-Working Providence* (J. F. Jameson, ed., *Original Narratives of Early American History*, N. Y., 1906-), 202.
[2] Cotton Mather, *Magnalia*, II, 27.

that my comrade could not converse with them. . . .
The minister of the place goes over there morning and
evening to make prayer, and has charge over them;
besides him, the students are under tutors or masters.[22]

However, nothing can be more misleading than the
superficial observations of a stranger. Two members of
the class who must have been present in the group afterwards became tutors in the institution, and one of them,
John Leverett, was elected president. Even though its
scope had been greatly restricted, Harvard was unquestionably still doing good work. Possessing the only
college in the colonies, with a good-sized reading public
and a creditable system of common schools, New England was well in advance in the matter of education.
Although illiteracy was by no means uncommon, the
percentage of those who could neither read nor write
was undoubtedly lower than elsewhere in the colonies.
But this superiority was in a measure offset by the close
supervision over education and thought exercised by the
clergy, and the consequent narrowing of the horizon of
intellectual interests.

In the tobacco colonies the prevalence of plantation
life made it impossible to establish effective school systems. It proved difficult enough to go ten or fifteen
miles to attend church through the forests, or in boats
on the rivers and creeks; to send children such distances
to school was not to be thought of. Even in the most
thickly settled parts, seldom could one find within a
reasonable radius enough children to make up a school or
provide a living for a competent teacher. The Vir-

[1] Jasper Dankers [or Danckaerts] and Peter Sluyter, "Journal of a
Voyage to New York and a Tour in Severall of the American Colonies
in 1679-80," L. I. Hist. Soc., *Memoirs*, I, 384-385.

ginians and Marylanders struggled earnestly with this problem, but found no way out of it.

In 1670, when the board of trade inquired of Sir William Berkeley what course was taken about the instruction of the people in Virginia, he replied, "The same course that is taken in England out of towns, every man according to his ability instructing his children." [1] Unquestionably thousands of planters, especially those of the yeoman class, were forced themselves to act as instructors, or induce some neighbor to do this service for them, paying in tobacco or other farm produce. The wills of the period show that parents and guardians often sought to make sure that the education of their children would be provided for. William Moseley of Princess Anne County, Virginia, left directions that his family should be "brought up in such learning as is most useful and necessary for this country's affairs," while Thomas Whitlock of Rappahannock made provision for placing his son in the care of a teacher. Prevost Nelson in his will charged the Reverend Thomas Teakle to instruct his two sons in reading and writing, and in 1686 David Williams directed his executors to keep his sons under a teacher's care until they could read the Bible with facility. [2] The planter considered himself fortunate who could get an indentured servant qualified to be a teacher for his children and those of the neighbors.

There were in existence in all parts of this region what were known as Old Field schools. This name originated from the custom of establishing schools in

[1] W. W. Hening, comp., *Statutes at Large of Virginia* (Phila., 1823), I, 517.

[2] P. A. Bruce, *Institutional History of Virginia in the Seventeenth Century* (N. Y., 1910), I, 299, 304-305.

abandoned fields located within walking distance of several plantations.   Here the children received instruction in reading, writing and the catechism.   The schools were small and inefficient.   In certain cases the parents in the neighborhood were numerous enough or rich enough to secure the entire time of a competent teacher, but it was more usual for the clergyman, the lay reader or the wife of one of the planters to preside over the school.   In cases where there were professional masters, they usually increased their meager stipends by putting out a crop of tobacco.[1]   The proud boast of Governor Berkeley in 1671 that there were no free schools in Virginia [2]—a statement which has been quoted far and near—gives a false conception of educational conditions.   It reflects, not the wishes and views of the people of Virginia, but solely those of the old governor himself.   Moreover, Berkeley's assertion was actually untrue.   At the time he wrote there were certainly two free schools in existence in Virginia, and probably more.   These institutions were not supported by taxes, however, but were endowed by public-spirited benefactors.[3]

"I may not forget to tell you we have a Free-Schoole, with two hundred acres of Land," wrote the author of the *Perfect Description* in 1649, "a fine house upon it, forty milch Kine, and other accommodations to it: his name Mr. Benjamin Symes, worthy to be Chronicled; other petty Schools also we have."   Symes's will, which was dated February, 1635, left the land together with eight cows, and provided that the income of the estate

[1] Bruce, *Institutional History of Virginia*, I, 331-342.
[2] Hening, *Statutes at Large of Virginia*, I, 517.
[3] G. F. Wells, *Parish Education in Colonial Virginia* (Teachers Col., Columbia Univ., *Contribs. to Educ.*, no. 138), chap. iii.

should be allowed to accumulate until there was enough
for the erection of a schoolhouse. Eight years later the
assembly passed a special act to carry out these directions,
and by 1647 the school was well-established and in active operation. In 1671, when Berkeley made his report, it was unquestionably still flourishing, for we have
frequent references to it afterwards.[1]

A similar school was set up in Virginia under the will
of Dr. Thomas Eaton. The endowment consisted of
five hundred acres, two Negroes, twelve cows, two bulls,
and twenty hogs, together with a furnished residence.
The school was placed under the control of a board of
trustees consisting of the clergyman and churchwardens
of the parish and the justices of the county court. The
master served as the manager of the estate, and in return
for the income derived from it, gave instruction to the
children residing in Elizabeth City County. In 1668 a
Mr. King gave a tract of land for the foundation of
another school,[2] while several years later Henry Peasley
left an estate consisting of six hundred acres, ten cows
and a mare for a similar purpose. The historian Robert
Beverley states that there were

> tracts of land, houses, and other things granted to free
> schools for the education of the children in many parts
> of the country; and some of these are so large that of
> themselves they are a handsome maintenance to a
> master; but the additional allowance which gentlemen
> give with their sons render him a comfortable subsist-
> ence. In all other places, where such endowments have
> not been made, the people join and build schools for

[1] W. A. Maddox, *The Free School Idea in Virginia before the Civil
War* (Teachers Col., Columbia Univ., *Contribs. to Educ.*, no. 93), 1.

[2] "Free Schools in Isle of Wight County," *William and Mary Quart.
Hist. Mag.*, V, 112-113.

their children, where they may learn on very easy terms.[1]

In view of these facts it is not surprising to find that illiteracy among the whites of Virginia was far less extensive than has been generally thought. According to a careful student of the subject, of 2160 men serving on one hundred and eighty juries in nine counties, 1166 were able to sign their names in full while 994 made their marks. In a list of 12,445 names of men attached to depositions and deeds of conveyance in fourteen counties in the period from 1641 to 1700, 7439 were signed in full. On the other hand, of 3066 women who signed deeds and depositions, all save 756, or about three fourths of the total, were forced to make their marks. Thus in a grand total of 15,511 men and women in these lists, 8195 could sign their names, as compared with 7316 who could not.[2] This constitutes a very fair record for a new country in which distances were so great and transportation facilities inadequate.

The Virginia planter who wished his son to receive a college education sent him across the Atlantic to one of the English universities. William and Mary, it is true, was chartered in 1693, but it was not opened until April, 1697, and then only as a grammar school. As a matter of fact, few young men actually undertook the journey to England, for the danger and expense of the voyage made many parents hesitate. Ralph Wormeley the younger, however, was matriculated at Oriel College, Oxford; John Lee, son of Colonel Richard Lee, entered

[1] Robert Beverley, *The History and Present State of Virginia* (London, 1705), 224.

[2] Bruce, *Institutional History of Virginia*, I, 450-459.

Queen's College; Henry Perrott was at Gray's Inn in 1674; William Byrd II studied in the Middle Temple.[1] But for all save a handful, instruction came to an end with the grammar school, and any education beyond that was obtained from private tutors, or from experience, observation and reading.

It is interesting to note that a project to erect a college was put on foot by the Virginia assembly in 1661. It was resolved "that for the advance of learning, education of youth, supply of the ministry and promotion of piety there be land taken upon purchases for a colledge and freeschoole and that there be with as much speede as may be convenient houseing erected thereon for entertainment of students and schollers."[2] The assembly hoped to "gather the charity of well disposed people in England," while they themselves subscribed "severall considerable sumes of money and quantityes of tobacco." Unfortunately this design came to naught, possibly because Governor Berkeley, although we find him among the subscribers, was at heart opposed to it, possibly because of the universal poverty and distress caused by the operation of the navigation acts. Three decades were to elapse before the attempt was repeated, and then the indomitable Blair, backed by the great Anglican prelates, pushed the project to completion.

Virginia was without a printing press through almost the entire century. In 1680, it is true, the merchant John Buckner brought in a press and received an order from the assembly to print the acts passed that year. Later he was accused of working without a license, summoned before the governor and forced to close his estab-

[1] Bruce, *Institutional History of Virginia*, I, 316-322.
[2] Hening, *Statutes at Large of Virginia*, II, 25.

lishment.[1]   So far as is known not a single book was
printed in the colony during the century.   This circum-
stance, along with the fact that the energies of the people
were turned chiefly to conquering the wilderness, rendered the literary output extremely meager.   Robert
Beverley's *History of Virginia*, which was written at the
end of the century, stands almost alone as a product of a
native-born Virginian of the period.   But the accounts
of the Rebellion of 1676 known as *Bacon's Proceedings*
and *Ingram's Proceedings*, together with Mrs. An.
Cotton's *Our Late Troubles in Virginia*, are written in
a vivid style and with a touch of humor which makes
them fascinating reading.[2]   The pamphlets descriptive
of Virginia and Maryland, intended to attract settlers,
are fluent, interesting and well-suited to their purpose.

Some of the ministers who came to Virginia were men
of scientific interests, and have left works relating to the
flora and fauna of the region.   The Reverend John
Banister of Appomattox Parish compiled a catalogue of
Virginia plants which was published in Ray's *Historia
Plantarum*.   He also contributed various papers to the
Philosophical Transactions of the Royal Society, among
them "Insects of Virginia," "Curiosities of Virginia,"
"On Several Sorts of Snails" and "Description of the
Snake Root."   The Reverend John Clayton of Jamestown was a member of the Royal Society and a friend of
Robert Boyle, the chemist.   He wrote a description of
the lightning bug; and his reflections on Virginia, in
which he describes the climate, soil, animals and natives
of the country, were published by the Royal Society.

More important than this meager grist of published

[1] Hening, *Statutes at Large of Virginia*, I, 518.
[2] All are reprinted in Force, *Tracts*, I.

works is the mass of private and public correspondence, official reports, petitions and journals which flowed from the pens of the planters. Many thousands of these manuscripts have been preserved, either in the British Public Record Office or in private collections, and denote no small degree of culture and literary skill. The replies of the council of state or the house of burgesses to the governors' addresses, the mass of evidence presented to the board of trade against Sir Francis Nicholson, the private letters of William Byrd II or William Fitzhugh, are all admirably clear, the choice of words is excellent, the structure of sentences good, while even the spelling is fairly correct according to the standards of the day. But in the fields of science, of poetry and the drama, of travel and of theology the tobacco colonies produced little of value.

If the people of Virginia published few books, they read extensively. It is by no means unusual for inventories of the seventeenth century to show, even among planters of the yeoman class, a considerable number of volumes. In Lower Norfolk County alone there have come down to us for the half century from 1640 to 1690 the names of more than one hundred persons who possessed from one volume to several hundred.[1] Among them was George Lock, with five books; Philip Felgate, who owned a "parcell of books;" Colonel William Moseley, whose library was valued at three thousand pounds of tobacco; Mrs. Sarah Willoughby, who had fifty-five books; and William Archer, with one hundred books. Before the end of the century some of the wealthier planters had collected really extensive libraries. The will of William Fitzhugh refers to a "study of

[1] Bruce, *Institutional History of Virginia*, I, 411.

books." [1]   From his correspondence with his London
agents we learn the titles of some of his works, such as
Buchanan's *De Jure*, Boyle's *Letters to a Friend Con-
cerning Specific Physic*, and the *Memorable Actions of
King William the Third*.   The library of Secretary
Ralph Wormeley, which was one of the largest in Vir-
ginia, contained three hundred and seventy-five titles;
that of William Colston, one hundred titles; that of
Arthur Spicer one hundred and two titles; and that of
Henry Willoughby about two hundred titles. [2]

Although in the Virginia libraries the same tendency
was noticeable as in New England to neglect the ablest
contemporaneous writers, on the whole they show a
considerable breadth of interest.   Colonel Wormeley
seems to have been acquainted with Ovid's works, with
Lord Bacon, with Plutarch, with Josephus and even
with Cervantes.   Colonel John Carter seems to have
read the *Iliad*, Josephus, Ovid, Virgil, Plutarch and
Bacon's *Natural History*, and even owned a copy of
William Penn's *No Cross, No Crown*.   Matthew
Hubbard possessed Ben Jonson's *Remains*, Donne's
Poems, Æsop's *Fables* and Purchas's *Pilgrims*.   In other
collections we find Hakluyt's *Travels*, Montaigne's
Essays, *Travels of Ulysses*, *Travels of Sir Francis Drake*,
together with many other volumes on religion, history,
law, agriculture, medicine and navigation. [3]

After all, neither books nor schools shaped the education of the Virginian or Marylander as much as life
upon the plantation.   The son of the poor planter was

[1] William Fitzhugh, "Will of William Fitzhugh," *Va. Mag. of Hist.
and Biog.*, II, 227.
[2] Bruce, *Institutional History of Virginia*, I, chaps. xiv-xv.
[3] Bruce, *Institutional History of Virginia*, I, chap. xv.

schooled in the arts of the woodsman: he knew how to
handle his ax and his gun, how to bring down the wild
turkey, the deer or even the occasional bear; he had to
assist his father in clearing away the great trees of the
virgin forest, in planting and tending the tobacco crop,
in cutting, curing and packing the ripened leaves, in
placing the hogsheads on shipboard; he must know how
to repair barns, work in the garden, care for the cattle.
It was a free, invigorating school—this practical school
of the pioneer life in the woods of America. No wonder
George Alsop speaks of the native Marylanders as "con-
veniently confident, reservedly subtile, quick in appre-
hending." The author of the *Sot-weed Factor* gives a
most unfavorable picture of

> . . . that Shoar, where no good Sense is found,
> But Conversation's lost, and Manners drowned.

Yet he was surprised to find that the uncouth son of a
planter had his own views upon so interesting a question as the origin of the North American Indians. The
youth supposed them to have been "Tartarians or
Chinese" who had migrated to Mexico and made their
way north by degrees.

> I Smil'd to hear my young Logician
> Thus reason like a Politician;
> Who ne'er by Fathers Pains and Earning
> Had got at Mother *Cambridge* Learning.[1]

As for the wealthy planters, even in the seventeenth
century they were being molded by the influences under
which they lived into that type of Southern gentleman

[1] Ebenezer Cook, "The Sot-weed Factor [1708]," Md. Hist. Soc.,
Fund Publs., no. 36, 11-32.

which in succeeding generations became so distinctive
a feature in the nation's history.   The boy who was
reared upon a plantation of several thousand acres, tilled
perhaps by forty or more slaves and servants, was taught
the various duties which were to fall to his lot when
he grew to be a man.   When still quite young he exercised authority over the workmen and directed them at
their tasks, so that he might develop the habit of command.   He acquired versatility by performing the hundred and one tasks required in the conduct of the plantation—the raising of stock, the planting and tending of
tobacco, the laying out of orchards, the building of
fences, the purchasing of goods from the English im-
porters, the care of the sick, the superintendence of plantation manufacture.   While his mind was thus trained
to business, his body was developed by an active out-of-
door life—by hunting, fishing, swimming and racing.
From his father and his guests he became acquainted with
the political life of the colony, and no doubt kept fairly
well abreast of the chief happenings in England.   All in
all, the plantation life tended to make him practical,
inquiring, robust and self-reliant, even though it seldom
instilled into him the inventive spirit or inspired him to
literary effort.

In forming our judgment of the intellectual activities
of the colonists we must remember that in the seventeenth century, British America constituted the extreme
western frontier of civilization.   The narrow fringe of
settlements from Maine to Carolina faced on the one
hand the vast expanse of the Atlantic Ocean, on the other
the trackless wilderness.   Despite constant communication with the mother country, a large degree of isolation
was inevitable.   There could be no personal touch with

the great minds which were taking the lead in science and literature, none of the inspiration which comes from companionship and emulation. It is true that the colonists could read the books of such men, but one usually peruses published works with the detached mind of the spectator, while personal acquaintance leads to intellectual stimulus. Even within the limits of the colonies themselves, distances were so great that it was difficult for men of like interests to commune with each other for the exchange of ideas and the quickening of creative ambition. Under the circumstances a literary or scientific circle was well-nigh impossible.

Equally important was the fact that no leisure class existed as yet in British America. The small groups in New England and the tobacco colonies who acquired wealth were composed of active business men. The Boston merchant and the Virginia planter were still in the stage of accumulation, and could devote little time to study and investigation. It is true, as we have seen, that these men, in an attempt to keep in touch with the great world of Europe, gathered libraries and read somewhat extensively. But they read not as scholars or creators, but as men whose chief interest lay elsewhere, in the spare moments snatched from the details of purchases and shipments and planting.

CHAPTER XI

PLANTER AND PURITAN AT PLAY

DESPITE the difference in the motives of their emigration, the early American colonists, north and south, were much more alike in tastes and deportment than has been commonly understood. The seventeenth century was the seventeenth century behind the Accomac Peninsula as well as behind Cape Cod—for instance, the government's concern in private conduct was not confined to either latitude. The first legislature in Virginia took measures which the Pilgrims, had the *Mayflower* brought them to that region the following year, would have cordially approved. There were laws against idleness, drunkenness and Sabbath breaking, laws placing heavy penalties on those who gamed at dice and cards, and laws against "excess in apparell," it being provided, as a deterrent, that each subject should be assessed for public contribution according to the degree of luxury in dress shown by himself and his family.[1] Yet the circumstances of life and the course of leadership in the two sections developed on such different lines that by the middle of the century the rules of right and wrong had grown quite different, and the tobacco planters, whatever the statute books might say to the contrary, felt free to

[1] T. H. Wynne and W. S. Gilman, eds., *Colonial Records of Virginia* (Richmond, 1874), 9-32, *passim.* Sumptuary laws regulating private conduct were not an American or a Protestant invention. See J. M. Vincent, "European Blue Laws," Am. Hist. Assoc., *Report for 1897,* 357-372. These laws in Virginia soon became dead letters.

follow pleasure as far as might be convenient. In Virginia and Maryland, racing, hunting, dancing and card playing, all found many enthusiastic devotees.

The Southerners were especially fond of horse racing. As soon as they passed through the pioneer stages, regular courses were laid off and matches were frequently held. Horses abounded. In 1649 the *Perfect Description* stated that in Virginia "there are of an excellent raise, about two hundred Horse and Mares," [1] and before many years the number had multiplied many times over. In the last quarter of the seventeenth century all save the very poorest planters had one or more horses, while the well-to-do possessed all that they could use. Although the breed of horses as a whole tended to deteriorate, on certain farms care was taken to uphold the highest English standards.

The sport of racing was at first indulged in only by the richer planters. In 1674 a tailor was fined by the court of York County, Virginia, for "haveing made a race for his mare to runn with a horse belonging to Mr. Mathew Slader for twoe thousand pounds of tobacco and cask, it being contrary to Law for a Labourer to make a race, being a sport for Gentlemen." [2] But with the breaking down of class distinctions among white freemen, which followed the introduction of slaves in large numbers, such restrictions were ignored. "The Common Planters leading easy lives do'nt much admire Labour," says the Reverend Hugh Jones, "or any manly exercise except Horse racing. . . . The

[1] Anon., "A Perfect Description of Virginia [1649]," Peter Force, comp., *Tracts and Other Papers* (Wash., 1836-1846), II, no. viii, 3.
[2] P. A. Bruce, *Economic History of Virginia in the Seventeenth Century* (N. Y., 1895), II, 473.

Saddle-Horses, though not very large, are hardy, strong
and fleet; and will pace naturally at a prodigious Rate.
They are such lovers of Riding, that almost every ordinary Person keeps a Horse." [1]

Henrico County in Virginia, while still a part of the
frontier, became famous for its races. Courses were
laid off at five places: Bermuda Hundred, where Dale
made his settlement in 1611, Conecock, Varina, Ware
and Malvern Hill. In the counties lying between the
Potomac and the Rappahannock were several courses,
of which the most important were the Coan Race Course
in Westmoreland; Willoughby's Old Field in Richmond,
Fair Fields Race and Scotland Race Ground in Northumberland, and the track at Yeocomico. There were
courses also at Smith's Feld in Northampton, at Rappahannock Church, at Devil's Field in Surry, and elsewhere. Although interest in racing was general, there
were special devotees of the sport whose names appear
in the records over and over again in connection with
disputes of one kind or another. In Henrico Richard
Liggon, Captain Thomas Chamberlaine, Stephen Cocke
and William Randolph were all ardent supporters of the
turf. [2]

Among the famous racers of the day was a pure white
horse named Young Fire, owned by John Gardiner of
Westmoreland. At a meet in 1693 at Willoughby's Old
Field, Gardiner offered to race any other horse on the
track for a stake of one thousand pounds of tobacco
and twenty shillings in coin. This sum was covered by
Daniel Sullivant, who borrowed a bay horse from John

---

[1] Hugh Jones, *The Present State of Virginia* (London, 1724), 48.
[2] P. A. Bruce, *Social Life of Virginia in the Seventeenth Century*
(Richmond, 1907), 195-210.

Baker, and the race was duly run. A dispute arose as to the winner, however, which had to be settled by a suit in court. Smoker, belonging at one time to Joseph Humphreys and later to Captain Rodham Kenner, was another famous racer. At the Coan Course this horse was defeated by Peter Contanceau's Folly, but only by the treachery of the rider, it was claimed, who purposely held him back. The dispute arising out of this incident was so bitterly contested that it finally came before the general court of the colony. At Yeocomico, Smoker ran against a horse named Campbell for a stake of five hundred and seventy-seven pounds of tobacco, but this time it was he who benefited from a foul, for when a brother of Rodham Kenner rushed forward with a loud shout, Campbell shied from the track. In 1695 Smoker defeated John Haynie's Prince on the Coan Race Course for a stake of four thousand pounds of tobacco and forty shillings. Joseph Humphreys seems to have been an indefatigable racer, for we find him engaged in another suit over a projected race in 1703.[1]

Not less popular in the South than horse racing, and even more universal, was the sport of hunting. Every planter had his gun and knew how to use it, for about him was game in great abundance. If he wished the excitement of bringing down really dangerous animals, the presence of wolves, bears and panthers gave him wide opportunity. If he took delight in hunting smaller game, he could find foxes, rabbits, squirrels, raccoons and opossums; if he went out in quest of wild fowl, he could make his selection from partridges, turkeys, geese and ducks. Tracking the raccoon or the opossum at night was a favorite sport and seems to have been con-

[1] See Bruce, *Social Life of Virginia,* 196-197.

ducted much as at present in the South.   Selecting a
bright night, the hunters took their dogs to woods where
these animals were known to live, and having located one
of them, drove it up a tree.   The nimblest member of
the party then climbed up and shook the creature down
among the yelping hounds.   On such nocturnal hunts it
was customary to take along a certain number of large
dogs to guard against attack by wildcats and wolves.[1]

In hunting deer the colonists trained their horses to
stand motionless so as to conceal them from the timid
animals until they had approached within gunshot.
More effective, although far less exciting, was the shoot-
ing of deer from blinds formed by felling trees near the
feeding grounds.   So numerous were deer and so easy
to kill that venison was said to be less esteemed than
mutton.   George Alsop stated that deer meat "in some
Places of this Province is the common provisions the inhabitants feed on." [2]   Rabbits were hunted with trained
dogs, which either caught them while running, or forced
them to take refuge in briar patches or hollow trees.
More interesting was the hunting of wild horses, which
in the last decades of the century abounded in the woods.
These animals, as they were unmarked, belonged to anyone who could capture them.   But to do this was no easy
matter, for they were so fleet and so difficult to follow
through the woods that one was more apt to ruin an old
mount than to gain a new.[3]   Wolves were usually caught
in traps.   In some localities it was customary to destroy these animals by placing bait near their habitats,

[1] Robert Beverley, The History and Present State of Virginia (London,
1705), 258.
[2] George Alsop, A Character of the Province of Maryland [1666]
(N. D. Mereness, ed., Cleveland, 1902), 38.
[3] Beverley, History of Virginia, 258.

with a loaded gun so arranged that the wolf, when it began to eat, pulled the trigger. Fishing was indulged in not only with nets but with lines. Often a very long line was used with a number of hooks placed at intervals of three or four feet, each sustained by a gourd.

Despite the proficiency of the Marylanders and Virginians with firearms, they seldom indulged in the practice of dueling. The legend of the Southern cavalier has led certain writers into the mistake of assuming that this custom, so popular with the English gentry of the seventeenth century, was universal among the tobacco planters. But the most painstaking investigation has failed to bring to light more than five or six duels in Virginia during the entire colonial period. In 1619 William Epes killed Captain Edward Stallings in a duel at Dancing Point. Five years later George Harrison crossed swords with Richard Stephens. "There was some words of discontent between him and Mr. Stephens with some blows. Eight or ten days after Mr. Harrison sent a challenge to Stephens to meet him in a place, which was made mention of, they meeting together it so fell out that Mr. Harrison received a cut in the leg which did somewhat grieve him, and fourteen days after he departed this life." [1] In 1661 a servant belonging to Christopher Calvert sent a challenge to Goslin Van Netsen, and in the resulting duel was badly wounded.

The few scattered cases of challenges and encounters gleaned from the records serve to prove that dueling was frowned upon by public sentiment. Not only was there no social stigma attached to ignoring a challenge, but in some instances the challengers were subjected to summary

[1] Alexander Brown, *The First Republic in America* (Boston, 1898), 582.

legal punishments. In 1643 a commissioner was dis-
abled from holding office for having challenged a member of the council. About 1653 Captain Thomas
Hackett sent a challenge by his son-in-law, Richard Denham, to Daniel Fox, who was then sitting on the Lancaster court. The message ended by declaring that if
Fox "had anything of a gentleman or manhood" in
him, he would meet Hackett with rapiers. Major Carter, one of the justices, at once spoke in terms of strong
condemnation of the challenge, and told Denham that
"hee knew not how his father would acquit himself of
an action of y't nature, w'h he s'd he would not be yᵉ
owner of for a wo'ld." Denham replied in an insulting
way that Hackett "would answer it well enough."
Thereupon the court, "conceiving yᵉ said Denham to
be a partye with his father-in-law," sentenced him to receive "six stripes on his bare shoulder with a whip."
So far from accepting the challenge, Fox requested the
court to arrest Hackett, "him to detain in safe custodie
w'thout baile or mainprize," until he should "answer
ye s'd crime" at the next session of the general court.
Even though Fox's course in this matter was dictated
in part by a desire to uphold the dignity of the court,
it shows clearly enough that the "code of honor" was
by no means accepted in colonial Virginia.[1]

In the Southern colonies dancing was a common form
of diversion. The music was usually provided by a female member of the family, but there were among the
servants and slaves some skilled fiddlers who were called
in at house parties or formal dances. The Jack Foresters
and Tubals of Thomas Nelson Page's stories had their

[1] "A Virginian Challenge in the Seventeenth Century," *Va. Mag. of
Hist. and Biog.*, II, 96-97.

predecessors on the plantations of the seventeenth century. The isolation of the life upon the farms was in part offset by frequent social gatherings at the homes of the planters, and on these occasions gayety was unrestrained. The guests often remained for several days, dancing, playing cards and partaking of the ample larder of their host. Such parties were considered harmless, and the parish clergyman not only graced them with his presence, but took a round or two with those who were drinking healths, or perhaps invited a partner to join him in the dance.[1]

The social instinct so thwarted by isolation caused the people to welcome to their homes visitors of all kinds, even total strangers. Robert Beverley states that the traveler in Virginia had no need of inns, for when seeking food and shelter he had only to ask the location of some planter noted for keeping a good table, and he could be sure of generous entertainment. So universal was this hospitable custom that, when leaving their homes for more than a day, gentlemen instructed their servants to regale chance visitors with all that the plantation afforded. Even the poorest yeoman would sit up all night, or sleep upon a hard bench, in order that the weary traveler might occupy his only bed. If there chanced to be some man who from stubbornness or ill nature would not conform to this custom, he was sure to be sharply censured by his neighbors.[2]

The love of the planters for card playing is evidenced by the frequent reference in the records to packs of cards. In 1665 Captain Jeremiah Fisher of York owned nine packs, and a few years later we find Jonathan Newell in

[1] Bruce, *Social Life of Virginia*, 180-185.
[2] Beverley, *History of Virginia*, 258.

possession of eight.   In 1678 the grand jury of Henrico
presented Joseph Royall for playing cards on the Sabbath.   The first assembly which met in Virginia passed
an act prohibiting gambling with cards and dice under
penalty of fine; but this law of 1619 certainly fell into
abeyance in later years, for the courts not only permitted these games but actually enforced the payment
of money bet on them.   In 1686 Captain Soane and
Richard Dearlove of Henrico indulged in a game of put
for fifteen hundred pounds of tobacco, which was won
by the former.   Dearlove refused to pay, and Soane
entered suit against him in court.   For betting to be upon
a legal footing it was necessary to draw up a written
contract or to place the stake in the hands of a holder.
In 1690 Allanson Clerk of Henrico, who had won four
pounds sterling in a game of put with Peter Rowlett,
could not collect the money because he had neglected
these requirements.[1]   Hardly less popular than cards
was ninepins.   This game was played usually at taverns
where there were especially constructed alleys, but at
times also in private residences.   Here too betting was
customary, in some cases resulting in quarrels and ap-
peals to the courts.

An occasion of great festivity in Maryland and Virginia was the wedding.   The Anglican church made an
effort to have all marriage ceremonies performed in the
church building, but this was impracticable.   When
guests came from many miles around it was necessary
to provide food and in many cases lodging for the night.
Such accommodations could not be had at the isolated
churches and chapels, and so it became the practice to
hold the ceremony at the home of the bride, where every

[1] Bruce, *Social Life of Virginia*, 192-193.

preparation was made for the entertainment of a large number of visitors. Although the records are singularly silent as to the details of the early wedding festivals, yet it is certain that it was the custom, as it was in other social gatherings, to indulge in dancing, drinking and feasting.[1]

The people of New York, although not so given to the quest of pleasure as their Southern neighbors, and more frequently kept indoors by the severity of the climate, had an advantage in the enjoyment of winter sports. Madam Knight, a visitor from Boston, wrote in 1704: "Their diversions in the Winter is Riding Sleys about three or four Miles out of Town, where they have Houses of entertainment at a place called the Bowery, and Some go to friends Houses who handsomely treat them. . . . I believe we mett 50, or 60 slays that day——they fly with great swiftness and some are so furious that they turn out of the path for none except a Loaden Cart."[2] When the tardy northern spring made its appearance the people turned eagerly to the open air for exercise and pleasure. A favorite diversion of young folk was to set out in canoes on rural excursions or picnics. After arriving at some sheltered spot where delicious wild fruits abounded or the fishing was good, they clambered ashore and with merry shouts chose their camping ground. In the forenoon the young men fished and hunted, while their companions busied themselves with their needlework and gathered dried branches for the fire. The ample luncheon basket contained tea, sugar, a little rum and

---

[1] Bruce, *Economic History of Virginia*, I, 223-238.
[2] *The Private Journal of a Journey from Boston to New York in the Year 1704. Kept by Madam Knight* (Albany, 1865), 70-71.

now and then some cold pastry from the home larder, but the party depended upon the fish they could catch or the game they could bring down for their more solid food. In the cool of the evening the picnickers, tired after their day's pleasure, resumed their canoes for the trip home.[1]

No sooner had the English secured possession of New Netherland than they introduced the typical British sports. Racing had not been popular with the Dutch, but Governor Nicolls announced in 1665 that a horse race would take place at Hempstead. He was interested in this matter not so much for "the divertissement of youth as for the encouraging the bettering of the breed of horses which through great neglect" had been impaired. Four years later Governor Lovelace directed that a race should be run each year in May and that the subscriptions would be received from all who were disposed to run for a crown in silver or the value thereof in wheat. The first course was laid off on Long Island in a level place called Salisbury Plains. Here, wrote Daniel Denton, that indefatigable seventeenth-century advertising man, in 1670, "lieth a plain sixteen miles long and four broad . . . where you shall find neither stick nor stone to hinder the horse-heels, or endanger them in their races." Once a year, horses of the best breed were brought to this course to test their speed and compete for two silver cups.[2] As in the South, the young people amused themselves with horse hunts. "They commonly turn their spare horses into yᵉ woods, where they breed

[1] Alice M. Earle, *Colonial Days in Old New York* (N. Y., 1896), 203-207.
[2] Daniel Denton, *Brief Description of New York* [1670] (Gabriel Furman, ed., N. Y., 1845), 2-6.

and become wild; and as they have occasion to catch up yᵉ colts, and break them for their use." [1]

In New England pleasure seeking was looked upon with something akin to suspicion, and was narrowly watched and circumscribed. Games and sports which in other English communities seemed innocent were here prohibited. "Those infamous Games of Cards and dice," especially condemned "because of the lottery which is in them," were placed under the ban of the law. "Stage-Players and Mixed Dancings" were frowned upon,[2] while even shuffleboard was condemned as an idle game which caused the youth to waste precious time. One of the duties of the tithing man, who had ten families under his care, was to see that no boy went swimming.[3] Toys might sell in New England, wrote the Reverend John Higginson to his merchant brother in England, "if in small quantity." [4]

Yet human nature demands recreation, and even the Puritans were not without their diversions. When the first harvest was gathered in at Plymouth, Governor Bradford sent out four men to kill wild fowl so that he could spread a feast for the members of the little colony. This celebration, the first Thanksgiving Day, was attended by the Indian chief Massasoit and his people, "whom for three days we entertained and feasted." [5] The first Thanksgiving in Boston was held February 22,

[1] Charles Lodowick, "New York in 1692," N. Y. Hist. Soc., *Colls.*, ser. 2, II, 245.
[2] See, however, John Cotton's defense of some kinds of dancing, Mass. Hist. Soc., *Colls.*, ser. 2, X, 183-184.
[3] Alice M. Earle, *Customs and Fashions in Old New England* (N. Y., 1893), 18.
[4] T. W. Higginson, *Travellers and Outlaws* (N. Y., 1889), chap. i.
[5] Cotton Mather, *Magnalia Christi Americana* (Hartford, 1853), I, 69.

1630, as an expression of gratitude for the safe arrival of ships from England bringing supplies of food and additional settlers. The next year Thanksgiving Day was held on November 4, and from that time until 1684 not less than twenty-two public days were appointed in Massachusetts for rendering thanks. But Thanksgiving Day did not become a fixed annual observance until many years later, and in times of deep gloom during the seventeenth century the feast was omitted. The harvesting of an abundant crop was not the only occasion for this celebration, for at various times it was held in gratitude for a victory over the Indians, for the success of the Protestant arms in Germany, the accession of a king, the abatement of epidemics, the "healing of breaches" in church congregations, or the suppression of pirates.[1] Nor was the celebration confined to any one month or any one day of the week. One year it was appointed for a Tuesday, another for a "Wednesday com fortnit," and it was only in after years that the custom of holding the feast on Thursdays became fixed.[2]

Training days offered other opportunities to break the monotony of New England life. When the Puritans began pouring into the Massachusetts Bay region in 1630, they came, as did the Israelites to the Promised Land, as an armed host. Cotton Mather tells us in his *Magnalia* that "their arms, ammunition and great artillery cost twenty two thousand pounds," quite enough

[1] John Cotton wrote, "We sometimes upon extraordinary occasions either of notable judgements do set apart a day of humiliation, or upon special mercies we set apart a day of thanksgiving." John Cotton, *The Way of the Churches in New-England* (London, 1645), 70. For an example of a Thanksgiving proclamation early in the eighteenth century, see plate vi in *A History of American Life*, III.

[2] W. DeL. Love, *The Fast and Thanksgiving Days of New England* (Boston, 1895), 239-255.

The Reverend John Cotton gives his views on playing cards and dancing.

to equip several thousand fighting men. The leaders were keenly alive to the possibility that they might have to battle in the New World as their fellow Calvinists were battling in the Old, and they were determined that this last retreat of God's people should not be carried by an enemy without a struggle. In order to keep the men proficient in military exercises special training days were held at regular intervals. Winthrop says that at the training at Boston in May, 1639, a thousand men took part, with arms of various shapes and sizes, while in the autumn of the same year the number was twelve hundred. The officers were usually chosen by the men.[1] In the sober life of the Puritan the training days offered an innocent diversion which was eagerly anticipated. Although the exercises were always preceded by prayers and the singing of psalms, the occasion was enlivened by a bountiful dinner on Boston Common. Equally enjoyable was the target practice with guns and cannon. A stuffed human form offered a realistic mark at which to shoot, and prizes were offered for the best marksmanship. These took the form of a silk handkerchief, a pair of silver shoebuckles, a silver cup, a silver-headed pike or some similar object.

Election day in New England also early assumed the character of a holiday, and was seized upon by the young as an occasion for gayety. Urian Oakes complained that it was becoming a time "to meet, to smoke, carouse and swagger and dishonor God with the greater bravery." The soberness of early New England life is further illustrated by the eagerness with which the people grasped at the rather arid bit of amusement afforded by the mid-

[1] For the regulation of defense, see H. L. Osgood, *The American Colonies in the Seventeenth Century* (N. Y., 1904-1907), I, chap. xiii.

week lecture, at the conclusion of which marriage engagements were announced, public notices posted, and once in a while some seditious or heretical book was burned. The young folks attended in great numbers, and actually went to neighboring towns in order to enjoy several of these "treats" during the same week. This seemed to the magistrates a form of dissipation so undesirable that in 1633 they attempted to limit each minister to one lecture in two weeks. But the law was not enforced, and in 1639 we find John Cotton complaining that the lectures were proving harmful to the people by diverting them from their necessary tasks.

The day was also signalized by the punishment of criminals. "At this very moment the constable has bound an idle fellow to the whipping-post and is giving him his deserts with a cat-o-nine-tails," writes Hawthorne in his description of the colonial lecture day. "Ever since sun rise, Daniel Fairfield has been standing on the steps of the meeting-house, with a halter about his neck, which he is condemned to wear visibly throughout his lifetime; Dorothy Talby is chained to a post at the corner of Prison Lane with the hot sun blazing on her matronly face, and all for no other offence than lifting her hand against her husband." [1]

Christmas the New Englanders hated as a "wonton Bacchanallian" feast. Any person who observed the day in Massachusetts not only incurred the disapproval of the clergy, but was subject to a fine of five shillings. On Christmas Day, 1621, the newcomers who had arrived at Plymouth on the *Fortune* excused themselves on the ground of conscientious scruples from going to

---

[1] Nathaniel Hawthorne, "Main Street," *The Snow-Image and Other Twice-Told Tales* (*Complete Works*, Boston, 1883, VI), 458.

work with the original Pilgrims. When Governor Bradford returned at noontime, he found them "pitching ye
barr" and playing "at stoole-ball." Thereupon he ordered them to stop "gameing or revelling in ye streets,"
declaring that it "was against his conscience that they
should play & others worke." [1] With the coming of
many Anglicans in the closing decades of the century, the
Puritan clergy became even more determined to permit
no observance of Christmas. On December 25, 1685,
at the time of the new régime instituted after the re-
voking of the Massachusetts charter, Judge Sewall wrote
in his *Diary*, "Carts come to town and shops open as
usual. Some somehow observe the day, but are vexed
I believe that the Body of the People Profane it, and
blessed be God no authority yet to compel them to keep
it." A few years later, when the Anglicans observed
Christmas under the protection of Governor Andros,
Sewall forbade his son to accompany a party of friends
to the services. But the temptation to join in the Christmas festivities soon proved too much even for members
of some of the most conservative congregations. "I hear
a Number of young People of both Sexes, belonging,
many of them, to my Flock, have had on the Christmas-
night, this last week, a Frolick, a revelling Feast, and a
Ball," wrote Cotton Mather, "which discovers their
Corruption, and has a Tendency to corrupt them yett
more, and provoke the Holy One to give them up unto
eternal Hardness of Heart." [2]

The Puritans abhorred May Day with its masks and
processions. In 1627 the pleasure-loving Morton and

[1] William Bradford, "History of Plymouth Plantation," Charles Deane,
ed., Mass. Hist. Soc., *Colls.*, ser. 4, III, 134-135.
[2] Cotton Mather, *Diary* (Mass. Hist. Soc., *Colls.*, ser. 7, VII-VIII),
II, 146.

his followers observed the day at Merry Mount in a way which shocked their stern neighbors. "They set up a May-pole," says Bradford, "drinking and dancing aboute it many days togeather, inviting the Indian women for their consorts, dancing and frisking togeather like so many fairies or furies rather." Endicott rode over to investigate matters, cut down the "idoll Maypole," and threatened to make the "merry mount but a woful mount," if there were a revival of such heathenish rites.[1] Yet from time to time Maypoles were set up in New England to the indignation of the Puritan clergy. "It is an abominable shame that any persons in a land of such light and purity as New England has been, should have the face to speak or think of practicing so vile a piece of heathenism," said Increase Mather in 1686.[2] The following year a Maypole was erected at Charlestown; but it was promptly cut down.

Commencement Day at Harvard was an occasion of such importance that visitors attended from various parts of New England. Judge Sewall recounts the happenings of this day: the presentation of degrees, the dinner, the Commencement cake. But Cotton Mather, especially after his estrangement from the college, frowned upon the whole proceeding. In one entry he speaks of "the Day of senseless Diversions, which they call the Commencement at Cambridge." "This day, being our insipid, ill-contrived, anniversary Solemnity, which we call The Commencement," he writes again, "I chose to

[1] C. F. Adams, jr., *Three Episodes of Massachusetts History* (Boston, 1892), I, 198-208.
[2] In 1686 Mather published at Boston his sermon entitled, *An Arrow against Profane and Promiscuous Dancing*. It was said to be by "The Minister of Boston," but Mather acknowledged it in his *Autobiography.* See K. B. Murdock, *Increase Mather* (Cambridge, 1925), 163.

spend it at home." Others, however, took a different view, and in 1699 Edward Ward spoke of this occasion as a holiday equal in importance to election day and training days.

Moreover, persons of means, whether they lived on the shores of Massachusetts Bay or the banks of the James, loved to adorn themselves with costly finery. Accepting the European standards in such matters, they seem to have been unaware of the incongruity of silver-laced coats and embroidered sleeves in the crude surroundings of the frontier. Robert Richbell of Massachusetts must have presented a striking figure indeed in his satin coat decorated with gold flowers, his blue breeches and gold buttons and his powdered wig. In New England ostentation in dress was, as we have seen, prohibited to the lower classes; but in the South the humblest person could indulge in all the finery his pocketbook could afford. "Our cow-keeper in Jamestown on Sundays goes accoutred in fresh flaming silk," wrote John Pory, "and the wife of one in England that had professed the black art, not of a scholar, but of a collier of Croyden, wears her rough beaver hat with a fair pearl hat-band and a silken suit thereto correspondent." [1]

The Virginia gentleman, when entertaining guests, attending church or sitting on the county court, might be seen in broadcloth coat with silver buttons and sleeves edged with ruffles or cuffs, colored waistcoat ornamented with Turkey-work, olive-colored plush or broadcloth breeches, silk stockings, shoes with silver buckles, deerskin gloves and, if the weather were sharp, a silk mantle or perhaps scarlet cloak. The inventories, even in the

[1] E. D. Neill, *Virginia Vetusta* (Albany, 1885), 111.

days when the colony was only a wilderness settlement, show a profusion of rich attire. Thomas Warnet, who died in 1629, bequeathed among other things a coif, a cross-cloth of wrought gold, a pair of silk stockings, a sea-green scarf edged with gold lace, a black beaver hat, a doublet of black camlet and a gold belt.

But Warnet, the Virginian, was not more richly attired than some of the settlers of the supposedly somber Puritan colonies.[1] Lechford tells us that Robert Keayne of Boston paid two pounds and ten shillings "for a silver laced coat and a gold wrought cap." Mistress Ann Hibbins in 1656 could boast of a diamond ring, a "taffaty" cloak valued at two pounds and ten shillings, and a black satin doublet. Mrs. Jonathan Corwin wore scarlet petticoats ornamented with silver lace, and silk-laced or black broadcloth gowns. It was in 1676 that the Connecticut government attempted to put an end to the practice of wearing gold and silver lace, silk ribbons, gold and silver buttons, silk scarfs and other superfluous finery. The New England gentleman wore baggy trousers tied with knotted garters and a doublet, and long-sleeved waistcoat.[2] The sleeves were often slashed and extravagantly embroidered; the neck was adorned with falling bands or with a deep linen collar. Those who dared to pose as dandies wore long hair, despite the proscription of St. Paul, the admonition of the pulpit, the solemn resolutions of the magistrates, and the definite prohibition by law. Trunk hose, shoes ornamented

[1] A good idea of the kinds of cloth imported may be seen in the "Wyllys Papers," Conn. Hist. Soc., *Colls.*, XXI, 30-60. There were silks, colored hats, tassels, "red Spanish Rash," as well as the coarser fustians and linseys.

[2] Sidney Perley, *The History of Salem, Massachusetts* (Salem, 1924), I, 321.

with rosettes, the beaver or felt hat, embroidered gloves, gold and silver lace, swords suspended from elaborately decorated shoulder belts conspired to make many a picturesque and elegant figure.[1]

It is not to be supposed, however, that sensible men and women who had to labor in home or field, especially upon the frontier, attired themselves in this gaudy fashion. Men could not fell trees and till the fields in broadcloth coats and silk stockings; silver-laced petticoats were hardly consistent with cooking by the sooty fireplace or sweeping the sanded floors. The laboring man, if he lived in the older settlements, was usually clad in a rough suit of canvas or leather, with cotton stockings, shoes with wooden heels, Monmouth cap and buttons of pewter; or, if his home was on the frontier, in a comfortable suit of buckskin.

It will be seen that the New Englander, although his pleasures were strictly circumscribed by law and custom, was not without amusements. He could not, like his Southern neighbors, dance freely or play cards or race horses without risking punishment, but he had his own holidays and his own recreations which no doubt he fully enjoyed. After all, pleasures are largely a matter of contrast; and to the Boston youth the weekly lecture or the training day seemed, in comparison with the somber religious cast of his everyday life, occasions of rare pleasure. Human nature was not wholly suppressed; there were some pleasures which were permitted to all and there were some stolen sweets. But the picture as a whole is not bright, and there is something unhealthful

[1] Waters, *History of Ipswich*, 35-44. Toward the end of the century periwigs came in—those "Horrid Bushes of Vanity." See also Alice M. Earle, *Two Centuries of Costume in America* (N. Y., 1903), I, chaps. i-ii.

in a social life which could make it possible for one of the leaders of public life to amuse himself by arranging the coffins in the family vault, and speak of the task as "an awful yet pleasing Treat."

CHAPTER XII

HOMES ALONG THE HIGHWAY

THE bitter struggle for existence which confronted these first Americans made it impossible for them to construct comfortable and permanent homes. While disease was taking its toll, while the Indian danger was ever present, while the little crop of wheat or corn alone stood between the people and starvation, they were forced to content themselves with the rudest and flimsiest shelters. "In foule weather we shifted into an old rotten tent," says Captain John Smith in his description of conditions at Jamestown, "for we had few better. . . . This was our church, till we built a homely thing, like a barne, set on Cratchets,[1] covered with rafts, sedge and earth, so was also the walls: the best part of our houses of like curiosity; but the most part farre worse workmanship, that could neither well defend wind nor rain." [2]   The colonists themselves often spoke of their first abodes as wigwams, although apparently they were modeled after crude English houses rather than the Indian huts. "They burrow themselves in the earth for their first shelter under some Hill side," wrote Edward Johnson, "casting the Earth aloft upon Timber . . . yet in these poor Wigwames they sing Psalms, pray and

[1] Crachets, or crochets, were posts with forked tops.
[2] John Smith, *Works* (Edward Arber, ed., Birmingham, 1884), II, 957. The two volumes are printed in one.

praise God till they can provide them houses." [1]   When Penn's Quakers established themselves on the banks of the Delaware, some of the poor families made similar shelters, with one chamber, half-underground, covered with rushes, bark and sod.

Captain Nathaniel Butler in his *Unmasked Face of Virginia,* written in 1622, declared that the "Howses are generally the worst that ever I sawe, the meanest Cottages in England being every waye equall (if not superior) with the most of the best." [2]   This evidence was corroborated later by the Virginia general assembly. "For our howses and churches in these tymes," they wrote, "they were so meane and poore . . . that they could not stand above one or two yeares." That log cabins of the familiar American type were constructed in any of the English colonies prior to 1660 is open to doubt. Isaac de Rasières declared that the Plymouth houses were of "hewn plank," but he gives no hint as to the way in which the timbers were put together. Some authorities are inclined to believe that the hewn logs were set vertically in the ground, and not horizontally after the manner of the American frontier of later times. [3]

In the continued use of thatch for roofing may be seen a remarkable instance of the survival of a practice long after new conditions rendered it uneconomical and unwise. English peasants of this period covered their

---

[1] Edward Johnson, *Wonder-Working Providence* (J. F. Jameson, ed., *Original Narratives of Early American History,* N. Y., 1906-   ) 83.   *Cf.* illustration showing a Kansas dugout about 1867, in *A History of American Life,* VIII.
[2] E. D. Neill, *Virginia Company of London* (Wash., 1868), 398, 409,
[3] Fiske Kimball, *Domestic Architecture in the American Colonies* (N. Y., 1922), 6-7.

humble homes with thatch, because the growing scarcity
of timber placed the cost of shingles beyond their means.
But in the colonies, with the erection of the first sawmills, all kinds of boards became exceedingly cheap. Despite this fact, despite the poor protection from the cold
afforded by thatch and its extreme combustibility, many
persons persisted in its use until into the next century.
Apparently they were reluctant to avail themselves of the
cheaper and better material, simply because they and
their fathers for generations had been unaccustomed
to it.

At Plymouth the first houses were thatched. Governor Bradford relates that during the winter of 1620-
1621 the common house of the tiny settlement was set
on fire "by a spark that flew into the thatch, which instantly burnt it all up." That the practice had not
been discarded forty-three years later is shown by one
of the incidents described by Increase Mather in his
Remarkable Providences. "A company of neighbors being met together at the house of Henry Condliff, in
North-Hampton . . . ," he says, "there came a ball of
lightning in at the roof of the house, which set the thatch
on fire. . . ." It was long the custom in New England
for the town government to assign certain lots for the
growing of thatch.[1] In the actual work of erecting the
thatched roof the colonists seem to have followed closely
the established practice in England. The rushes or straw
were gathered and made into bundles about six inches
in diameter. The bundles were then placed upon the
framework of the roof, in even rows, one overlapping
the other in the manner of shingles, and securely fastened

[1] Men of considerable estates in the colonies maintained their own
thatch beds. See, for example, N. Y. Hist. Soc., *Colls.,* (1892), 411.

with short willow sticks. It was customary to lay the thatch six or eight bundles deep.

No sooner had the people of each colony overcome the initial difficulties of settlement than they began building substantial frame houses. "The Towne itself by the care and Providence of Sir Thomas Gates . . . is reduced into a handsome forme," wrote Ralph Hamor concerning Jamestown in 1615, "and hath in it two faire rowes of howses all of framed Timber, (two stories, and an upper garret, or corn loft, high)." At Henrico, Virginia, there were three streets of "well framed houses," besides "a faire framed parsonage house," which was occupied by the Reverend Alexander Whitaker.[1]

Later in the century, with the advent of prosperous times, the construction of comfortable homes became general in the colony. "Pleasant in their building," wrote John Hammond in 1656, "which although for the most part they are but one story besides the loft, and built of wood, yet contrived so delightfully that your ordinary houses in England are not so handsome, for usually the rooms are large, daubed and whitelimed, glazed and flowered, and if not glazed windows, shutters which are made very pritty and convenient." "They have Lime in abundance for their houses," said another writer in 1649, "store of Bricks made, and House and Chimnies built of Brick, and some of Wood high and fair, covered with *Shingell* for *Tyle*." [2]

The typical residence of the tobacco country in the seventeenth century was a rectangular framed building

[1] Alexander Brown, *The First Republic in America* (Boston, 1898), 208-210.

[2] Anon., "A Perfect Description of Virginia [1649]," Peter Force, comp., *Tracts and Other Papers* (Wash., 1836-1846), II, no. viii, 7.

with shingled roof and a chimney at each end.   The small planters, who constituted the bulk of the population, contented themselves with little houses averaging perhaps twenty by sixteen feet, with but one room on the main floor, a loft or attic and no cellar.   The "great houses" of the wealthy group, while seldom large or handsome when measured by modern standards, were far more pretentious.   The residence of Nathaniel Bacon, the elder, contained seven or eight rooms, that of Ralph Wormeley eight rooms, that of Richard Willis eight, that of Adam Thoroughgood six.   Green Spring, the home of Sir William Berkeley, was divided into six rooms, while William Fitzhugh's house had no less than twelve or thirteen.

In New England the lowly hovels which for a time sheltered the newcomers were also soon discarded for more comfortable abodes.   Upon his arrival at Charlestown in 1630, John Winthrop ordered his house to be cut and framed, and when the colonists moved to Boston, the "frame of the Governor's house" was carried to that place.   In 1636 Samuel Symonds at Ipswich gave directions for the erection of a frame dwelling, with wooden chimneys at each end lined with clay, the stairs to be "close by the door," the windows provided with "draw-shutters," the cellar extending under the entire structure, the sides covered with "very good oake-hart inch board." [1]   Men of more moderate means built smaller houses.   William Rix, a weaver, signed a contract in 1640 for a frame house, "16 foot long & 14 foote wyde, with a chamber floare finisht, summer & ioysts, a cellar floare with ioysts finisht, the roofe and

[1] *The Winthrop Papers* (Mass. Hist. Soc., *Colls.*, ser. 4, VII), 118-120.

walles Clap boarded on the outsyde, the Chimnay framed without dawbing to be done with hewen timber." [1]

In the South few frame houses remain which can be positively identified as belonging to the seventeenth century. Less sturdily constructed than the homes of New England, apparently they have succumbed sooner to the ravages of time. Some, no doubt, were converted into slave quarters when the owners built more pretentious residences, and so lost their identity. On the other hand, a number of frame houses now standing in New England are known to have been built in the years from 1650 to 1700. These old houses show that the builders of early colonial times followed the traditions of the Middle Ages in structure, form and details, but stressed those features well-adapted to their situation. All were originally simple rectangular houses, with a steep gable roof to deliver the snow, a single chimney rising through the middle so as to conserve the heat, the main frame of heavy timber with elaborate jointing, the walls covered with wooden boards, the roof shingled, the plain interior set off by winding stairs, and the huge fireplace spanned by one great beam. In some cases where the building originally had had but one room in each of two full stories, it was substantially enlarged by the construction either of a room beyond the chimney or a lean-to in the rear. An element of picturesqueness was lent to these New England houses by the projecting second story, recalling cramped medieval streets, but especially esteemed here in the garrison houses as affording better defense against the Indians.

Just as the thatched roof eventually gave way to the shingled roof, so brick and stone superseded timber

[1] Thomas Lechford, "Note-Book," Am. Antiq. Soc., *Trans.*, VII, 302.

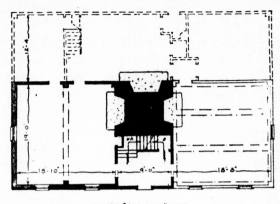

ORIGINAL HOUSE.

* * *   LATER ADDITION.   * * *

LEANTO ADDITION.

*Above: The
Hempsted House,
New London,
1643-.
Center: A
Betty lamp.*

*Below: The
Kitchen in the
"Old Ordinary"
1649-,
Hingham,
Massachusetts.*

daubed with clay for chimneys. So early as 1631 Thomas Dudley wrote that in the "new town [Boston] intended this summer to be builded; we have ordered that no man there shall build his chimney with wood." [1] It is true that this order was not always obeyed, yet the ever present danger of fire gradually brought about the elimination of wooden chimneys, even in the rural districts. Brick chimneys are mentioned in the records of Hartford so early as 1639. In various parts of New England chimneys were built of stone, but in tidewater Maryland and Virginia, where stones were scarce, brick, certainly by 1690, came into almost universal use.

The windows were built small to minimize the cold draft from without. It is probable that the "shutting draw windows" of the first settlers remained in use in the humbler homes throughout the century, but from the first glass was used to some degree. "Be sure to furnish yourselves with . . . glass for windows," wrote Francis Higginson in 1629 to intended immigrants to Massachusetts. The glass casements, which seem to have been universal in the better class of houses in the first part of the century, were hinged sashes, provided with leaded panes, diamond-shaped in some cases, oblong in others. Doors were made of wide boards in two thicknesses, vertical on the outside and horizontal inside. The interior walls and partitions were frequently sheathed with boards, grooved together and molded at the joints. Some, however, were plastered with clay or perhaps white-limed. The stairs began with a few steps which wound around the newel post, continued with a

[1] Governor Thomas Dudley, "Letter to the Countess of Lincoln [1631]," Mass. Hist. Soc., *Colls.*, ser. 1, VIII, 46.

short straight run, and ended with another wind at the top.

Although most of the seventeenth-century houses were constructed of wood, brick was not unknown even in the earliest days. Bricklayers were included among the settlers at Jamestown in 1607, and it was stated that the first story of the houses at Henrico, erected in 1611, was of brick. In Massachusetts brickmaking was in progress in 1629, in Maryland in 1653, and in Pennsylvania in 1684. Among the few brick houses which have survived to the present day are the unpretentious Warren house (or Smith's Fort) and Bacon's Castle in Virginia; Peter Tufts' house and the Usher house, Medford, Massachusetts; and the William Penn house in Philadelphia. Of equal interest was "Fairfield" (or "Carter's Creek"), built by Major Lewis Burwell in 1692, in Gloucester County, Virginia, recently destroyed by fire. The massive walls of this house, the narrow windows with their small panes, the groups of high, diamond-shaped chimneys, the heavy arches of the cellar gave the distinct impression of an English manor. Here it was that the charming Lucy Burwell lived with her father, and here came Sir Francis Nicholson from the capital at Williamsburg to sue in vain for her hand. In New York the Dutch tradition was followed in a freer use of brick and stone. The stone manor house of the Van Cortlandts built before 1681 at Croton on the Hudson was an example of a house built for defense, its thick walls pierced with narrow slits for guns.

In Philadelphia the settlers soon learned the advantages of brick residences. "Now as to the Town of Philadelphia," wrote Robert Turner to William Penn in 1685, "it goeth on in Planting and Building to admiration." His own house, the first to be built of brick, he said, he "did design after a good manner to incourage others, . . . and some that built wooden Houses, are sorry for it; Brick Building is said to be as cheap. Brick are exceeding good, and better than when I built." He added that he was engaged in putting up a new house, "three large Stories high, besides a large Brick cellar under it, of two Bricks and a half thickness in the wall, and the next story half under ground, the cellar hath an Arched Door for a Vault to go to the River, and so to bring in goods, or deliver out." As for the results of the good example he was setting, he recorded: "Humphrey Murray, from New York, has built a large Timber house, with Brick Chimneys. John Test has also finished a good Brick house, and a Bake House of Timber. John Day a good house, after the London fashion, most Brick, with a large frame of Wood, in the front, for shop Windows; all these have Balconies." [1]

An interesting description of a New Jersey brick house of this period appears in the biography of Christopher White.

> The main building was thirty feet by twenty feet, two stories high; the stories were nine feet in height. At the east end of the house was a wing ten feet square in the form of a tower, in that was the stairway leading to the second story and garret. . . . The cellar was only three feet underground. It was paved with pressed brick six inches square, made of the finest clay. . . . Six stone steps, six feet in length and one foot in thickness, led up to the main entrance of the building. . . . The partitions and doors were made of heart yellow pine. There were two rooms on the first floor and

[1] Quoted in J. T. Faris, *The Romance of Old Philadelphia* (Phila., 1918), 53.

three on the second floor; the garret was not plastered. There was one chimney in the main building near its centre, the fireplace in the hall or parlor was eight feet in length, the breast plate of the chimney being of heart yellow pine and full of carvings. There were five windows in the front of the house two in the lower story and three in the upper; also two windows in the gable ends of each story.[1]

The early public buildings of the colonists, like their residences, were simple and unpretentious. The first assembly of Virginia, elected in 1619, for lack of a state house convened in the church at Jamestown. Later, when the government acquired a building of its own, it seems to have been nothing more than a small courthouse. At the end of the century the state house, the successor of the famous structure burned by Bacon's rebel band, was a plain brick house, seventy-four feet in length and twenty wide. It contained the council chamber, secretary's office and one other room on the lower floor, and the assembly hall and clerk's office above. In the room occupied by the secretary the interior walls seem to have been covered with "sawen boards smoothed and battened," while the windows were protected with shutters or window leaves, of half inch board with a "crosse barr to each."[2]

The Boston town house, occupied in 1658, while not built of brick, was considerably larger than the Virginia capitol. The specifications called for "a very Substantiall and Comely building . . . sixty-six foot in Length and thirty-six foot in Breadth from outside to outside, set upon twenty-one Pillers of full ten foot high . . .

[1] Barclay White, "Christopher White," *Pa. Mag. of Hist. & Biog.*, X, 164-165.
[2] S. H. Yonge, *The Site of Old James Towne, 1607-1698* (Richmond, 1914), 94.

the whole Building to Jetty over three foot." The structure was to be a story and a half in height, with three gable ends on each side, on the roof a walk fourteen or fifteen feet wide protected with turned banisters. The churches in New England were plain, unadorned, rectangular frame buildings, with truncated pyramidal roofs, the wood being left to the coloring of age. The interior was severely plain, and the raftered walls, sanded floors, stiff benches and elevated pulpit overhung by a high sounding board gave the impression of coldness and austerity. The pews, when there were pews, had high partition walls and narrow, uncomfortable seats. The bell rope usually hung down to the floor in the center of the aisle. The "Old Ship," as the church at Hingham, Massachusetts, is called, is the best surviving example of these places of worship.

In Virginia the use of brick in the construction of churches dates to the first half of the seventeenth century. The famous old Jamestown church, whose tower has withstood the ravages of more than two centuries and a half, seems to have been built about 1647. It was a rectangular building, 50.6 feet by 22.7 feet within the walls, with high pitched roof, the aisle paved with brick, the chancel with tiles. The walls were made with English bond, quaintly embellished with glazed headers. The tower was eighteen feet square, with walls three feet thick at the base, forty-six feet high, surmounted by a spire. Near the top of the tower were six loopholes, intended no doubt to make it defensible against Indian attack. Hardly less interesting is St. Luke's, near Smithfield, Virginia. This charming structure is probably the oldest standing Protestant church in the New World. The tradition which assigns the date of erec-

tion to 1632 cannot be substantiated, but the buttressed
walls, the round-headed windows with lancet lights, the
massive square entrance tower and the great east window, all contribute to the conclusion that it was built
early in the seventeenth century.

It will be seen that the typical buildings of the colonists in the seventeenth century, private and public, followed closely prevailing types in England and the continent. The early residences, with their steep gables and
leaded casements, represent merely a survival of medieval
architecture, the Anglican churches adhered to the Gothic
style still common in England outside London, while
the Puritan meetinghouse imitated the Protestant type
of churches so widely diffused in France after the Edict
of Nantes. In architecture, as in other arts, the colonists
showed little creative power.

Naturally, too, the cabinetmaker's art was imitative.
Though but little furniture could be crowded into the
tiny ships that brought the early immigrants,[1] the old
tastes were a part of their mental outfit, and the home
environment was reproduced as nearly as could be. During the seventeenth century the Gothic tradition persisted, though dwindling rapidly toward the end—a tradition of architectural form in oaken furniture, of large
and heavy cupboards and paneled solid-back chairs, save
where lightened by the use of spindles. The inventories
of the time reveal a considerable range in the degrees of

[1] The *Mayflower* was less than one hundred feet long and about
twenty-five feet wide. The *Speedwell*, its companion, which had soon
to return to the English port because of a leak, was one third as large.
See William Bradford, "History of Plymouth Plantation," Charles Deane,
ed., Mass. Hist. Soc., *Colls.*, ser. 4, III, 85. See also Azel Ames, *The
May-Flower and Her Log* (Boston, 1901), chap. iv, for the fullest
description of the ship.

comfort. The parlor, or best bedroom, of the affluent pastor of Ipswich, Massachusetts, the Reverend Nathaniel Rogers—with its great chairs, its livery cupboards (having grills for ventilation), its framed pictures, window curtains, clock and violin—must have astounded some of his parish, even in the sixteen-fifties. His neighbor Ensign Whittingham had a canopy bed and gear, which without counting linen was worth twenty pounds, exactly twice the sum that represented the entire outfit of William Averill who lived among the humbler houses down toward the river.[1]

In the South there was somewhat more luxury, at least in the last half of the century when the tobacco plantations were fully developed. To transport the bulky crop it was necessary to send good-sized ships from England, whose outward cargoes, valuable as they might be, left space for furniture in part payment for the staple. The home of Nicholas Wyatt in Maryland, whose inventory bears the date of 1676, may stand as an example. In the hall, or dining room, there were seven framed pictures, an oblong table covered with a "carpet," and six joint stools, that is with corners mortised. But though such stools and short forms were still the more common furniture for sitting,[2] Master Wyatt had in this same room a complement of twenty-three chairs, covered with leather and Turkey-work upholstery. The splendid post beds, the looking-glasses, the elaborate hangings and capacious chests throughout

[1] T. F. Waters, *History of Ipswich in the Massachusetts Bay Colony* (Ipswich, 1905), 24, 30, 32, 121, 362, 367, 489, 500-501.
[2] L. V. Lockwood, *Colonial Furniture in America* (N. Y., 1913) II, 4-5. Dr. Lyon, searching the inventories of seventy-five householders between 1641 and 1659, found an average of two chairs each. I. W. Lyon, *Colonial Furniture of New England* (Boston, 1891).

the eight-room house all marked it as typical of the well-to-do planters.[1]   It was after 1680, for the most part, that the use of cane and lacquer, and some imported china dishes, showed the influence of European contacts with the East.   The advent later of the Jacobean chair with the rudiments of structural curves indicated the beginning of a period of more grace and comfort.

The homes of the seventeenth-century Americans, it may be said in summary, were simple but not crude, at least among the well-to-do in the later decades.   One qualified authority maintains that in point of design the houses and furnishings between 1670 and 1700 were better than those which followed; going further he says that the men and women of that time "were better clad, and spoke better English than has been the case at any time since."[2]

The settlers did not often leave their homes on long journeys.   Distances were too great, the means of transportation too primitive.   Had the settlements not been usually located upon navigable waters, communication between widely separated colonies would have been almost impossible because of the lack of good roads and bridges and the precarious character of the ferries.   If the tobacco planter of the James or the Potomac had an important reason for visiting New England, he waited perforce until a merchant vessel bound for Boston or New London came into his river, and then made arrangements with the master for his passage.   Even for

[1] Esther Singleton, *The Furniture of Our Forefathers* (N. Y., 1900), I, 58-60, gives this among many examples.   The Reverend John Cotton had twenty-six chairs, thirty stools, six forms and a couch.   *Ibid.*, 185, 191.
[2] Wallace Nutting, *Furniture of the Pilgrim Century, 1620-1720* (Framingham, Mass., 1924), 190-191.

short distances boat travel was popular. On every river,
bay and creek could be seen the shallop, the ketch, the
sloop or the bateau. The planter took his family to
church by boat, the burgess journeyed to the assembly
by boat, the farmer transported his produce to market
by boat, the militiaman came to muster by boat. At
first the English were inclined to sneer at the canoe as a
"cockling fly-boat," in which Europeans could "scarce
sit without a fearful tottering," but they were not long
in discovering its many advantages. For long inland
trips, or for quick passage up and down the rivers, it
soon came into universal use.

The first roads followed the old Indian trails, cut
through the dense underbrush and "blazed" upon the
trees.[1] In time the trails were widened to permit the
passage of horse and rider, and eventually became regular roads suitable for vehicles. Poor affairs they were,
however, even in New England where the population
was less scattered—used chiefly for short hauls or local
visits. The land route from New York to Canada, according to a report in 1694, was practically impassable,
the way "being extream steep and Rocky, mountains or
else a meer morasse cumbred with underwood, where
men cannot goe upright, but must creep throu Bushes for
whole days' marches, and impossible for horses to goe at
any time of ye year." [2]

The rivers and creeks, which were so great an aid to
travel by boat, proved serious obstacles to travel on foot
or by horse. It was in 1631 that Governor Endicott re-

[1] Seymour Dunbar, *A History of Travel in America* (Indianapolis,
1915), I, 19.
[2] William Pinhorne and Nicholas Bayard to Benjamin Fletcher, July
25, 1694 (N. Y. Hist. Soc.).

fused to go from Salem to Boston to visit John Winthrop because he was not strong enough to wade across the fords. Winthrop himself the next year, when he went to Plymouth, overcame this difficulty by crossing the streams on the back of his Indian guide. We are not surprised, then, to learn that so early as 1630 permission had been granted for the establishment of a ferry from Boston to Charlestown, and that three years later a "cart bridge" over Muddy River was built at the joint charge of Boston and Roxbury. In time both bridges and ferries multiplied. Often the ferryman took his passengers across in a canoe, forcing the horses, if there were any, to swim behind. The bridges were usually flimsy wooden structures designed for pedestrians only, but in 1634 the Massachusetts court gave permission to Israel Stoughton to "keep a horse bridge at Neponset." Nearly three decades later a new era began in New England bridge building with the opening of the Great Bridge over the Charles River at Cambridge on pile bents from fifteen to twenty feet apart.[1]

Despite the gradual development of roads the number of vehicles in the colonies was very small even at the end of the century. It was a matter of pride in Philadelphia in 1697 that there were "thirty carts and other wheeled vehicles" in town. In New England, Maverick noted in 1660 a "comone trade carrying & recarrying goods by land in Cart and on Horseback." In Virginia and Maryland overland travel by horseback long continued the rule. We know, however, that Governor Berkeley was in possession of a coach in 1677 in which he sent King Charles's commissioners to their landing after an official visit at Green Spring. In Virginia in-

[1] H. J. Tyrrell, *History of Bridge Engineering* (Chicago, 1911), 123.

ventories saddles and pillions were among the most common items, but coaches or vehicles of any kind were rare.[1]

In all the colonies the ordinary or tavern was a center of life. In the North it was to be found, not only in almost every village, but also along the more frequented highways. Here the weary traveler secured rest and refreshment; here the villager enjoyed his "beare and cracks" at noontime; here the shivering people thronged from the icy meeting house to warm themselves between services; here the jolly good-natured crowd gathered on training days. The water of Plymouth was wholesome, wrote Governor Bradford, though not, of course, as wholesome as good beer and wine; in proper quantities these formed an element of diet whenever they could be had.[2] As for the tavern keeper, he was an important figure in every community.[3] We find him running a ferry near his ordinary, or leading the singing on Sunday, or serving as selectman, or heading the local militia, in addition to regaling his guests with rum and food and tidbits of gossip. Typical of the old New England hosts was Captain Marshall, whose ordinary lay halfway between Boston and Salem. "Here I staid to refresh nature with a pint of sack and a good fowl," says the book dealer, John Dunton. "Capt. Marshall is a hearty old gentleman, formerly one of Oliver's soldiers, upon which he very much values himself. He had all the history of the civil war at his fingers end, and if we may believe him Oliver did hardly anything that was considerable with-

[1] Dunbar, *History of Travel in America*, I, 48.
[2] Bradford, "History of Plymouth Plantation," 194-195.
[3] J. A. Krout, *The Origins of Prohibition* (N. Y., 1925), 44-45.

out his assistance, and if I'd have staid as long as he'd have talked he'd have spoiled my ramble at Salem." [1]

Taverns were established in New England with the first coming of the Massachusetts Bay settlers. We know that the famous "Anchor," at Lynn, whose hospitable sign was hailed with joy by travelers for nearly two centuries, was in existence as early as 1630. A few years later taverns were open for business in Boston, Salem, Dorchester, Newbury, Charlestown, Duxbury, Portsmouth and other places. Some of the inns were small, cheerless places with but two or three rooms and scant furnishings. Such was the house of John Whipple at Providence, which consisted of "yᵉ lower room" and "yᵉ chamber," containing in all little more than one bedstead, three feather beds, four chairs and a chest. [2] In the larger towns the taverns were more pretentious. It was a common custom to give each of the rooms a separate name. The "King's Arms," at Boston, kept by Hugh Gunnison, boasted of the "Exchange," the "Court Chamber," the "London" and the "Star." The "Blue Anchor," also a Boston institution, contained the "Cross Keys," the "Green Dragon," the "Anchor and Castle Chamber," and the "Rose and Sun Low Room."

In the South the eagerness of the planters to entertain guests made taverns less necessary than in the North. Nevertheless, they were often to be found at the county seats and other places where the people were accustomed to assemble. At the time of Bacon's Rebellion Jamestown is described as a village of "som 16 or 18 howses

[1] John Dunton, *The Life and Errors of John Dunton* (London, 1705), 126.
[2] Edward Field, *The Colonial Tavern* (Providence, 1897), 27-28.

. . . and in them about a dozen families getting their liveings by keeping ordnaries at extraordnary rates." [1] In 1668 taverns and tippling houses in Virginia had increased so rapidly that the assembly passed an act strictly limiting the number in each county.   In case of urgent need, however, additional taverns were permitted at ports, ferries or the crossings of important roads.   Any person who conducted a tippling house without license was liable to a fine of two thousand pounds of tobacco.

The history of architecture and travel during the seventeenth century illustrates admirably the play of forces in the transit of civilization from the Old World to the New.   So far as they could, the Pennsylvanians or New Englanders or Virginians clung to the customs and practices of the mother country; but when conditions made this impossible, they adjusted themselves to their new surroundings.   Reluctantly they substituted shingles for thatch and weatherboarding for half-timber filled in with clay or bricks; reluctantly they accepted the canoe or the pack horse for inland travel.   In these things, as in all others, they were compelled to yield to the forces which were slowly operating to change them from Englishmen to Americans.

[1] Bacon's *Proceedings*, reprinted in Force, *Tracts*, I.

CHAPTER XIII

THE PROGRESS OF A CENTURY

THE outstanding accomplishment of the seventeenth century in American history was the planting of the colonies. In the year 1600 America north of the Floridas was inhabited by savage beasts and hardly less savage Indians; in 1690 the Atlantic Coast from Charleston to Nova Scotia was dotted with flourishing villages and towns, while many of the river valleys were covered with farms where comfortable homesteads nestled among fields of tobacco and wheat and corn. When the Virgin Queen passed on the English throne to James of Scotland, the Spaniards and the Portuguese alone had secured a hold upon the New World; a century later Englishmen were firmly planted in the Carolinas, around Chesapeake and Delaware bays and in New England; the French had taken possession of the Valley of the St. Lawrence; while the Hudson, as a reminder of its original possessors, was lined with the hamlets and farms of the Dutch.

America and the world in general must always be grateful to the men and women who braved the Atlantic to establish European civilization in the New World. The business of conquering the wilds was full of hardship, toil and peril. It required courage, physical endurance and an iron will to desert a safe and comfortable home, to risk starvation, disease and the tomahawk, to hew out a clearing, build a rude cabin and face the task of rearing a family under wilderness conditions.

What President Eliot said of Puritan women might have been remarked quite as truly of all colonial women. "We are apt," he wrote, "to think of the men who bore these hardships as stout and tough. . . . But what of the tenderer women? Generations of them cooked, carried water, washed and made clothes, bore children in lonely peril, and tried to bring them up safely through all sorts of physical exposure without medical or surgical help, lived themselves in terror of savages, in terror of the wilderness, and under the burden of a sad and cruel creed, and sank at last into nameless graves, without any vision of the grateful days when millions of their descendants should rise up and call them blessed." [1]

The typical New Englanders or Virginians of three hundred years ago may have contributed little to the advance of science, art or literature, but they did their part in a work no less important, that of adding a vast continent to the civilized world. While they were founding homes and tightening their grip on the country, they were also steadily advancing the cause of liberty. They were frontiersmen, and frontiersmen are proverbially haters of tyrannical restraint. It was in vain that the English kings sought to crush out the representative system in America, that the Dutch and the founders of Maryland attempted to introduce the manorial system, or the Carolina proprietors to establish Locke's constitutions in the South. Equally futile was the effort of theocratic or aristocratic groups to prevent the growth of democracy. The isolation from Europe, the life in the woods, the contest with the forces of nature, tended to make men impatient of restraint. The seventeenth cen-

[1] C. W. Eliot, *American Contributions to Civilization* (N. Y., 1897), 358.

tury brought not only the first representative assembly in America, not only the first American rebellion against despotism, but a long, persistent and successful struggle for liberalism in government.   The vigilance with which the assemblies, in the royal and proprietary colonies, defended their control over taxation is in itself a stirring theme of our early history.   The liberty George Washington and Samuel Adams and Thomas Jefferson fought to preserve in the years from 1765 to 1783 in no small degree was won by their ancestors in the colonial legislative halls.

From the womb of this century was also born a new order of men—the first Americans.   John Cotton, John Winthrop, Peter Stuyvesant, Sir Thomas Gates and Sir Thomas Dale were Europeans, and remained Europeans to the day of their death.   William Byrd II, Robert Carter, Cotton Mather and Sir William Phips were Americans.   The vast distance between the two continents, the development of distinct interests, the adoption of an imperial policy which subordinated the welfare of the colonies to that of the mother country, the growth of separate customs, points of view, dialects, occupations and religious organizations—all tended to this end. Thus, while the white settlers were transforming America, America was transforming the settlers.   It found them Englishmen and by its irresistible alchemy, it made them Americans.

The transplanting of European culture to North America forms perhaps the most significant chapter in the epic story of the expansion of European influences to the rest of the world, and forms a theme for study by the social historian which has not yet received adequate attention.   Men, like plants, cannot be uprooted from their native soil and set again in some distant land without undergoing profound changes.   Thus, in the case of the famous Havana tobacco of Cuba—small of leaf, rough to the touch and exceedingly delicate in flavor— it has been found that, if the seeds are planted in the Connecticut Valley, they produce in a very few seasons an entirely different leaf—large, thin and remarkably fine and silky.   The Cuban product is modified by different conditions of soil and climate.   In like manner the institutions, manners, morals, religious beliefs and thoughts of the European settlers underwent a change in the soil of America.

In none of the colonies was this more marked than in Virginia and Maryland.   Here the settlers were brought under the influence of an economic system which had no counterpart in Europe.   The culture of tobacco entailed methods of work and conditions of life to which the newcomers were strangers.   If they were men of means and purchased or developed considerable estates, they had to take upon themselves the responsibility of controlling, directing and caring for their servants and slaves.   This developed in them a sense of self-reliance, self-respect and the power of command.   The planting, tending and curing of tobacco made them practical farmers; the marketing of crops and the purchase of merchandise from Europe made them business men; the building and repair of houses and barns, the manufacture of beer and wine, the making of clothing for the workers, the care of the horses and cattle, combined to make them efficient managers.   The mild climate and out-of-door life gave them a love of sport.

The galaxy of great Virginians who played so important a rôle in the Revolutionary War was the product of the tobacco plantation. It is futile to argue that these men displayed such remarkable leadership and statesmanship because of qualities inherited from distinguished English ancestors. They were unlike anything which England ever produced, whether at the time when their ancestors migrated, or, later, in their own day. The widespread belief that during the years from 1645 to 1660 Virginia was the refuge of large numbers of English Cavaliers is entirely without foundation in fact; but had wealthy adherents of the unhappy Charles I flocked thither, the tobacco plantations would in a few generations have transformed them from Cavaliers into Marylanders and Virginians. The small farms which covered the tidewater section had upon their owners an effect no less significant. The English farm laborer who found himself in possession of two hundred acres, who raised his own tobacco and sold it to the exporters, who prided himself on his right to vote, who cut his own firewood from his own woods, became a responsible, self-respecting, prosperous man—a free American, no longer a European peasant. He too was the product of soil, climate and geographic conditions.

In like manner the fur trade developed a class of men peculiar to itself. The traders of New York, like the famous *coureurs de bois* of Canada, became creatures of the wilderness, setting their traps in distant places, driving their bargains with the Huron or the Illinois, pushing their slender canoes through lake and river, wandering along the tangled forest trails, enduring hunger, cold and fatigue. Generous, open-handed, improvident, given to the use of strong liquor, in their dress and manner of life they closely resembled the Indians. As for the merchants of Manhattan, the manor lords along the

Hudson, the rice planters of South Carolina, the ship-builders, traders, and fishermen of New England, they too, in varying degree, felt the molding influence of the New World of which they had become a part.

These first Americans were deeply affected by the proximity of the frontier. Even in later days, when not a few native-born colonists were rounding their seventh or eighth decade, when Boston, Portsmouth, New York and Charleston had become thriving towns, when well-to-do merchants and planters were building substantial homes and fitting them out with every comfort of the old country, even then the fresh scent of the forest came strong with every breeze from the west, while the toma-hawk and the scalping knife continued menacingly near. In the Virginia house of burgesses, when it assembled in the charming new state house at Williamsburg, were to be seen not only the wealthy planter of Gloucester or Middlesex, impressive in periwig, silk stockings, plush breeches and broadcloth coat with ruffled cuffs, but also the rude frontiersman of the upper James or the Pamun-key, clad in canvas or buckskin.

As we have seen, the frontier in the seventeenth, as in the eighteenth and nineteenth centuries, was an ever active school of democracy. The free life of the back-woods, the common struggle to conquer the forest and wring a living from the soil, the common peril from the savages, tended to break down social distinctions and make all men, in fact, equal. From the first the frontier districts have been prompt to raise a strident voice against privilege, injustice and the creation of artificial distinc-tions in government. When Virginia was suffering from the navigation acts, when Sir William Berkeley had so corrupted the assembly as to make it the mockery of a representative body, it was the frontiersmen who raised the standard of rebellion and drove the governor into exile. The aristocratic clique sneered at Bacon's men as "rag, tag and bobtayle," but their rough garb concealed true lovers of liberty, and the laws which these men wrung from the reluctant assembly and the still more reluctant governor mark an epoch in the history of liberty in the New World. In its essential features Bacon's Rebellion was a wind of democracy blowing from the west, a wind that was to come again and again as the frontier receded.

The influence of the Indians upon the life and customs of the colonists was profound. In every practical concern the English learned more from the Indians than the Indians learned from them. For centuries the red men had lived in the forest, and their civilization, such as it was, had been shaped to meet its needs. So long as the Europeans built their homes or hunted, or made war in the shadows of the great trees, they found it necessary to turn to the savages for instruction. Englishmen and Frenchmen might despise the squalid life of the aborigine, they might abhor his religion; but in woodcraft they became his imitators. In the course of time, as the forests disappeared, the white men abandoned many of the Indian customs, but others remained with them throughout the eighteenth century, a few until the present day.

It required only a few years for the English settlers to discover that in the forest the Indian method of fighting was superior to their own. Before the seventeenth century had run half its course they were pursuing the savage enemy in the woods in small bands unencumbered with baggage trains, sleeping in the open, bringing down

their food with their guns, creeping through the underbrush to catch the foe by surprise, making use of every
bit of natural shelter when once the battle had begun.
In September, 1676, when a report reached Virginia that
two thousand redcoats were on their way to restore peace
to the distracted colony, Nathaniel Bacon expressed con-
fidence in his ability to beat them with five hundred men.
Our use of ambushes, our knowledge of the country, our
skill in forest fighting, our marksmanship, will render
their discipline of no avail, he said.   Had the rebel leader
been alive and at the head of his veteran band when the
British troops actually arrived, it is not improbable that
he would have driven them into Chesapeake Bay within
a month.   His estimate of the helplessness of disciplined
troops under wilderness conditions was strikingly vindicated three quarters of a century later by Braddock's defeat on the Monongahela.

The white men learned from the Indians not only the
art of fighting in the forests, but also the art of living in
them.   They copied their methods of trapping the
beaver and the fox, of hunting the deer and the bear,
of blazing a way through the trackless wilds, of building fires, of signaling with smoke columns, of using wild
herbs for medicines, of making maple sugar, dressing
skins, cooking food, detecting the approach of enemies.
Most important of all, they learned from the Indians
how to make and use that merchant vessel of primeval
America—the canoe.   It was the canoe, put together
skillfully with birch bark, which made possible the fur
trade with the interior, and it was the fur trade which
laid the foundation of some of the colonies.   "A moca-
cin's the best cover a man ever had for his feet in the
woods," said an old New England peddler, " the easiest

to get stuff for, the easiest to make, the easiest to wear. And a birch-bark canoe's the best boat a man can have on the river. It's the easiest to get stuff for, easiest to carry, the fastest to paddle. And a snowshoe's the best help a man can have in the winter. It's the easiest to get stuff for, the easiest to walk on, the easiest to carry." [1]

The white man adopted as his own the maize of the Indian, imitated his method of cultivating it—including the efficacious herring in the seed hill—and accepted his way of preparing it for the table. [2] The Indian words, pone, succotash and hominy, bear testimony to his obligation to the aborigine. [3] The early settler, in imitation of the Indian, often heated water by dropping hot stones in it, he lighted his cabin with the pine-knot torch, caught fish in a fishweir and solaced his idle hours by smoking the Indian weed, tobacco.

Unfortunately many of the frontier dwellers copied the Indian's vices as well as his useful arts. At times they repaid treachery with treachery, cruelty with cruelty. The backwoodsman whose wife had been scalped before his eyes or whose children had been carried off into captivity was not slow to take a terrible revenge whenever the opportunity presented itself. From the day when John Pott, the convivial physician of Jamestown, poisoned large numbers of Indians until Chief Logan uttered his famous remonstrance because

[1] Alice M. Earle, *Home Life in Colonial Days* (N. Y., 1898), 202-203.

[2] The suspension of the pestle from the elastic bough or sapling as an aid in grinding corn was also in imitation of the Indian. See H. R. Schoolcraft, *Information Respecting the History, Condition and Prospects of the Indian Tribes* (Phila., 1854), IV, plate 21.

[3] Among other Indian words which have found a place in English are opossum, raccoon, skunk and woodchuck. G. P. Krapp, *The English Language in America* (N. Y., 1926), I, 104.

of the murder of his relatives, the white men were almost the equals of their savage foe in deception and cruelty.

While the settlers were falling under the spell of the frontier, the life and thought of Europe were making upon them an ever fainter impression. As quiet pools often form near the river's bank while the current rushes on, so these dwellers on the outskirts of civilization missed the main trend of progressive thought. In medicine there was deterioration; in literature almost nothing of value was created, while there was little real appreciation of the best contemporaneous English productions. Painting and graphic art were rare indeed, and sculpture was almost unknown.[1]

The America of three centuries ago offered a limitless opportunity for the poet's pen or the painter's brush. But the settlers were too much engrossed with the bitter struggle for existence to revel in the beauty of the scenery or to appreciate the romantic features of wilderness life. Newcomers from Europe, it is true, were wont to give expression to their admiration and wonder as the grandeur of the new continent for the first time broke upon their eyes. Some of the most interesting pictures of the American scene in the seventeenth century came from the pens of those who merely sojourned in this country, like John Smith and John Josselyn; but they devoted more space to nature than to man. It may be said in passing that the writings of such seventeenth-century observers helped to turn the attention of philosophers to the earth

[1] There was a crude beginning of the graphic arts, as is evidenced by Foster's woodcut of Richard Mather. Frank Weitenkampf, *American Graphic Arts* (N. Y., 1924), 112-113. See also C. K. Bolton, *The Founders; Portraits of Persons Born Abroad Who Came to North America before the Year 1701* (Boston, 1919-1926).

itself and its wonders, an interest so elaborately indulged in the *Encyclopedie* of the following century.[1] When the *Sarah Constant*, the *Discovery* and the *Goodspeed* sailed into Chesapeake Bay in 1607, the adventurers were entranced with the fair meadows, sweet with the smell of spring, with the bits of woodland, the song of birds, the rivulets dappled with sunlight. But the rigors of frontier existence soon robbed the settlers of their æsthetic appreciation. Jeremiah Dummer, silversmith and engraver and a man of standing in the society and politics of Boston, had somewhere and somehow learned to paint by the end of the sixteen-eighties; at least, in 1691 he did such creditable portraits of himself and his wife that he may take his place, as far as the record shows, as the first native American painter of competence.[2] He had few rivals.

The vast leafy ocean stretching out as far as the eye could see seemed to the settlers only a tremendous barrier to settlement; the picturesque savages were a deadly enemy to be subdued and swept aside; the broad rivers were of interest chiefly as obstacles or avenues of transportation. They lived too close to the mighty forces of nature to paint them or sing about them. Their task was to fight, to conquer, to labor and to build.

In material progress the accomplishment of the seventeenth century was not great; as compared with that of the eighteenth century it was almost insignificant.

[1] Geoffroy Atkinson, *Les Relations de Voyages du XVII Siècle et l'Évolution des Idées* (Paris, 1925).

[2] F. W. Coburn, "Newly Discovered Painter of the Puritans," *N. Y. Times Book Review and Magazine*, July 24, 1921. Dummer (1645-1718) was son of Richard Dummer, a prominent immigrant, and father of Jeremy Dummer, agent in England of Massachusetts and Connecticut, and also of Lt.-Gov. William Dummer of Connecticut. Unlike most colonial painters he was a man of family and influence.

Jeremiah Dummer,
by himself.

A group from the Metropolitan Museum

A high chair   A leather-back
(left),   (right).

An oak court cupboard.   A high chest of drawers.

The Touch of Art.

Despite the continued migration to the various colonies the growth of population was slow and halting. The census figures for the time are unsatisfactory. The pious New Englanders believed, on the authority of I Chronicles xxi., that God's wrath would follow any enumeration. This fear, which they carried to New Jersey and New York, forced Governor Hunter to ingenious shifts to get an estimate. Yet there were reckonings based often upon the tax lists or the strength of the militia.[1] In 1649, forty-two years after the founding of Jamestown, Virginia had but 15,000 people. The prosperity which attended the economic freedom of the Commonwealth period brought about a sudden increase to 40,000 in 1662, but the navigation acts of 1660 and 1663 put a halt to this movement. In 1698 Governor Nicholson placed the number of people in the colony at 58,040; within the century to follow it was to increase nearly twelvefold. The story is similar in the other colonies. In 1643 Massachusetts boasted of a population of about 16,000;[2] in 1658 the number was about 30,000; in 1700, perhaps 60,000. In 1643 Connecticut had possibly 5500 people; in 1689, from 17,000 to 20,000. New York grew from 7000 in 1664 to 18,067 in 1698; Maryland, from 8,000 in 1660 to 32,000 in 1701; Rhode Island, from some 1200 in 1658 to 7181 in 1708. All in all the colonies grew from about 25,000

[1] E. B. O'Callaghan and Berthold Fernow, eds., *Documents Relating to the Colonial History of the State of New York* (Albany, 1853-1887), V, 339, 459.

[2] The source of this immigration is interesting. Anders Orbeck took the pioneers of Plymouth, Watertown and Dedham as a sample and found that approximately two thirds came from the region along the English coast between London and the Wash, mostly from the southern part. Anders Orbeck, *Early New England Pronunciations* (unpublished thesis, Columbia Univ.), chap. v.

in 1640 [1] to about 80,000 in 1660, and to over 200,000 in 1689.[2]

Though the population was still small at the end of the century, though the forest in places stretched unbroken almost to the ocean shore, in social well-being and the comforts of life the advances were impressive. The most successful planters of Virginia and Maryland and the leading merchants of New England and New York had, by the year 1690, acquired a considerable degree of wealth,[3] built substantial homes, bought silver cups and candlesticks, and surrounded themselves with servants.   Even the humbler classes—small planters, artisans, shopkeepers—had discarded the huts of the earlier days for larger and better constructed homes. The life of the settlers of 1620 or 1630 was one of hardship and incessant labor; in 1690 their descendants enjoyed comforts which the well-to-do of England itself might have envied.

Nor were other indications of material progress lacking. The Indian trails which in the early days served as routes of travel were gradually giving way to roads suitable for horse-drawn vehicles; over many of the rivers and creeks bridges were supplementing the primitive ferries; the two-wheel cart was beginning to challenge the ascendancy of the pack horse and the canoe. The tiny rude churches where the first settlers had worshiped were now replaced by larger buildings, solidly constructed.

[1] Only about twice as many as had gone to the island of St. Christopher alone. See map-chart in J. T. Adams, *The Founding of New England* (Boston, 1922), 120.

[2] These estimates and reports are taken from W. R. Rossiter, ed., *A Century of Population Growth* (Wash., 1909), 3-10.

[3] William Fitzhugh estimated that he had made three times as much in Virginia as he could have made in England. William Fitzhugh, "Letters," *Va. Mag. of Hist. and Biog.*, I, 395-396.

Well-laid-out race courses, handsome state houses, comfortable inns, likewise bore testimony to the transformation which, in the older communities, was taking place. Though the tender plant of European civilization had not yet grown large in American soil, it had taken firm root, was healthy and vigorous. The way had been prepared for the remarkable growth of succeeding decades.

The American of 1690 no doubt often pictured his pioneer grandfather as he went about the work of subduing the wilderness. He could see him, broadax in hand, hewing away at the great oaks or pines or sycamores to make a first clearing in the forest. He pictured him erecting his little cabin, while his wife cared for the baby or cooked the food in the open; or breaking the ground with his spade or clumsy hoe for his crop of maize or tobacco. He could see him alone in the forest bringing down the wild turkey or the deer with his bell-mouthed musket; barricaded in his house, holding off the bloodthirsty savages; hastening over the forest trail to bring the distant pastor-physician to sick wife or child; wending his way by boat or horse many miles to attend church. He thought of the perils of those early days, of the thousands who succumbed to malaria or the plague; of those who perished of hunger, privation and cold; of those who fell beneath the tomahawk of the Indian; of the ever-present dread of the hated Spaniard.

Then he turned his vision to the America of his own day, and smiled at the pleasing contrast. If he were a well-to-do planter, he thought of his estate of a thousand acres, three hundred of them cleared and under cultivation; of his comfortable dwelling house, its great hall hung with tapestry, its chambers provided with all kinds of furniture; of his cellars stocked with wines, his crops of tobacco and corn, his servants and slaves, his cattle, horses and sheep. If he were a prosperous merchant, his mind perhaps dwelt on his swift sloop, beating its way to the West Indies laden with provisions, timber, fish and rum; his warehouse at the water's edge filled with sugar and molasses; or his commodious dwelling house in Boston or Portsmouth.

All in all the men of the seventeenth century did well the task which fate assigned them. Their failures, such as they were, are readily explained by the peculiar conditions of their life. When the inventory of their accomplishment is taken, it bulks large in the history of American life. Their arduous labors in conquering the wilderness, their hardships and sufferings, were not in vain, for they planted firmly on the northwestern shores of the Atlantic the standard of European civilization, and laid the broad foundations of nationality upon which future generations were to erect the mighty structure of the United States.

CHAPTER XIV

CRITICAL ESSAY ON AUTHORITIES

PHYSICAL SURVIVALS

THE century of beginnings has left comparatively few nonliterary remains of historical importance, though fortunately a considerable portion of those which exist are passing into the control of historical societies or other institutions which will preserve them for public benefit. The houses of the seventeenth-century South, built rather loosely of wood, have nearly all disappeared, yet some in whose construction masonry played a larger part still stand along the shores of the sea, Chesapeake Bay and the watercourses. As examples may be mentioned "Long Point," in Talbot County, Eastern Shore, Maryland; "Bacon's Castle" (before 1676), Virginia; and the Jenkins house (1683), Edisto Island, South Carolina, the last, despite its early date, a harbinger of the eighteenth-century classical forms. A little of the atmosphere of Virginia in the reign of William and Mary may be realized among the old houses of Yorktown.

There are scores of wooden houses built in this period still standing in excellent condition in New England where the climate made better construction essential. Notable among towns which possess good specimens are Guilford, Connecticut, and Ipswich, Newburyport and Salem, Massachusetts. The Society for the Preservation of New England Antiquities has acquired twelve houses, seven of which are dated in the century here under review, these being located in Newbury, Cambridge, Saugus, Watertown and Rowley, Massachusetts, Portsmouth, New Hampshire, and Lincoln, Rhode Island. Its magazine *Old Time New England* (title varies; Boston, 1910-) specializes in the description of existing old houses, a field which the architectural magazines likewise

increasingly cultivate. Seventeenth-century houses in Connecticut may be readily identified by the traveler who carries
Rawson Haddon, *Tourists' Guide to Connecticut* (Water-
bury, 1923), and J. F. Kelly, *Early Domestic Architecture
of Connecticut* (New Haven, 1914)—each a model of its
kind. The Colonial Dames of Connecticut, with some
professional assistance, have photographed, measured and
described about five hundred early houses in that state,
depositing their portfolios in the state library; Bertha C.
Trowbridge, editor, in *Old Houses of Connecticut* (New
Haven, 1924) presents about sixty such little monographs
on specimens. Technical drawings of the Scotch-Boardman
house (Saugus, 1650), the Ward house (Salem, 1684) and
the Capen house (Topsfield, 1683)—all of them still standing—can be found in Donald Millar, *Measured Drawings
of Some Colonial and Georgian Houses* (N. Y., 1916).
Many houses have been altered by reconstruction and addition, such as the Whitefield house in Guilford (1639, the
oldest stone house in New England), the Fairbanks house in
Dedham, Massachusetts (1636, probably the oldest house
built by Englishmen in America), and the famous "House
of Seven Gables" in Salem (1669) ; so that the assigned date
applies only to a portion.

Among the few surviving structures built in New York
during the first forty years of English rule may be mentioned the Van Cortlandt manor house at Croton. It was
built sometime between 1665 and 1681 and is of stone, a
material more used here than to the eastward, often in combination with wood and brick. Though built shortly after
1700 and by French immigrants, the stone houses along the
quiet elm-shaded Huguenot Street in New Paltz suggest a
picture of the late seventeenth century as effectively as can
any place in New York state. The house which William
Penn built for his daughter about 1683, now removed to
Fairmount Park, Philadelphia, is an illustration of the brick
houses of the period. A sample of old New Jersey churches
is found in the Reformed Church of Hackensack.

The so-called "Old Ship Church" (1681) at Hingham,

Massachusetts, is the only specimen of seventeenth-century churches in New England—a relic of the days before gables and end spires. St. Luke's (1632) at Smithfield, Isle of Wight County, is the most famous building of the century existing in Virginia, showing Gothic forms giving way to new influences. Old Trinity, built about 1680, in Dorchester County, Maryland, though subsequent to St. Luke's, reveals the older type more rigidly persisting.

A number of the houses mentioned above are maintained as public museums. Some of them are distinguished for their display of seventeenth-century furnishings, implements and the like, as the Whipple house in Ipswich and the Hyland-Wilder house in Guilford. Pilgrim Hall in Plymouth, though not a seventeenth-century building, has a unique collection. The Ward house (1684) in the rear of the Essex Institute at Salem, Massachusetts, is rich in kitchen material. A recent and notable reconstruction, with genuine plenishings, is the suite on the third floor of the American Wing of the Metropolitan Museum of Art in New York City. The larger historical societies, such as those located in Boston, Providence, New Haven, New York and Philadelphia, together with the Smithsonian Institution in Washington, maintain museums well furnished with seventeenth-century items. Of special importance in this connection is the Pocumtuck Valley Memorial Association at Deerfield, Massachusetts. The Bucks County Historical Society collection at Doylestown, Pennsylvania, has the largest display of agricultural and industrial implements for the period. There has been no satisfactory survey of historical museums since that recorded in the *Annual Report* of the American Historical Association for 1905, I, 249-325, and that of P. M. Rea, *A Directory of American Museums* . . . (Buffalo, 1910). For those who cannot view the actual objects, an attractive short cut is afforded by the pictures brought together in R. H. Gabriel, ed., *The Pageant of America* (15 vols., of which seven have appeared, New Haven, 1926-), which, though not so complete as for later periods, nevertheless illuminates many phases of the life of the time.

GENERAL BIBLIOGRAPHIES

Charles Evans, comp., *American Bibliography* (9 vols., Chicago, 1903-1925, in progress), lists year by year the entire output of American presses throughout this period, and will probably be found the most convenient of the general works on the subject. Justin Winsor, ed., *Narrative and Critical History of America* (8 vols., N. Y., 1884-1889), describes most of the important sources. One valuable body of source material on social history is found in diaries; Harriette M. Forbes, *New England Diaries* (Topsfield, Mass., 1923), is the best guide.

The literature *about* the seventeenth century is disproportionately large. Besides the special bibliographies to which reference is made later, the student will, of course, for this and subsequent volumes of this series, consult Edward Channing, A. B. Hart and F. J. Turner, eds., *Guide to the Study and Reading of American History* (Boston, 1912); J. N. Larned, ed., *Literature of American History* (Boston, 1902), containing helpful critical estimates; and the *Writings on American History* (N. Y., 1904-1925, in progress) compiled by different editors, these annual volumes since 1918 being in charge of Grace G. Griffin. Early history has had a fascination for historical societies, and it would be unsafe for any serious student to leave unexamined A. P. C. Griffin, comp., *Bibliography of American Historical Societies* (Am. Hist. Assoc., *Ann. Rep. for 1905*, II), though this unfortunately has not been brought up to date. The characteristics and tendencies of the times are abundantly displayed in local history. An old but serviceable guide to this material is A. P. C. Griffin, comp., *Index of Articles upon American Local History in Historical Collections in the Boston Public Library* (Boston Pub. Libr., *Bull.* no. 3, 1883), which is supplemented by his *Index of the Literature of American Local History in Collections Published in 1890-1895* (Boston, 1896). Bibliographies covering this field for Massachusetts, Connecticut and New York have been prepared by C. A. Flagg, comp., *A Guide to Massachusetts Local History* (Salem, 1907) ; same comp., *Reference List on Connecticut Local History* (N. Y. State Libr., *Bull.* no. 53, Albany, 1900) ; and same comp., with J. T. Jennings, *Bibliography of New York Colonial History* (N. Y. State Libr., *Bull.*, no. 56, Albany, 1901). Others useful for the seventeenth century are: anon., *List of Books Relating to the State of New York* (Albany, 1916) ; O. G. Hammond, comp., *Check List for New Hampshire Local History* (Concord, 1925) ; D. B. Hall, *Reference List of Maine Local History* (Albany, 1901) ; anon., *A Check List of Pennsylvania County, Town and Township Histories* (Harrisburg, 1892) ; E. G. Swem, comp., *A Bibliography of Virginia* (2 vols.,Richmond, 1916-1919) ; and S. B. Weeks, comp., *A Bibliography of the Historical Literature of North Carolina* (Justin Winsor, ed., *Harvard Libr. Bibl. Contribs.*, no. 48, 1895).

DOCUMENTARY SOURCE COLLECTIONS

By far the most complete and valuable collection of documentary material covering the period from 1607 to 1690 is W. N. Sainsbury and others, eds., *Calendar of State Papers, Colonial Series, America and West Indies* (27 vols., covering 1574-1714, London, 1860-1926, in progress). This great work is sadly in need of a complete and serviceable index. Moreover, no abridgment can take the place of the complete documents, and at times even the most abridged form is lacking, so that one has to content himself with the bare mention of indispensable journals or reports. Fortunately many of the documents have been printed in full in America, and are available in most libraries. These volumes may be supplemented by W. L. Grant and James Munro, eds., *Acts of the Privy Council* (4 vols., Hereford, Eng., 1908-1911), I-II; and Joseph Redington, ed., *Calendar of Treasury Papers* [1556-1728] (6 vols., London, 1868-1889).

Among the collections of papers which have been published are Peter Force, comp., *Tracts and Other Papers* (4 vols., Wash., 1836-1846) ; A. B. Hart, ed., *American History Told by Contemporaries* (4 vols., N. Y., 1897-1901— fifth volume in progress) ; Massachusetts Historical Society, *Collections* (75 vols., in progress) ; and the collections of statutes, legislative journals and administrative correspondence for the various colonies, published for Virginia, New York, New Jersey, North Carolina, Pennsylvania, Rhode Island and other states. See J. T. Adams, *Provincial Society, 1690-1763* (*A History of American Life,* III), chap. xii, where the major collections of published colonial documents are listed. I. N. Phelps Stokes, *Iconography of Manhattan Island* (6 vols., of which five have appeared, New York, 1915-   ), has collections of source extracts referring to New York in the period under our review.

Hundreds of papers which throw light upon the civilization of the period have been printed in the various state historical magazines, notably the *Virginia Magazine of History and Biography* (Richmond, 1893-   ), the *William and Mary College Historical Quarterly* (Williamsburg, 1892-   ), the *Pennsylvania Magazine of History and Biography* (Phila., 1877-   ) and the *Maryland Historical Magazine* (Balt., 1906-   ). The *Publications* of the Prince Society (Boston, 1865-   ), of which thirty-eight volumes have appeared, contain reprints of many rare seventeenth-century works. In volume xx (1890), 333-340, is an interesting account of the society and its accomplishments. The Gorges Society, *Publs.* (5 vols., Portland, Me., 1884-   ), are similar in character, though chiefly relating to Maine. Inaccessible to the general reader, but invaluable for the scholar, are the manuscript collections in the public archives of the various states, counties and towns.

ECONOMIC CONDITIONS

The best survey of the economic relations of the colonies is to be found in the works of G. L. Beer, *The Origins of the British Colonial System* (N. Y., 1908), and *The Old Colonial System, 1660-1754* (2 vols., N. Y., 1912). Treating the colonies from the imperial standpoint, these books give a perspective which is necessary for a clear understanding of their relations with the mother country and with foreign nations. Edward Channing, *A History of the United States* (6 vols., N. Y., 1905-1926, in progress), deals with economic and social forces in seventeenth-century life in his first two volumes. The works on economic history published by the Carnegie Institution in the series called *Contributions to American Economic History* are of great value not only in their text but in the appended book lists as well: E. R. Johnson and others, *History of Domestic and Foreign Commerce* (2 vols., Wash., 1915); V. S. Clark, *History of Manufactures in the United States, 1607-1860* (Wash., 1916); P. W. Bidwell and J. I. Falconer, *History of Agriculture in the Northern United States before 1860* (Wash., 1925); and B. H. Meyer and others, *History of Transportation in the United States before 1860* (Wash., 1917). On farming methods the most valuable work is Lyman Carrier, *The Beginnings of American Agriculture* (N. Y., 1923). A description of the processes of textile making and other domestic industries in the seventeenth century is given in Alice Morse Earle, *Home Life in Colonial Days* (N. Y., 1898), chaps. viii-xi. See also C. A. Beard and Mary Beard, *The Rise of American Civilization* (N. Y., 1927), chap. iii.

For conditions in the tobacco colonies a storehouse of information will be found in P. A. Bruce, *Economic History of Virginia in the Seventeenth Century* (2 vols., N. Y., 1896). Other works touching the subject are Alexander Brown, ed., *The Genesis of the United States* (2 vols., Boston, 1890); and same author, *The First Republic in America* (Boston, 1898); W. A. Crozier, ed., *Virginia County Records* (5 vols., N. Y., 1905-1908); T. J. Wertenbaker, *The Planters of Colonial Virginia* (Princeton, 1922); Meyer Jacobstein, *The Tobacco Industry in the United States* (Columbia Univ., *Studies*, XXVI, 1907, no. 3); A. O. Craven, *Soil Exhaustion as a Factor in the Agricultural History of Virginia and Maryland, 1606-1860* (Univ. of Ill., *Studies*, XIII, 1926, no. 1); E. I. McCormac, *White Servi-*

tude in Maryland, 1634-1820 (Johns Hopkins Univ., *Studies*, XXII, 1904, nos. 3-4); J. C. Ballagh, *White Servitude in the Colony of Virginia* (Johns Hopkins Univ., *Studies*, XIII, 1895, nos. 6-7); J. T. Scharf, *History of Maryland* (Balt., 1879). On slavery one should read the early chapters of U. B. Phillips, *American Negro Slavery* (N. Y., 1918); source items may be found in L. D. Scisco, "Rolfe's Story of the First Slave Cargo," *Magazine of History*, XIII, no. 3. For a study of the motives for the settlement of America by the British, one should turn to Richard Hakluyt, *A Discourse on Western Planting* [1584] (Charles Deane, ed., *Doc. Hist. of the State of Maine*, ser. 2, II, 1877), and Samuel Purchas, *Pilgrims* (London, 1613).

The most comprehensive work on economic conditions in colonial New England is W. B. Weeden, *Economic and Social History of New England, 1620-1784* (2 vols., Boston, 1890). The book is replete with information, but is poorly organized and very uneven in literary merit. The local histories, which abound for New England, contain much that is pertinent to this subject. Especially valuable are George Lincoln and others, *History of the Town of Hingham*, (3 vols., Hingham, 1893); W. De L. Love, *Colonial History of Hartford* (Hartford, 1914); Frances M. Caulkins, *History of New London* (New London, 1895); Sylvester Judd, *History of Hadley, Massachusetts* (Springfield, 1905); T. F. Waters, *History of Ipswich in the Massachusetts Bay Colony* (2 vols., Ipswich, 1905); W. I. Munro, *History of Bristol, Rhode Island* (Providence,1880); J. T. Adams, *History of Southampton, Long Island* (Bridgehampton, 1918); J. U. Usher, *History of Medford* (Boston, 1855); Justin Winsor, ed., *Memorial History of Boston* (3 vols., Boston, 1880-1881); and J. G. Palfrey, *History of New England* (5 vols., Boston, 1858-1890). Thomas Lechford, *Note-Book* [1638-1641] (E. E. Hale, jr., ed., Am. Antiq. Soc., *Trans.*, VII, 1885), is rich in material for the economic history of New England. New England's part in maintaining the royal navy is treated in R. G. Albion, *Forests and Sea Power* (*Harvard Econ. Studies*, XXIX,

1926). See, also, J. S. Marais, *The Colonization of New England* (N. Y., 1927).

For a study of colonial manufactures the student should read R. M. Tryon, *Household Manufactures in the United States, 1640-1860* (Chicago, 1917); C. J. H. Woodberry, *Textile Education among the Puritans* (Boston, 1917); J. B. Pearse, *A Concise History of the Iron Manufacture of the American Colonies to the Revolution* (Phila., 1876); and A. H. Cole, *The American Wool Manufacture* (2 vols., Cambridge, 1926). General accounts are found in J. L. Bishop, *A History of American Manufactures, 1608-1860* (2 vols., Phila., 1861), and V. S. Clark, *History of Manufactures in the United States, 1607-1860* (Wash., 1916). Light is thrown upon the methods of distributing wares to the scattered inhabitants by Richardson Wright, *Hawkers and Walkers in Early America* (Phila., 1927), though the book is not as full as for later periods.

Land ownership and control in New England are treated in the following special works: R. H. Akagi, *The Town Proprietors of the New England Colonies* (N. Y., 1925); Anne B. Maclear, *Early New England Towns* (N. Y., 1908); Melville Egleston, *The Land System of the New England Colonies* (Balt., 1886); C. M. Andrews, *The River Towns of Connecticut* (Balt., 1889); and H. L. Osgood, *The American Colonies in the Seventeenth Century* (3 vols., N. Y., 1904-1907), particularly I, chap. xi. In his second volume, chap. ii, Professor Osgood treats of the land system of the later proprietary provinces. See also Amelia C. Ford, *Colonial Precedents of Our National Land System* (Univ. of Wis., *Bull.*, no. 352, 1910).

RELIGION

Though no adequate bibliography has been compiled of colonial Christianity, the following manuals are distinctly useful: W. H. Allison, comp., *Inventory of Unpublished Materials for American Religious History* (Wash., 1911); and P. G. Mode, ed., *Source Book and Bibliographical Guide* for *American Church History* (Menasha, 1921). Philip Schaff and others, *The American Church History Series* (13 vols., N. Y., 1893-1897), is especially good on the colonial beginnings of the leading sects and denominations. In the thirteenth volume L. W. Bacon gives a general view of the subject under the title *A History of American Christianity* (N. Y., 1897). H. K. Rowe, *The History of Religion in the United States* (N. Y., 1924), is an interesting interpretative study in brief compass.

For the Massachusetts theocracy, Cotton Mather, *Magnalia Christi Americana* (2 vols., Hartford, 1820), is indispensable. The work is a glorification of the early leaders, whom Mather frankly regarded as saints, but it sheds light upon their motives, ideals and hopes. J. T. Adams, *The Founding of New England* (Boston, 1921), is scholarly, readable and stimulating. Its treatment of the Massachusetts leaders is unsympathetic, a tendency which is shared by Brooks Adams, *The Emancipation of Massachusetts* (Boston, 1887). Osgood, *The American Colonies in the Seventeenth Century*, I, chaps. iii-v, also gives a picture of religious conditions in Massachusetts. Of value is J. B. Felt, *Ecclesiastical History of New England* (2 vols., Boston, 1855-1862), though annalistic in form. The Massachusetts theocracy has been the occasion of so much controversy and has been depicted in such contrasting lights that the student should form his own judgment as far as possible from a reading of contemporaneous writers. For this purpose he will find useful: William Bradford, *History of Plymouth Plantation* (Charles Deane, ed., Mass. Hist. Soc., *Colls.*, ser. 4, III, 1856); John Winthrop, *History of New England* (J. K. Hosmer, ed., 2 vols., in J. F. Jameson, ed., *Original Narratives of Early American History*, N. Y., 1908-); George Bishop, *New England Judged by the Spirit of the Lord* (London, 1703); Edward Johnson, *Wonder-Working Providence of Sions Saviour, or a History of New England* (Jameson, ed., *Original Narratives of Early American History*); Samuel Sewall, *Diary* (Mass. Hist. Soc., *Colls.*, ser. 5, V-VII, 1878-1882); and Cotton Mather, *Diary* (Mass. Hist. Soc., *Colls.*, ser. 7, VII-

VIII, 1911-1912). Interesting works by later writers are Williston Walker, *History of the Congregational Churches in the United States* (Schaff, ed., *American Church History*, III); C. F. Adams, *Three Episodes of Massachusetts History* (2 vols., Boston, 1892); R. P. Hallowell, *The Quaker Invasion of Massachusetts* (Boston, 1883); Edward Eggleston, *The Beginners of a Nation* (N. Y., 1897); E. H. Byington, *The Puritan in England and in New England* (Boston, 1896); Elizabeth D. Hanscom, ed., *The Heart of the Puritan* (N. Y., 1917); W. De L. Love, *The Fast and Thanksgiving Days of New England* (Boston, 1895)— including bibliography, 515-602; S. H. Cobb, *The Rise of Religious Liberty in America* (N. Y., 1902); H. M. Dexter, *The Congregationalism of the Last Three Hundred Years* (N. Y., 1880); Alice M. Earle, *The Sabbath in Puritan New England* (N. Y., 1891); G. E. Ellis, *The Puritan Age and Rule in the Colony of Massachusetts Bay* (Boston, 1888); and M. L. Greene, *The Development of Religious Liberty in Connecticut* (Boston, 1905). Specimens of early New England character may be examined in R. C. Winthrop, *Life and Letters of John Winthrop* (Boston, 1869); Alice M. Earle, *Margaret Winthrop* (N. Y., 1896); E. J. Carpenter, *Roger Williams* (N. Y., 1909); and K. B. Murdock, *Increase Mather* (Cambridge, 1925). An attractive picture of a type is to be found in F. S. Child, *The Colonial Parson* (N. Y., 1896).

A standard authority on the Anglican church is J. S. M. Anderson, *History of the Church of England in the Colonies* (London, 1848). More scholarly and up-to-date is A. L. Cross, *The Anglican Episcopate and the American Colonies* (*Harvard Hist. Studies,* IX, 1902). Other works dealing with the subject are: S. E. Baldwin, "The American Jurisdiction of the Bishop of London in Colonial Times," Am. Antiq. Soc., *Proceeds.,* new ser., XIII (1899), 179-221; F. L. Hawks, *Contributions to the Ecclesiastical History of the United States* (2 vols., N. Y., 1836-1839); William Meade, *Old Churches, Ministers and Families of Virginia* (2 vols., Phila., 1857); H. R. McIlwaine, *The Struggle of*

Protestant Dissenters for Religious Toleration in Virginia (Johns Hopkins Univ., *Studies,* XII, 1894, no. 4) ; S. B. Weeks, *Church and State in North Carolina* (Johns Hopkins Univ., *Studies,* XI, 1893, nos. 5-6). For an exhaustive study of early Anglicanism in Virginia, one must rely chiefly on the original documents. P. A. Bruce devotes much space to the subject in his *Institutional History of Virginia in the Seventeenth Century* (2 vols., N. Y., 1910), but his treatment is not exhaustive. Most of the papers and reports relating to this subject are to be found in the British Public Record Office in London. Valuable published sources are W. S. Perry, ed., *Historical Collections Relating to the American Colonial Episcopal Church* (4 vols., Hartford, 1870-1878) ; R. H. McIlwaine and J. P. Kennedy, eds., *Journals of the House of Burgesses of Virginia, 1727-1776* (8 vols., Richmond, 1905-1910) ; Peter Force, comp., *Tracts and Other Papers* (cited earlier) ; extracts in the *Virginia Magazine of History and Biography* and the *William and Mary College Historical Quarterly;* and W. W. Hening, comp., *The Statutes at Large of Virginia, 1619-1792* (13 vols., Phila., 1823). A scholarly defense of the earliest established church in English America is now available in the Rev. E. L. Goodwin, *The Colonial Church in Virginia* (Milwaukee, 1927), 1-104; the book also contains a biographical list of the clergy from 1607 to 1785 (241-319).

For the minor denominations one should consult Isaac Backus, *A History of New England with Particular Reference to the Denomination of Christians called Baptists* (Newton, 1871) ; A. H. Newman, *A History of the Baptist Churches in the United States* (N. Y., 1915) ; J. G. Shea, *The Catholic Church in Colonial Days,* being the first volume of his *History of the Catholic Church within the Limits of the United States* (4 vols., N. Y., 1880-1892) ; and R. M. Jones, *The Quakers in the American Colonies* (London, 1911).

LITERATURE AND EDUCATION

There has been no extensive essay at a general bibliography of the history of American education since 1902, that of E. P. Cubberley; but the reading lists following the chapters in the same author's *Public Education in the United States* (Boston, 1919) represent a good selection. Probably the best collection of early American children's books, starting with *Spiritual Milk for Boston Babes* (Boston, 1681), is that formed by Dr. A. S. W. Rosenbach, New York City. Perhaps the most comprehensive work on intellectual culture in the colonies is M. C. Tyler, *A History of American Literature* (2 vols., N. Y., 1879). E. G. Dexter, *A History of Education in the United States* (N. Y., 1922), and Cubberley's book (cited earlier) give concise treatments of educational conditions. All classes of printed material fall within the catholic range of treatment of the contributors to *The Cambridge History of American Literature* (4 vols., N. Y., 1917-1921), edited by W. P. Trent and others. Various aspects of seventeenth-century literary culture are dealt with in E. E. Slosson, *The American Spirit in Education* (Allen Johnson, ed., *The Chronicles of America Series*, 50 vols., New Haven, 1918-1921, XXXIII) ; Edward Eggleston, *The Transit of Civilization* (N. Y., 1901) ; Alice M. Earle, *Customs and Fashions in Old New England* (N. Y., 1894) ; same author, *Child Life in Colonial Days* (N. Y., 1899) ; and Isaiah Thomas, *The History of Printing in America* (Am. Antiq. Soc., *Trans.*, V-VI, 1874). S. A. Green has included monographs on Stephen Daye, the first American printer, and Benjamin Tompson, the first native poet, in his *Ten Facsimile Reproductions Relating to New England* (Boston, 1902), and has published another on *John Foster, the Earliest American Engraver and the First Boston Printer* (Boston, 1895).

The intellectual culture of New England has received far more study than that of the other colonies. T. G. Wright, *Literary Culture in Early New England* (New Haven, 1920), is an excellent work, marred somewhat by a tendency to special pleading. Valuable for a study of New England reading tastes and opportunities are: W. C. Ford, *The Boston Book Market, 1679-1700* (Boston, 1917); C. A. Duniway, *The Development of the Freedom of the Press in Massachusetts* (*Harvard Hist. Studies*, XII, 1906); G. E. Littlefield, *The Early Massachusetts Press, 1638-1711* (2 vols., Boston, 1907); same author, *Early Boston Booksellers* (Boston, 1900); and same author, *Early Schools and School Books in New England* (Boston, 1904). The educational system is treated in G. H. Martin, *The Evolution of the Massachusetts Public School System* (N. Y., 1894); Josiah Quincy, *History of Harvard University* (2 vols., Boston, 1840); E. J. Young, "Subjects for the Master's Degree in Harvard College from 1655 to 1791," Mass. Hist. Soc., *Proceeds.*, XVIII (1881), 119-151; R. F. Seybolt, *Apprenticeship and Apprentice Education in Colonial New York and New England* (Teachers Col., Columbia Univ., *Contribs. to Educ.*, no. 85, 1917); W. H. Small, *Early New England Schools* (Boston, 1914); Harlan Updegraff, *Origin of the Moving School in Massachusetts* (Teachers Col., Columbia Univ., *Contribs. to Educ.*, no. 17, 1908); and E. E. Brown, *The Making of Our Middle Schools* (N. Y., 1903). The articles on colonial education by M. W. Jernegan, in the *School Review*, XXIII (1915) and XXVI-XXVIII (1918-1920), are studies preliminary to a comprehensive treatment of the subject. A. W. Tuer, *The History of the Horn-book* (London, 1896), describes the kinds of textbooks used in the colonies as well as in England.

Indispensable for a study of education in colonial Virginia is Bruce, *Institutional History of Virginia in the Seventeenth Century* (cited earlier), which contains pioneer chapters on libraries, schools and illiteracy. The reader would do well to consult also C. J. Heatwole, *A History of Education in Virginia* (Paul Monroe, ed., *Home and School Series*, N. Y., 1916); W. A. Maddox, *The Free School Idea in Virginia before the Civil War* (Teachers Col., Columbia Univ., *Contribs. to Educ.*, no. 93, 1918); G. F. Wells, *Parish Education in Colonial Virginia* (Teachers Col., Columbia

Univ., *Contribs. to Educ.*, no. 138, 1923); H. B. Adams, *The College of William and Mary* (U. S. Commissioner of Educ., *Circular of Information*, no. 1, 1888); and "Papers Relating to Governor Nicholson and to the Founding of William and Mary College," *Va. Mag. of Hist. and Biog.*, VII-IX (1899-1902), *passim*. D. E. Motley, *Life of Commissary James Blair* (Balt., 1901), obviously made no use of the great mass of manuscript material on the subject in the British Public Record Office, and is of doubtful value. Several excellent articles on education in Virginia have been published in the *William and Mary College Historical Quarterly*, V-VII. Information concerning libraries will be found in the *Virginia Magazine of History and Biography*, II-III; the *William and Mary College Historical Quarterly*, II-III; and the *Lower Norfolk County Antiquary* (5 vols., Balt., 1895-1906), I.

THE SUPERNATURAL

For the English background of witchcraft the best work is Wallace Notestein, *Witchcraft in England* (Wash., 1911). Important for any study of the subject are W. E. H. Lecky, *History of the Rise and Influence of the Spirit of Rationalism in Europe* (2 vols., N. Y., 1866), and Eggleston, *The Transit of Civilization* (cited in the preceding section). The standard collection of sources on superstition and witchcraft in the American colonies is G. L. Burr, ed., *Narratives of the Witchcraft Cases, 1648-1706* (J. F. Jameson, ed., *Original Narratives of Early American History*, cited earlier), which contains extracts from Increase Mather's *An Essay for the Recording of Illustrious Providences;* Richard Chamberlain's *Lithobolia;* Cotton Mather's *Memorable Providences Relating to Witchcraft and Possessions;* Deodat Lawson's *A Brief and True Narrative of Witchcraft at Salem Village;* Cotton Mather's *Wonders of the Invisible World;* Robert Calef's *More Wonders of the Invisible World;* and other papers relating to witchcraft. The preface and the introductions to the various documents are scholarly and illuminating. Other materials bearing on the subject are S. G. Drake,

Annals of Witchcraft in New England and Elsewhere in the United States (Boston, 1869); J. M. Taylor, *The Witchcraft Delusion in Connecticut* (N. Y., 1908); C. H. Levermore, "Witchcraft in Connecticut," *New Eng. Mag.*, new ser., VI (1892), 636-644; C. W. Upham, *Salem Witchcraft* (2 vols., Boston, 1867)—which treats fully the local setting; Thomas Brattle, "Account of the Delusion Called Witchcraft, which prevailed in New-England [1692]," Mass. Hist. Soc., *Colls.*, V (1798), 61-80; S. P. Fowler, *Samuel Parris* (Salem, 1857); S. A. Greene, *Groton in Witchcraft Times* (Groton, 1883); Ebenezer Turell, "Detection of Witchcraft," Mass. Hist. Soc., *Colls.*, ser. 2, X (1823), 6-22; "Salem Witchcraft [extracts from the records of the church in Danvers]," Mass. Hist. Soc., *Colls.*, ser. 3, III (1833), 169-180; Joshua Coffin, *History of Newbury* (Boston, 1864); W. E. Woodward, *Records of Salem Witchcraft* (Boston, 1864); Amelia M. Gummere, *Witchcraft and Quakerism* (Phila., 1908); and W. F. Poole, "Cotton Mather and Salem Witchcraft," *N. Am. Rev.*, CVIII (1869), 337-397. Pertinent information is also to be found in Cotton Mather's *Diary* and Samuel Sewall's *Diary* (both of which have been referred to earlier), and in the court records of Massachusetts and Connecticut. John Fiske has an interesting chapter on the Salem witchcraft cases in his *New France and New England* (N. Y., 1902), which is marred by an obvious attempt to clear the clergy of guilt in the matter. See also Winsor, "The Literature of Witchcraft in New England," Am. Antiq. Soc. *Proceeds.*, n. s., X, 351-373.

Bruce, *The Institutional History of Virginia in the Seventeenth Century* (already cited), has a chapter on witchcraft in Virginia. Additional data in regard to the colonies south of the Hudson are to be found in the publications of the *Virginia Magazine of History*, IV and XXVI; *William and Mary College Historical Quarterly*, III-IV; *Lower Norfolk County Antiquary*, I; *Maryland Historical Society*, XXII-XXV; and in O'Callaghan, ed., *Documentary History of New York* (cited earlier), IV.

MAN'S TREATMENT OF MAN

Punishment for crime is a subject that has been largely overlooked by colonial historians. Students must therefore go to the original court records or glean the information from articles on criminal law and procedure. For New England the most important original sources are: John Noble, ed., *Records of the Court of Assistants of Massachusetts, 1630-1692* (2 vols., Boston, 1901-1904) ; W. H. Whitmore, ed., *The Colonial Laws of Massachusetts* (Boston, 1889) ; C. F. Gray, "The Body of Liberties of 1641," Mass. Hist. Soc., *Colls.*, ser. 3, VIII (1843), 216-237; Force, *Tracts and Other Papers* (cited earlier), III; and the published collections of the historical societies of that section. Secondary sources of value for New England are Adams, *The Founding of New England*, and Eggleston, *The Transit of Civilization* (both cited before) ; Alice M. Earle, *Curious Punishments of Bygone Days* (Chicago, 1896) ; John Noble, "Notes on the Trial and Punishment of Crimes in Massachusetts," Col. Soc. of Mass., *Publs.*, III (1895-1897), 51-66; C. F. Gray, "Remarks on the Early Laws of Massachusetts Bay," Mass. Hist. Soc., *Colls.*, ser. 3, VIII (1843), 191-215; G. Myers, *Ye Olden Blue Laws* (N. Y., 1921).

For colonies other than New England, material can be found in Hening, *Virginia Statutes at Large* (cited earlier) ; *Virginia Magazine of History and Biography*, IV, XI, XIII-XIV; W. H. Browne, ed., *Archives of Maryland* (30 vols., Balt.,1883- , in progress) ; H. L. Osgood and others, eds., *Minutes of the Common Council of New York, 1675-1776* (8 vols., N. Y., 1905) ; Alice M. Earle, *Colonial Days in Old New York* (N. Y., 1899) ; Philip Klein, *Prison Methods in New York State* (Columbia Univ., *Studies*, XC, 1920, no. 1) ; Scharf, *History of Maryland* (cited earlier) ; and H. E. Barnes, *A History of the Penal Reformatory and Correctional Institutions of the State of New Jersey* (Trenton, 1918). A comparative study of punishment for crime in England may be made by a perusal of Sir J. F. Stephen, *History of the Criminal Law of England* (London, 1883).

For the treatment of servants and slaves one should turn to J. C. Ballagh, *A History of Slavery in Virginia* (Johns Hopkins Univ., *Studies,* extra vol., XXIV, 1902); same author, *White Servitude in the Colony of Virginia* (Johns Hopkins Univ., *Studies,* XIII, 1895, nos. 4-5); J. R. Brackett, *The Negro in Maryland* (Johns Hopkins Univ., *Studies,* extra vol., VI, 1889); J. S. Bassett, *Slavery and White Servitude in the Colony of North Carolina* (Johns Hopkins Univ., *Studies,* XIV, 1896, nos. 4-5); Bruce, *Economic History of Virginia in the Seventeenth Century* (cited earlier); K. F. Geiser, *Redemptioners and Indented Servants in the Colony and Commonwealth of Pennsylvania* (New Haven, 1901); C. A. Herrick, *White Servitude in Pennsylvania* (Phila., 1926); and E. I. McCormac, *White Servitude in Maryland* (cited before). U. B. Phillips in the early chapters of his *American Negro Slavery,* discusses the introduction of slaves.

MEDICINE

A. H. Buck, *The Growth of Medicine from the Earliest Times to about 1800* (New Haven, 1917), supplies a background for an understanding of seventeenth-century medicine in America. Equally interesting, but far less reliable, is A. D. White, *A History of the Warfare of Science with Theology in Christendom* (2 vols., N. Y., 1896). A comprehensive though ill-digested account of medicine in the colonies is found in F. R. Packard, *The History of Medicine in the United States before 1800* (Phila., 1901). James Thacher, *American Medical Biography* (2 vols., Boston, 1828), has many sketches, though no references are given.

Contemporaneous writings containing much information upon the subject are: Cotton Mather's *Diary* (cited previously); G. L. Kittredge, ed., "Letters of Samuel Lee to Dr. Nehemiah Grew," Col. Soc. of Mass., *Publs.,* XIV (1911-1913), 142-186; George Alsop, *A Character of the Province of Maryland* [London, 1666] (reptd., N. D. Mereness, ed., Cleveland, 1902); and *William and Mary College Historical Quarterly,* XIV. The student should also consult the following secondary treatments: O. W. Holmes, "The Medical Profession in Massachusetts," in his *Medical Essays* (Boston, 1883), 312-369; Harriet S. Tapley, "Early Physicians of Danvers," Danvers Hist. Soc., *Colls.*, IV (1913), 73-88; F. H. Brown, "The Practice of Medicine in New England before 1700," Bostonian Soc., *Publs.*, VIII (1911), 94-120; G. W. Russell, *Early Medicine and Early Medical Men in Connecticut* (Hartford, 1892); Stephen Wickes, *History of Medicine in New Jersey* (Newark, 1879); and S. A. Green, *History of Medicine in Massachusetts* (Boston, 1881).

AMUSEMENTS

No comprehensive study has yet been made of colonial amusements in the seventeenth century. The writings of Alice M. Earle, however, treat this subject in various chapters, and abound in illustrations from contemporaneous writers. They include: *Customs and Fashions in Old New England* (cited earlier); *Home Life in Colonial Days* (N. Y., 1898); *Colonial Days in Old New York* (cited earlier); *Child Life in Colonial Days* (N. Y., 1899); and *Colonial Dames and Goodwives* (N. Y., 1900). Similar in character are Mary C. Crawford, *Social Life in Old New England* (Boston, 1914); and same author, *In the Days of the Pilgrim Fathers* (Boston, 1920). S. G. Fisher treats this among other subjects in his *Men, Women & Manners in Colonial Times* (2 vols., Phila., 1898). The most comprehensive treatment for the South is to be found in P. A. Bruce, *Social Life of Virginia in the Seventeenth Century* (Richmond, 1907). C. M. Andrews, *Colonial Folkways* (*The Chronicles of America Series*, IX), contains a brief general treatment. Much incidental material of importance will be found in William Meade, *Old Churches, Ministers and Families of Virginia*, and W. De L. Love, *Fast and Thanksgiving Days in New England* (both cited earlier); and in Robert Beverley, *History of Virginia* (London, 1705); Hugh Jones, *The Present State of Virginia* (London, 1724); Daniel Denton, *A Brief Description of New York* (London, 1670); and in many of the other contemporaneous writings that have been referred to, such as those by Sewall, Alsop and Cotton Mather.

MORALS

Essential for a study of morality and relations between the sexes is A. W. Calhoun, *A Social History of the American Family* (3 vols., Cleveland, 1917). This should be supplemented by readings in the standard works by Bruce on seventeenth-century Virginia, and by the volumes of Alice M. Earle cited in the preceding paragraph. Of more limited scope is "Some Phases of Sexual Morality and Church Discipline in Colonial New England," by C. F. Adams, in Mass. Hist. Soc., *Proceeds.*, ser. 2, VI (1891), 477-516. For a more thorough grasp of the subject it is necessary to go to the colonial laws and court records. An interesting compilation based on such sources is John Noble's "Notes on Trial and Punishment in Massachusetts" (cited before). Additional light is thrown upon the subject by the writings of Governor Bradford, Cotton Mather and Samuel Sewall, by the published sermons of the New England ministers, and by Ebenezer Cook, "The Sot-weed Factor," B. C. Steiner, ed., Md. Hist. Soc., *Fund Publ.*, no. 36 (1900), 11-32. An interesting but unreliable picture of morals in Boston at the end of the century is given in Edward Ward, "A Trip to New-England [1699]," reptd., G. P. Winship, ed., *Boston in 1682 and 1699* (Providence, 1905), 29-70. A wealth of information is to be had from local and town histories, notably W. De L. Love, *History of Hartford;* Frances M. Caulkins, *History of New London;* and Charles Brooks, *History of the Town of Medford*—all cited earlier. Consult also the works referred to under Man's Treatment of Man.

ARCHITECTURE

Perhaps the best work on architecture in the colonies is Fiske Kimball, *Domestic Architecture of the American Colonies and of the Early Republic* (N. Y., 1922). Of great value also are L. A. Coffin, jr., and A. C. Holden, *Brick*

Architecture of the Colonial Period in Maryland and Virginia (N. Y., 1919); R. A. Lancaster, *Historic Virginia Homes and Churches* (Phila., 1915); J. M. Hammond, *Colonial Mansions of Maryland and Delaware* (Phila., 1914); W. J. Mills, *Historic Houses of New Jersey* (Phila., 1902); S. H. Yonge, *The Site of Old "James Towne"* (Richmond, 1907); H. D. Eberlein, *The Architecture of Colonial America* (Boston, 1921); J. E. Chandler, *The Colonial House* (N. Y., 1916); N. M. Isham and A. F. Brown, *Early Connecticut Houses* (Providence, 1900); and the books on Connecticut mentioned under Physical Survivals. There are a number of good books on the Eastern cities which devote much space to architecture in this period. I. N. Phelps Stokes, *The Iconography of Manhattan Island* (6 vols., N. Y., 1915-1926), is foremost; Justin Winsor, ed., *Memorial History of Boston* (cited earlier), is not yet superseded. Philadelphia has been written up from this point of view by E. P. Oberholtzer, *Philadelphia* (Phila., 1912); J. T. Faris, *Old Churches and Meeting-houses in and around Philadelphia* (Phila., 1926); Thomas Westcott, *The Historic Mansions and Buildings of Philadelphia* (Phila., 1877); H. D. Eberlein and H. M. Lippincott, *Colonial Homes of Philadelphia and Its Neighborhood* (Phila., 1912); and Frank Cousins and P. M. Riley, *Colonial Architecture of Philadelphia* (Boston, 1920). W. N. Black has an interesting article on "Colonial Building in New Jersey" in *Architectural Review*, III (1893-1894), 245-262.

Among the many books on early American furnishings one may mention L. V. Lockwood, *Colonial Furniture in America* (2 vols., N. Y., 1913); I. W. Lyon, *Colonial Furniture of New England* (Boston, 1891); and Esther Singleton, *The Furniture of Our Forefathers* (2 vols., N. Y., 1900). Miss Singleton's volumes make almost a source book because of the many inventories reproduced; her latest book, *The Collecting of Antiques* (N. Y., 1926), considers chiefly American material. An increasing periodical literature is devoted to old furnishings. Wallace Nutting, *Furniture of the Pilgrim Century, 1620-1720* (Framingham, Mass., 1924) has in addition to its scholarly text about fifteen hundred excellent illustrations.

HABILIMENTS AND TRAVEL

On conditions of travel, roads, bridges and taverns much information may be had from Seymour Dunbar, *History of Travel in America* (4 vols., Indianapolis, 1915); Weeden, *Economic and Social History of New England*, and Bruce, *Economic History of Virginia in the Seventeenth Century* (both cited before); Edward Field, *The Colonial Tavern* (Providence, 1897); Alice M. Earle, *Stage Coach and Tavern Days* (N. Y., 1900); Mary C. Crawford, *Little Pilgrimages among Old New England Inns* (Boston, 1907); and W. H. Bayles, *Old Taverns of New York* (N. Y., 1895); Elise Lathrop, *Early American Inns and Taverns* (N. Y., 1926), richly illustrated and an excellent reference book; and J. A. Krout, *The Origins of Prohibition* (N. Y., 1925), for early tavern legislation.

For the manner in which the people of the colonies attired themselves, the standard treatments by Elizabeth McClellan, *Historic Dress in America, 1607-1800* (Phila., 1904), and Alice M. Earle, *Two Centuries of Costume* (N. Y., 1903), may be supplemented by M. N. Stanard, *Colonial Virginia, Its People and Customs* (Phila., 1917), and the works by Bruce and Weeden.   J. B. Felt, *Customs of New England* (Boston, 1853), has special interest as the pioneer work covering the subjects of this section.

INDEX

A-B-C'S, in schools, 246.
Abigall, brings epidemic to Virginia, 179.
Adultery, punishments for, 216, 218.
Agriculture, in New England, 11; in Middle colonies, 12; in South, 12-13; tobacco, 22-47; methods in South, 37-39; equipment for, 40-41; navigation acts, 42-43; plantation economy, 40-47; in New England, 55-59, 84; tools, 58; slaves in New England, 62; indentured servants in New England, 67-68; books on, 323.
Ague, remedy for, 169.
Alsop, George, on indentured servants, 28; drives off hostile "humors," 169-170; physician cures, 176; on future of female servants, 206-207; calls colonists law-abiding, 214; on colonial prisons, 223; on treatment of servants, 229; on intellectual activity in colonies, 259; on deer, 266.
America, cargo of ship stores, 81.
Amusements, horse-racing, 263-265, 272-273; hunting in South, 265-267; dancing, 268-269; cards, 269-270, 273; in New York, 271-273; in New England, 273-279; Thanksgiving day, 273-274; training day, 274-275; election day, 275; mid-week lecture, 276; Christmas, 276-277; May day, 277-278; Harvard commencement, 278-279; books on, 335-336.
Anatomy, 165.
Anderson, Charles, Virginia minister, 128.
Andros, Edmund, tyranny in New England, 107; conflict with

James Blair, 134-135, 136; observes Christmas, 277.
Anglican church, Puritan claims to have true, 89; Massachusetts forbids warship of, 106; decline of, 115-117; large parishes in Virginia, 117-119; clergy poorly paid, 120-124, 136; glebes, 122-123; liturgy of neglected, 124-126; government of in Virginia, 126-127; Bishop of London, 127; commissaries of, 127; character of clergy, 127-131; plans to reform in Virginia, 132-134; ecclesiastical discipline in, 137; decline of, 138; books on, 325-328.
Anthropogeography, in American history, 21.
Appalachians, influence of, 2; westward expansion, 8.
Apprentices, in New England, 63-64.
Architecture, in New England villages, 85; of first settlers, 283-286; houses in South, 286-287, 317; in New England, 285-286, 287-288, 317-318; chimneys, 288-289; windows, 289-290; brick houses, 290; at Philadelphia, 290-291; in New Jersey, 291-292; state houses, 292-293; churches, 293-294; European models followed, 294, 301; books on, 336-337. *See also* Houses, Churches, etc.
Aristocracy, in Virginia, 26-27, 34-36, 44-48; in New England, 69, 70-71, 75, 97; dress of, 73-74, 279-281.
Arson, punishments for, 221.
Artisans, in New England, 61-65; wages, 69; property of, 70. *See also* Labor, Manufactures.

339

limited scope of, 240-241; libraries in New England, 240-242; publishing in New England, 242-244; poetry, 243-244; Harvard, 247-250; Virginians at Oxford, 254-255; books in Virginia, 255-258; factors shaping, 258-261.

Ipswich, fishing, 51; trade, 55; fulling mill, 79, 81; typical house, 287; old houses, 317.

Iron, in Va., 18; in New England, 82.

JACKSON, ANDREW, Virginia minister, 128.

Jails. See Imprisonment, Prisons, Punishment.

Jamaica, New England trade to, 54.

James I, believes in witchcraft, 143-144.

James II, dethroned, 107.

Jamestown, 5; manufactures, 18-19; tobacco in streets of, 22; hygiene at, 166-167; epidemics at, 178-179; houses of, 283-286, 290; state houses, 292; church, 293; taverns at, 300-301.

Jennings, Colonel, quoted, 214.

Johnson, Edward, on shipbuilding, 52; on indentured servants, 66; fear of heresy, 91; opposes commercialism, 112; *Wonder-Working Providence*, 242; on Harvard, 248-249; on first Massachusetts houses, 283-284.

Johnson, Mary, witch, 152.

Johnson, Samuel, on colonists, 213.

Jones, Hugh, quoted, 45; on racing in Virginia, 263-264.

Jones, Margaret, hanged as witch, 152.

Josselyn, John, account of New England, 65, 311.

KEMP, RICHARD, a planter, 47.

Kempis, Thomas à, read in New England, 240.

Kirby, F., bookseller, 242.

LABOR, dear, 11; in South, 23-26; indentured servants, 24-26; distribution of servants, 32; future of servants, 33-34; slave influx, 43-44; of wealthy planters, 44-47; skilled, 61-64; slaves in North, 63-68; domestics in New England, 65; on farms, 67-68; sound in New England, 68-69; wages, 69; democracy of, 75; in homes, 76-78. See Indentured servants, Slavery.

Land, size of Southern plantations, 26-31; grants of in South, 29-30; transfers of in South, 30; a typical plantation, 46-47; New England town system of, 55-59; books on, 325

Language, obsolete words, 56.

Latin, in Harvard, 247-249.

Lawn's Creek Parish, Va., 130.

Lawrence, Richard, accused, 204.

Laws Divine and Martiall, at Jamestown, 166-167; harsh enforcement, 211.

Leah and Rachel, on treatment of servants, 229-230. See also Hammond, John.

Lechford, Thomas, cited, 63; *Note Book* of, 71; his *Of Prophesie*, 238-239.

Leddra, William, Quaker, hanged, 104.

Lee, Samuel, quoted, 177.

Leisure class, none in colonies, 261. See also Aristocracy.

Leverett, John, at Harvard, 250.

Libraries, in New England, 240-242; of Harvard, 247; in Virginia, 257-258.

Lighting. See Illumination.

Lightning, Increase Mather on, 140-141; an omen, 162.

Lincoln, Daniel, of Hingham, Mass., 61.

Linen manufacture, 76.

Literature, of Puritans, 239; publishing in New England, 242-244; poetry, 243-244; of Virginia, 256-257; libraries of Virginia, 257-258; books on, 329-330. See also Books, Publishing.

358 INDEX

Witches, execution of in Europe, 143; in England, 143-144; in Scotland, 144-145; in Virginia, 145-148; in Maryland, 148-149; in Pennsylvania, 149; in New England, 150-162. *See* plate vii.

Woburn, class distinctions in, 74.

Women, work of, in New England, 84-85; vital statistics of at Hingham, 181-182; sex offenses on plantations, 203-207; part of in founding colonies, 303.

Wood, William, quoted, 58.

Wood, needed by England, 13. *See also* Forests, Naval stores.

Wooden ware, in New England, 83; in homes, 84-85.

Wool. *See* Sheep, Spinning.

Worcester, bishop of, 133.

Wormeley, Christopher, a planter, 47.

Wormeley, Madam, books of on medicine, 177.

Wormeley, Ralph, home manufacture, 45; slaves of, 47; library of, 258; residence, 287.

Wright, Goodwife, accused of witchcraft, 145-146.

YATES, BARTHOLOMEW, Virginia minister, 128.

Yellow fever, Cotton Mather on, 141; on immigrant vessels, 166; in Virginia, 178-179.

Yeomanry, formation of, 32-34; future of yeoman, 35; resist crown, 36-37; farm methods, 37-39; food, 39-40; inventories, 40-41; prosperity, 41-42; navigation acts, 42-43; migration from South, 43; slaves affect, 43-44.

Young, Achsah, hanged as witch, 152.